Postdramatic Theatre and India

Methuen Drama Engage offers original reflections about key practitioners, movements and genres in the fields of modern theatre and performance. Each volume in the series seeks to challenge mainstream critical thought through original and interdisciplinary perspectives on the body of work under examination. By questioning existing critical paradigms, it is hoped that each volume will open up fresh approaches and suggest avenues for further exploration.

Series Editors
Mark Taylor-Batty, University of Leeds, UK
Enoch Brater, University of Michigan, USA

Titles

Brecht and Post-1990s British Drama
Anja Hartl
ISBN 978-1-3501-7278-4

Contemporary Drag Practices and Performers: Drag in a Changing Scene Volume 1
Edited by Mark Edward and Stephen Farrier
ISBN 978-1-3500-8294-6

Drag Histories, Herstories and Hairstories: Drag in a Changing Scene Volume 2
Edited by Mark Edward and Stephen Farrier
ISBN 978-1-3501-0436-5

Performing the Unstageable: Success, Imagination, Failure
Karen Quigley
ISBN 978-1-3500-5545-2

Drama and Digital Arts Cultures
David Cameron, Michael Anderson and Rebecca Wotzko
ISBN 978-1-472-59219-4

Social and Political Theatre in 21st-Century Britain: Staging Crisis
Vicky Angelaki
ISBN 978-1-474-21316-5

Watching War on the Twenty-First-Century Stage: Spectacles of Conflict
Clare Finburgh
ISBN 978-1-472-59866-0

Fiery Temporalities in Theatre and Performance: The Initiation of History
Maurya Wickstrom
ISBN 978-1-4742-8169-0

For a complete listing, please visit
https://www.bloomsbury.com/series/methuen-drama-engage/

Postdramatic Theatre and India

Theatre-Making Since the 1990s

Ashis Sengupta

Series Editors

Mark Taylor-Batty and Enoch Brater

methuen | drama
LONDON · NEW YORK · OXFORD · NEW DELHI · SYDNEY

METHUEN DRAMA
Bloomsbury Publishing Plc
50 Bedford Square, London, WC1B 3DP, UK
1385 Broadway, New York, NY 10018, USA
29 Earlsfort Terrace, Dublin 2, Ireland

BLOOMSBURY, METHUEN DRAMA and the Methuen Drama logo are trademarks of Bloomsbury Publishing Plc

First published in Great Britain 2022
This paperback edition published 2023

Copyright © Ashis Sengupta, 2022

Ashis Sengupta has asserted his right under the Copyright, Designs and Patents Act, 1988, to be identified as the Author of this work.

For legal purposes the Acknowledgements on pp. ix–x constitute an extension of this copyright page.

Series design by Louise Dugdale
Cover image © Ajith Kumar O., International Theatre Festival Kerala 2019. Production title: *Dark Things*. Directed by Deepan Sivaraman and Anuradha Kapur. Based on the text by Ari Sitas. Dramaturgy by Purav Goswami and Ari Sitas. Music composers: Sumangala Damodaran, Chandran Veyattummal and Reza Khota.

All rights reserved. No part of this publication may be reproduced or transmitted in any form or by any means, electronic or mechanical, including photocopying, recording, or any information storage or retrieval system, without prior permission in writing from the publishers.

Bloomsbury Publishing Plc does not have any control over, or responsibility for, any third-party websites referred to or in this book. All internet addresses given in this book were correct at the time of going to press. The author and publisher regret any inconvenience caused if addresses have changed or sites have ceased to exist, but can accept no responsibility for any such changes.

A catalogue record for this book is available from the British Library.

A catalog record for this book is available from the Library of Congress.

ISBN: HB: 978-1-3501-5408-7
PB: 978-1-3502-8439-5
ePDF: 978-1-3501-5410-0
eBook: 978-1-3501-5409-4

Series: Methuen Drama Engage

Typeset by RefineCatch Limited, Bungay, Suffolk

To find out more about our authors and books visit www.bloomsbury.com and sign up for our newsletters.

For my wife Mitra, who wanted me to write this book; and for my daughter Pipli (Tirna), who made it possible.

Contents

List of Illustrations   viii
Acknowledgements   ix

Introduction
Hans-Thies Lehmann and Since: Debates in Postdramatic Theatre and Performance   1

1. Theorizing and Contextualizing India's Postdramatic   15
2. The Non-Dramatic Turn in Indian Theatre: Early Adaptations and Devised Plays   47
3. India's Postdramatic I: 'Telling Stories Across Forms', Theatre and the New Political, Theatre of Scenography   57
4. India's Postdramatic II: Monologies and Theatre Solos   91
5. India's Postdramatic III: Theatre-as-Event, Reality Theatre, Theatre Installations   117
6. Activism in India's Postdramatic Theatre   147

Conclusion
Postdrama and Theatre-Making in India   167

References   183
Index   197

Illustrations

1 *Midnight's Children* (2005), directed by Abhilash Pillai, presented by National School of Drama (NSD), New Delhi. Photo credit: S. Thyagarajan — 36
2 *The Job* (1996), directed by Anuradha Kapur, presented at Max Mueller Bhavan, Mumbai. Photo credit: Prakash Rao — 53
3 *The Legends of Khasak* (2015), directed by Deepan Sivaraman, presented by KMK Smaraka Kalasamithi, Trikkaripur. Photo credit: Ameer Ali Olavara — 84
4 *Are You Home, Lady Macbeth?* (2010), conceptualized and performed by Maya Krishna Rao, presented by Vismayah. Photo credit: S. Thyagarajan — 99
5 *Black Hole* (2019), conceptualized and performed by Jyoti Dogra, presented by Prithvi Theatre. Photo credit: Jazeela Basheer — 114
6 *Sleep Series* III (2014), conceptualized and directed by Amitesh Grover and Frank Oberhausser, produced by Heimathafen Berlin and Goethe-Institut India. Photo credit: Amitesh Grover — 120
7 *Propositions: On Text and Space I* (2010), directed by Zuleikha Chaudhari, based on Ibsen's *John Gabriel Borkman*, texts by the Raqs Media Collective, presented by Khoj International Artists' Association, New Delhi. Photo credit: Zuleikha Chaudhari — 139
8 *Active Space* (2012), design scene-work by Muzamil Hayat Bhawani, presented by National School of Drama. Photo credit: S. Thyagarajan — 143
9 *409 Ramkinkars* (2015), conceptualized by Vivan Sundaram and executed by a large group of arts practitioners, produced by Vivadi Cultural Society. Photo credit: S. Thyagarajan — 175
10 *409 Ramkinkars* (2015). Photo credit: S. Thyagarajan — 176

Acknowledgements

This book has happened in the face of overwhelming odds. My fieldwork began the day India suddenly announced demonetization, and I practically found myself penniless in a city thousands of miles from home. I wrote the book's last chapter during prolonged lockdowns in the wake of Covid-19, with little access to resources that were essential to my work. In between, a series of health emergencies in the family literally brought me to my knees. As I now wonder how the book could still happen, my heart becomes filled with gratitude for the people who in fact made this possible.

I would like to thank the following theatre-makers most sincerely for the conversations we have had over the years and for all the help they have extended to my research by sharing video clips, pictures, (unpublished) scripts and performance texts: Muzamil Hayat Bhawani, Zuleikha Chaudhari, Neelam Mansingh Chowdhry, Jyoti Dogra, Purav Goswami, Amitesh Grover, Anamika Haksar, Kirti Jain, Anuradha Kapur, Abhilash Pillai, Gowri Ramnarayan, Maya Krishna Rao and Deepan Sivaraman. I am very much thankful to each of them – special thanks to Anuradha and Neelam for their encouragement all through. At the same time, I regret that I could not cover the works of a few other prominent theatre-makers for various unavoidable reasons. I take this opportunity to express my admiration for Ari Sitas's significant contribution to the making of *Dark Things*. I should also mention that part of the source material for the production, Sitas's long oratorio, was published by Tulika Books, New Delhi, in December 2020 under the title *Notes for an Oratorio on Small Things that Fall* (*like a screw in the night*).

Performance documentation is not at all strong in India. I am thankful to Santanu Bose of the National School of Drama (NSD), New Delhi, for his help with some rare material, without which the book might not have seen the light of day. I also thank Katerina Delikonstantinidou for sending a soft copy of an indispensable but out-of-print book at an early stage of my research. I am very grateful for the feedback from Conrad Alexandrowicz, Michael Shane Boyle and Matt Cornish at different stages of writing. I also remember fondly the conversations I had with Rustom Bharucha, Soumyabrata Choudhury and Bishnupriya Dutt at the School of Arts and Aesthetics, Jawaharlal Nehru University, on postdramatic theatre.

I thank my doctor friend, Anandabrata Bose, and his wife, Nilika, most sincerely for their unfailing, affectionate help in hours of need through the years, without which I could not have continued my work. Joydeep

Bhattacharyya and Pinaki Ranjan Das, thank you for being there whenever I needed your assistance. Special thanks are also due to my old friend Dipankar Dasgupta for his constant encouragement and to Avijit Solanki who offered me accommodation when I visited NSD in 2016.

Working with Anna Brewer, Meredith Benson and Sam Nicholls at Bloomsbury Methuen Drama has always been a great pleasure – a big thank you to all of them. I would also like to thank series editors Enoch Brater and Mark Taylor-Batty for the hard work they put in for the volume. I look forward to the earliest opportunity to correct any inadvertent errors and oversights the book may still have.

Finally, I am thankful to the University of North Bengal for the modest grant awarded for the project, coupled with research leave for nearly a year.

My apologies in case I have left out anyone whose help might have sustained me in other ways during the long sojourn.

Siliguri, December 2020

INTRODUCTION

Hans-Thies Lehmann and Since: Debates in Postdramatic Theatre and Performance

Lehmann and this book

Hans-Thies Lehmann's book, *Postdramatic Theatre* (originally published in 1999 and translated into English in 2006), continues to stimulate debate in theatre studies over its 'clean of context' approach to theatre aesthetics (Fuchs 2008b: 179) – over the 'real', in other words, in performance practice. *Dramatic and Postdramatic Theatre: Ten Years After* (2011), edited by Ivan Medenica; *Postdramatic Theatre and the Political* (2013), edited by Karen Jürs-Munby, Jerome Carroll and Steve Giles; *New Dramaturgy* (2014), edited by Katalin Trencsényi and Bernadette Cochrane; Liz Tomlin's *Acts and Apparitions* (2016); and *Postdramatic Theatre and Form* (2019), edited by Michael Shane Boyle, Matt Cornish and Brandon Woolf are the most important critical texts of recent times that at once build on Lehmann and go beyond by critiquing his perspectives on theatre. Lehmann built his concept of postdrama mostly on the basis of European (and US) theatrical experiments since the 1970s, and with little or no reference to theatre practices in other parts of the world. But it is important to note that Fuchs, despite her serious reservations about his book, admitted in 2008 that Lehmann's 'postdramatic' 'will set the terms of discussion of much contemporary theatre for at least the next generation' (Fuchs 2008a: 19).

The relationship between postdrama and India being the subject of the present study, the introduction takes on board the debates in postdramatic theatre and performance ever since the publication of Lehmann's book with a view to expanding on his formulation of the paradigm and reading its ramifications in theatre's wider cultural and aesthetic contexts in the chapters that follow. The debates that continue have mostly centred on the understanding of the 'post' as a prefix, and therefore its relationship to 'dramatic', the reality status of performance and its connection to the world outside, the nature of presence and the changing course of mimesis/representation in theatre, and lastly, on the scope of the political in postdramatic aesthetics. It is important to engage with the debates because in its transcontinental, transcultural journey postdramatic theatre has augmented and reconfigured itself both as a concept and in practice. While the practice part in reference to India is extensively explored in the rest of the book, the debates revisited and rethought here should create fresh perspectives from which to probe contemporary theatre-making protocols in general. This will entail a critique of both Lehmann's thesis and the responses it has elicited so far, helping us appreciate postdramatic theatre beyond a rigid understanding of it and see its intriguing relationship with India in particular. The introduction is also necessary for readers and audiences in India because 'postdramatic' is still a much-misunderstood term in the subcontinent.

The passage towards postdramatic

Lehmann develops his concept of postdramatic against the backdrop of Peter Szondi's Hegelian 'archeology of drama' (Fuchs 2011: 64) and the latter's acceptance of epic theatre as a tentative solution to the 'historical crisis' of the dramatic form. But Brecht cannot be considered a revolutionary counter-model to the dramatic tradition, Lehmann writes, because his theatre is rather 'a completion of the classical dramaturgy' in that it works within the triad of text, action and plot. Brecht considered story, after Aristotle, to be the soul of drama in spite of his anti-Aristotelian position on the art of representation and his concern for a new act of spectating. Although the German 'fabel' must be differentiated from the English 'fable', the former as an analytical-dramaturgical category in Brecht could not transcend the conventions of the '*theatre of stories*', Lehmann observes (2006: 33). Brecht exposed the mechanics of illusionist theatre which he thought hide the reality of capitalism, especially of the bourgeois means of production that exploit the proletariat. Yet postdramatic theatre is post-Brechtian because it discards, in the words of Denise Varney (2007: 136), 'the Brechtian gestus of showing … and communicating the social relations of class' since the 'truth' Brecht aimed at by pulling down the fourth wall goes missing in the late capitalist, postmodern world. The reality and meaning of theatre now lie in the process of performance itself, which is nonetheless influenced by the material conditions of theatre's production but no longer by any dogmatic understanding of rationality and freedom. Lehmann sees the real solution to the crisis of drama in going beyond Brecht's inquiries about representation, in theatre's theatreness or in its turn to performance. Nevertheless, one must not fail to realize that the 'post', in this case, does not imply a complete disjunction with Brecht but a 'productive tension' with his vision and practice.

Theatre as performance remains inseparable from prevalent socioeconomic conditions, but in new ways and forms as discussed below.

The emergence of poststructuralism as a movement in philosophy and criticism that drew on linguistic theories, the 'end of history' thesis dominating the discourses on the economic and the political, the steady technological progress and a wholesale mediatization of society – these interlaced developments demanded a new theatre language in Europe (and the US) through the last few decades of the twentieth century and have also altered the theatre landscape elsewhere gradually since the collapse of the Soviet Union. With reality and meaning being decentred in the world outside of the stage, stage reality became of primary importance in theatre practice. Theatre's 'emphatic relationship with itself' (Stegemann 2008: 12) does not, however, dismiss external reality; but its self-referentiality has undergone continued experimentation during the postdramatic's decades-old journey, replacing the metanarrative on stage with little, non-linear and unsynthesized narratives and the referent with the sign's materiality. As this does not mean that theory has finally come to dominate performance, it is equally important to see that representation did not go out of the theatre altogether. Mimetic representation was nearly out; mimesis became performative instead. To perform an aesthetic moment within a theatrical frame is also to plan and organize the material for it and thus to represent, but this organization is very different from the ordering logic of dramatic theatre that naïvely passes off fiction as truth. Postdramatic theatre seeks to present reality or real-time action with an acceptance of what S. J. Bailes calls 'a poetics of failure' (in Tomlin 2016: 47) – the failure of re/presentation.

We should be careful not to conflate postdramatic and postmodern theatre because the former can be both modern and postmodern, though more postmodern than modern since the late twentieth century because it shares postmodernism's disbelief in a teleological view of the world. Lehmann says that the elements which characterize postdramatic theatre – non-linearity, hypernaturalism, ambiguity and heterogeneity of style – may also be found in productions that belong to modern (dramatic) theatre. Conversely, many traits of postmodern theatre practice – from the randomness of styles and forms to multiple codes of action and behaviour to mixed-media performance – do not automatically reject 'modernity on principle' (Lehmann 2006: 24–6). When a performance progresses with no 'internal logic' of a story, when a dramatic composition is perceived 'as an artificially imposed' structure, as Lehmann adds, then theatre acquires the potential to go beyond drama but not necessarily beyond modernity. The reading of 'a stylistic moment', whether dramatic or postdramatic, depends in the end only on 'the constellation of elements' engendering the moment (25).

In its attempt to avoid the internal logic of dramatic theatre, postdramatic theatre can be modern by presenting the unpresentable in a form that constitutes art's autonomous world and be postmodern by showing the sublime to be 'the unpresentable in presentation itself' and therefore with no 'solace of good forms' (Ray 2018: 115). Form in either case thus plays a vital role; we have rather a celebration of formlessness in the latter.

The dramatic–postdramatic 'binary'

The 'new' theatre paradigm does not thrive purely on the binaries it allegedly creates between text and non-text, narrative and non-narrative, theatre and performance, making the second term in each mandatory for contemporary theatre practitioners (unless, of course, institutional funding is biased against a certain type of theatre, for that matter). In fact, text-based theatre written for the contemporary stage can be postdramatic just as theatre with a 'new performative turn' (Fischer-Lichte 2005: 224) may well be treated as performance. Lehmann himself seems to have apprehended exploitation of an incorrect binary between dramatic and postdramatic after the publication of his 1999/2006 book and, therefore, wrote a sort of postscript elsewhere: a close understanding of one's 'actual dramatic theatre tradition' is essential for a better survey of their contemporary theatre landscape, although the emerging theatre idioms will tend to be postdramatic (Lehmann 2016: online). The implication is that the 'dramatic theatre tradition' of a place may very well show signs of a pending conversation with its posterior rather than standing disconnected from it.

Tomlin's thesis that Lehmann's book plays out the dramatic–postdramatic binary 'in various calibrations' (2016: 8) is, therefore, subject to debate. It is interesting to see how Lehmann takes pains to make it clear at the beginning of his book that postdramatic theatre did not grow strictly in terms of its binary opposition to dramatic theatre:

> [P]ostdramatic theatre ... most definitely, does *not* [original emphasis] mean a theatre that exists 'beyond' drama, without any relation to it. It should rather be understood as the unfolding and blossoming of a potential of disintegration, dismantling and deconstruction within drama itself. This virtuality was present, though barely decipherable, in the aesthetics of dramatic theatre; it was contemplated in its philosophy, but only, as it were, as a current under the sparkling surface of the 'official' dialectical procedure.
>
> Lehmann 2006: 44

Lehmann clarifies the point better in his 2009 paper at a Belgrade conference, published as '"Postdramatic Theatre," a decade later' in 2011: postdramatic theatre is 'not simply about the "death" of the drama (or the text or the author ...), but about a shift of viewpoint on contemporary theatrical realities' (2011: 42). This 'shift' is not a total break with dramatic theatre, but about recognizing more acutely the difference between drama and theatre. A historical/chronological reading of the 'post' in 'postdrama' should be discouraged because the postdramatic does not follow the dramatic in time; it is not epochal. The dramatic had always contained its postdramatic moments. While postdramatic theatre distinguishes itself from the diverse dramatic theatre forms, social-realist as well as non-realist, it does not take them as its binary oppositions. Rather it contemplatively looks at its birth out of the crumbling edifice of dramatic theatre which nevertheless continues to be taken as the 'natural' model of theatre in most countries and cultures. The new 'birth' does not necessarily imply the death of the old model (Lehmann puts 'death' in inverted commas) or a break between the past and the present of theatre practice. The (hi)story of postdrama is an ongoing process of dismantling the structural logic of drama. From this perspective, productions that look apparently dramatic in character may self-referentially show the dramatic in its decomposing state.

Even when the dramatic and the postdramatic are taken as binaries, no binaries can operate by ignoring each other since one gives the other its existence, thus allowing leakage and traffic that contaminates the presumed exclusivity of either entity. More importantly, when a theatre practice adopts a deconstructionist approach to its predecessor, it develops its capacity for self-criticality that accepts aporia and reconfigurations as conditions of the relatively new identity. The prefix 'post', or the 'postness' of the 'post', does not operate in 'either-or' terms but in 'both-and'. Lehmann insisted on this both-and, and not on 'one of [the] two things' Tomlin would like him to choose for theatre-making: *either* dramatic (text-based) theatre indeed goes 'beyond the representational strategies of social-realism' *or* 'the postdramatic framework ... include[s] text-driven practice' (2016: 62). The 'post' in our context suggests that the new paradigm has grown out of the subversion of dramatic theatre's narrative logic, catalysing in the process a burgeoning set of non-realist/non-mimetic forms more self-reflexive than before – the reason why postdrama is often viewed as a direct or indirect descendant of avant-garde categories. However, even this metaphor of genealogy is wrong, as hinted at above, because the 'post' operates in a liminal space of its own anterior ('pre-postdramatic' which is not exactly 'dramatic' but partly 'non-dramatic') and its own posterior ('post-postdramatic' which is not 'after-postdramatic' but partly 'more-than postdramatic'). Postdrama is a continuous act of revising drama into theatre-as-performance in diverse ways, of emphasizing the processual fabric of contemporary theatre that has not ceased drawing on social 'reality' or simply abandoned text.

If we take the postdramatic as an outcome-in-process of drama's hidden potential for self-subversion, we can perhaps also think of it in more *formal* iterations than Lehmann did staying within his own world of experience. For example, postdramatic theatre currently includes installation, live art, guided walks, staged trials, public debates and dance among other forms which were kept out of its orbit by Lehmann himself initially. They show theatre within an expanded frame of performance and beyond the literariness of drama. They are postdrama also because they do not ask us to take the 'there-and-then' for a 'here-and-now'. Yet they entertain flirtations with drama and its properties while trying to move beyond its 'lying' tradition. Lehmann sounds convincing as he locates the postdramatic in the ambiguous space of 'dramatic' and 'non-dramatic' in theatre, ruling out both 'the common reduction of the aesthetic to social positions' and the inefficacy of the 'aesthetic practice of theatre' that 'does not recognize the *reflection* [my italics] of social norms of perception and behavior' (2006: 19). In theorizing experiments in theatre, modernist as well as postmodernist, during the latter half of the twentieth century, Lehmann was looking into the works of those who were constantly expanding the scope of theatre beyond the 'aesthetic logic' of the dramatic stage. A great bulk of twenty-first-century theatre may be viewed as a realization or furtherance of that experimental spree.

The poetics of presence

One of the most controversial points about Lehmann's theory is postdramatic theatre's actual capacity to go beyond representation, or its nature of engagement with the aesthetics of presentation. Lehmann himself sounds ambiguous on this issue at many places in his *Postdramatic Theatre*. His notion of a self-referential theatre, which he explains vis-à-vis the mimetic, representational dramatic theatre, or his (over)emphasis on presence in theatre as the opposite of representation, seems laboured at times and also betrays some conceptual contradictions when read with his definition of 'postdramatic' as 'beyond but not without representation' (71). Yet Lehmann cannot perhaps be faulted on this count for the same reason as Tomlin cites. She argues that much of the postdramatic theatre which claims itself to be presentational, or which is a practice based on real time and real event on stage, can be pre-rehearsed and pre-conceived in the way dramatic theatre is and thus (equally) representational. One thing should be made clear and accepted – life is life and theatre, theatre. But in postdramatic theatre the nature of theatrical signs becomes the primary issue of concern. Theatre *is* ultimately 'a type of sign usage', Lehmann acknowledges (85). What is important here is the self-referencing of signs or their oblique relation to the world outside rather than the signs mimetically standing for things referenced. This precisely explains Lehmann's 'beyond but not without' position on re/presentation in postdrama, although it may not justify his defence of postdrama elsewhere in the book as capable of providing an 'unmediated experience' (134).

To think of theatre as a pure, unmediated art is not possible because no presentation on stage can be a state of full presence. Lehmann compares the presence in postdramatic theatre to Hans Ulrich Gumbrecht's 'production of presence': 'Gumbrecht draws on nothing short of the Eucharist, in which bread and wine are not the signifiers for Christ's body and blood but real presence in the act of communion, not something designated but substance: the model of a "presence" that refers to itself and joins the gathered congregation in a ritual ceremony' (Lehmann 2006: 135, 141). But what happens once the ritual is robbed of its setting? Lehmann does not answer, but the answer can be well inferred from his argument about sign usage in ritual as well as in all theatre. The bread and wine are shorn of their 'real presence', and with it 'the act of communion' is gone. What is produced as 'real' may ultimately bear traces of organization and repetition since in the 'loss of the untutored ... innocence of human perception', as Vincent Pecora says (2013: 44), all things between the heavens and the earth are mediated and 'nothing is given to us as a simple presence' (Bevir 2013: 55). Presence, including the materiality of things, may not be *pure* because any material, including the human body, can bring in a train of traces of 'outside' onto the stage. Besides, vision as an act of seeing is 'never neutral' (Johnson 2012: 10) and has its own history or spatiotemporal specificity that disrupts any (presumed or projected) state of purity and presence. Yet Lehmann must be appreciated for his notion of postdrama as the theatre of the present.

Postdramatic theatre is 'a *theatre of the present*', Lehmann argues, where '[t]*he present is necessarily the erosion and slippage of presence*'. The present here (presence reformulated as present) is 'a floating, fading presence' (2006: 143–4). What is more remarkable about such theatre is that it aims at an art of the impossible by seeking to dismiss representationalism and become 'the presentation of an *atmosphere*' or of '*a state of things*'. This presence means process and manifestation more than signification and interpretation (Lehmann 2006: 74, 84). It is performative in character because it is produced, as Gumbrecht would say, as something present by being tangible in space and appealing primarily to the human senses. It means a moving away from the 'linguistic turn', a refusal of thematic, interpretive, sustained meaning-making, or rather locating meaning in experience. Tomlin does not sound wholly convincing again when she cites Derrida's call for a theatre which will 'no longer *re*-present a present that would exist elsewhere and prior to it' (2016: 71) in order to advance her own argument that the postdramatic 'does not constitute an evasion of representation but an alternative manipulation of representation ... to shape a theatrical aesthetic which offers a distinct but equally illusory "presence" to that offered by the dramatic model' (71). Postdramatic theatre cannot be accused of lying 'equally' because it begins with the prior knowledge of its incapacity for proffering life's self-presence. Instead, it aspires to recuperate presence in terms of formal reflexivity (see Boenisch 2013: 116) and not as a foundationalist essence. If one goes through Lehmann's *Postdramatic Theatre* and studiously marks every context of his use of the word 'presence', it is not very difficult to understand that he is anxious, despite his occasional conceptual vagaries, to underscore what kind of presence he means: 'integration of the real presence of the viewer ... into the work' (53), self-presentation of actor (125), 'production of presence' rather than an already-there presence (135), presence as electronic instant (170) and presence as 'real virtuality' (172). Presence, in this sense, also implies strategies of encounter with things and people, multiplicity of time and 'performative schemes', '*traces* of performance', 'acts of construction and reconstruction', unstable spectatorship, and dynamics of documentation (Giannachi, Kaye and Shanks 2012: 2–21). The *for*mal mobilization of presence as present in postdramatic theatre makes time appear as 'an object of direct experience' that is pitted against historical or futuristic temporality, not necessarily to promote the late-capitalist market logic of the instant, whereas dramatic (or bourgeois) theatre prevents the present from disrupting the fictitious past on stage or does not allow time to appear as time, however fleeting (see Watkinson 2019).

With regard to the poetics of presence in contemporary theatre, a few words on mediation and hypermediacy may be in order since their relationship is a crucial issue in intermedial theatre. There is a need to understand that the use of media – 'live video relay' in postdramatic theatre, for example – challenges the conventional ideas of liveness and immediacy in performance. Ana Tasić argues after Greg Giesekam that mediatized action interrogates the common notions of presence and authenticity by problematizing the issues of 'real' and its representability and by showing 'that all performance is an act of mediation' because no performance can be immediate (2011: 124–5). When it comes to the issue of simultaneity of live and mediatized action, as Philip Auslander notes, 'mediatised performance derives its authority from its reference to the live or the real, [and] the live now derives its authority from its reference to the mediatized, which derives its authority from its reference to the live etc'. (in Tasić 2011: 125). Auslander also contends that the 'mechanical [read: mediatized] reproduction' (Benjamin's phrase) of the 'original' in action can provide greater intimacy and immediacy of watching to the spectator, primarily by pronouncing the element of visibility. Drawing on Bolter and Grusin, Tasić evokes the notion of hypermediacy to clarify this further: 'art *always* involves mediation of some sort' and every 'medium is a medium' of another medium (125). Postdramatic theatre, in this respect, reworks the notions of immediacy, presence and liveness into the concept of intermediality as a process that generates 'the conditions for the [simultaneous] emergence of subjects and objects' (Grusin 2015: 129), or of 'two producing subjects', rather than reinforces 'the resemblance between a representation (or mediation) and its object' (Derrida, in Grusin 2015: 131).

Postdrama and politics

The central issue about postdramatic theatre is its perceived uneasy and ambiguous relationship with the political, which keeps returning for discussion by different routes. Lehmann's observation at the 2009 Belgrade theatre conference, held ten years after the publication of his *Postdramatic Theatre* in the original German, that some momentous events across the world reopened 'the dialogue between theatre and society by taking up more directly political and social issues' (2011: 34), has apparently made his position more problematic. He refers in his address to 9/11 of 2001, new wars, 'the rise of rightist populist leaders in Europe, [and] the restructuring of the whole ideological and political field after the "Wende"' (34). One may add to the list collapse of the US debt market in 2008, the Arab Spring in the Middle East, the ethnic conflict in South Asia and the widening gap between the rich and the poor all over the world. Lehmann now admittedly feels the need for theatre 'to deal more directly' with external realities, but also makes it clear that it still has 'no solutions or perspectives to offer' for social crises (34). No theatre, especially postdramatic, offers 'solutions'. But Lehmann sounds partly self-contradictory by conflating it with 'perspectives' because *form*, which he considers after George Lukács as the 'truly social dimension of art', grows out of external reality and provides critical perspectives, however tentative, on it (35). This understanding of 'perspective' would make better sense of Lehmann's observation that postdrama is not doing political theatre but *doing* theatre politically.

I do not agree with Lehmann that while the political sets the rules, art is transgressive, and, therefore, should avoid the political. I would argue that while the political in its deconstructive posturing can help break the law in art, art may not change its *status quo* and be transgressive necessarily. 'Theatre as an aesthetic behaviour' is surely unthinkable without transgression, but can the political as such be necessarily conceived as *not* 'an infringement of prescriptions' or 'interruption of the law' (Lehmann 2006: 178-9)? The 'political' in theatre, as I understand it, can surely rupture the received notions of reality by not allowing stabilization of their signification on the stage, or by being disruptive of long-held aesthetic rules, and thus change the way we *look at* things. More importantly, as Borowski and Sugiera maintain, the divide between art and politics from the time of Friedrich Schiller down to the mid-twentieth century is rather false (2013: 72). Jacques Rancière, who is critical of 'critical art' that lacks transformative strategies, also maintains that art can be political by reorganizing or redistributing the sensible, shared by people, within its aesthetic schema and serve as an analogue of social action by breaking down its formal hierarchies. This is surely different from the thematization of politics in theatre that may blunt the political potential of the aesthetic as well as from the 'aestheticization of politics' that normalizes the market logic of late capitalism extending into neoliberalism. It is 'the politics of aesthetics' that possibly better explains the complex relationship between postdrama and the political, but not shunning content or context as such. This 'new' political is achievable by effecting what Rancière describes as 'a sensory rupture within the continuity of the representative cause-effect schema' (in Woolf 2013: 46), but now mostly in tandem with an ideological steer that is not above interrogation. The political, as deconstructed or transgressive content in this case, is ultimately manifest in the form, thus shifting the focus on to the spectators and their relationship to theatre as performance.

Boyle, Cornish and Woolf maintain that form is central to contemporary works in theatre and performance – and form is no longer treated as ornamental to a production, merely illustrating action that is, in Lehmann's words, 'laden with suspense' or perpetuating the old relationship between 'drama's literary form (namely dialogue) and content' (2019: 3). Formalism in postdramatic theatre is not 'a celebration of "art for art's sake"' nor does it betray political indifference by championing apolitical elitist presentism (7–8, 16). This formalism, in spite of its own kind of self-reflexivity, is not 'ahistorical' (Martin Puchner) but rather grows out of the historical crisis of drama as noted by Szondi. Postdramatic formalism does not shift the focus from 'social text' to 'medium specificity'; it widens our idea of theatrical form 'in all its social complexity' (Boyle et al. 2019: 2, 11). It tries to bring the social and the aesthetic together in the face of all tension between them and show in the act of performance how form is both constituted by and constitutive of social formations. This encourages a whole reviewing of the relationship of form with content or context – which helps see how economy, power, culture, organizational structure of theatre bodies, emergent technologies, performance space and prevalent 'modes of labour and spectatorship' determine theatrical forms (15). Postdramatic formalism foregrounds theatre's own 'conditions of production and reception', which as a political act is not altogether separable from Brecht's focus on the material conditions of a dramatic situation (3–4) but which now stresses *form*'s historicity above everything else. This relates the 'experience of performance' to the process of theatre-making that is not disconnected from social and cultural conditions.

Lehmann seeks to overcome the polarity between the political and art (theatre included) in his 2009 lecture via Nicolas Bourriaud's 'relational aesthetics': 'Postdramatic theatre does not lose its aesthetic dimension as art if it gives up the notion of its autonomy and negotiates hybrid alignments with social, political, and other practices' (Lehmann 2011: 45). Lehmann's position on doing theatre politically becomes more concrete in the entry he writes for *In Terms of Performance*:

> I believe that the theater and art in general are moving away from a once highly productive value, the autonomy of art, and moving toward a different idea: to see art and theater as a 'mixing' [Legierung] of aesthetic praxis with other social forms of praxis that cannot be judged or even discussed in purely aesthetic terms. Therefore I welcome ... the understanding of theater abandoning a purely aesthetic silo and that is able to perceive without prejudice art and theater in pedagogical, social, political forms of praxis.
>
> 2016: online

This also enables a different reading of Lehmann's description of theatre as 'afformance art' (Lehmann 2006: 179). Following the world events mentioned earlier in this section, theatre has aligned itself with society in more ways than was envisioned in *Postdramatic Theatre*. Lehmann later locates theatre in a 'twilight zone between political activism and aesthetic practice' (Lehmann 2013: 87). This 'grey' zone of 'art and the political' is still fairly different from their relationship in conventional political theatre. There is no return to the coupling of drama and society since no social or individual crisis is perceived any more in the form of a well-defined conflict owing to the invisible operation of power and incessant spectacularization (or normalization) of issues by the media. The theatrical political now exists in 'moments of performance' outside the dramatic structure (89). If theatre still pretends to perform, it does so by being aware of its pretence; or else it flags the 'conflict' in a non-dialectical, discursive way where multiple political perspectives are inserted into the spectatorial experience to build up a discourse on 'action'. Dramaturgies and spectatorship in such theatre are often conceived in the tension between the post-Marxist logic of equivalence on one hand and the neoliberal logic of individual autonomy on the other (see Tomlin 2016).

The chapters

Taking its cue from the introduction that participates in the ongoing debates on the definition and scope of postdramatic theatre, Chapter 1 argues that the theatre paradigm has of late gone beyond the parameters and matrixes as identified by Lehmann within its generative European (and North American) contexts by travelling 'through different cultural and theatrical traditions' (Mazzilli 2017: 6) and thus augmenting itself. This chapter builds up a historical and conceptual premise for understanding India's nuanced relationship with this theatre form. The contemporary postdramatic, the regional going global and the global influencing the regional 'accounts for a variety of styles and influences' (6–7) in today's theatre. In the case of India, it means appropriating the European paradigm, cross-pollinating it with 'indigenous' performance traditions, pushing the boundaries of its ideological and cultural identity, and acquiring a mobility that would put the country's present theatre and performance culture in a complicated conversation with contemporary global performance aesthetics. Art forms cannot stay insulated in a porous, hybrid world of capital, culture and movement; nor do they completely lose their 'local' identity in the globalized space. This is a time of belonging between roots and routes. The chapter takes on board the theatre-makers' views and opinions; local contexts and occasions for the emergence of India's postdramatic; and lastly charts the evolving phases of India's postdramatic that are elaborately discussed in the subsequent chapters.

Chapter 2 deals with early adaptations and devised theatre (the distinction made between them is more fluid than fixed), which dwell between the dramatic and the postdramatic, but have the predominance of non-dramatic, and often non-textual, elements in them – such as visual dramaturgy, dance and music, materials that bracket animate body with inanimate objects, spatial experiments and the use of multimedia. These productions of the 1990s are made or devised from non-dramatic texts, literary as well as non-literary. While the adaptations discussed here have a storyline somewhere to begin from, the devised production I have chosen for this chapter ensued from no existing stories as such. The latter was made out of anecdotes and published interviews, although it reached the stage after 'rehearsals' that actually means a long process of devising.

Chapters 3, 4 and 5 are close critical analyses of a wide variety of postdramatic theatre and performance in twenty-first-century India. Chapter 3 discusses theatre between-the-arts, theatre and the new political, and theatre of scenography – de-dramatization of theatrical texts or non-dramatic performances of non-theatrical texts by combining word with a variety of other performance languages. Chapter 4 deals with theatre solos that are distinctive for single-artist performance and the performer's self-presentation. Chapter 5 takes into account theatre-as-event (theatre-as-walk included), theatre of the real, and theatre/performance installations – a cluster of works where the story element is nearly conspicuous by its absence and theatre as live art and real-time action take over. Chapter 6 is a reassessment of activism in contemporary Indian theatre and performance, balanced between ideological content and autonomous spectating. Each of these chapters studies radically new productions that show an increasingly postdramatic turn in the theatres of India since the beginning of the twenty-first century.

The conclusion discusses the multi-layered theatre-making in India from postdramatic perspectives, now under the separate heads of devising, writing, designing/dramaturging and directing, although such departmentalized understanding of theatre as an art form is nearly abandoned in contemporary training and practice and the ultimate aim is to arrive at an understanding of their interconnectedness.

By traversing the debate on theatre and performance since the publication of Lehmann's *Postdramatic Theatre* and placing contemporary Indian theatre in the middle of larger discourses on the re/presentation of the real, this volume is the first to add India to the 'postdramatic' conversation. It is an attempt to look beyond the 'dramatic' varieties of theatre in India, paying attention to the new performative turn that began in the 1990s and has since proliferated steadily in the direction of postdrama. The book strives to strike a balance between theory, contextualization and praxis. It should change the idea of Indian theatre that currently engages with social and political reality in ways beyond the conventions of the stage that primarily thematize issues.

1

Theorizing and Contextualizing India's Postdramatic

Adaptation as contribution

The translation into several European languages of Lehmann's *Postdramatisches Theater* (1999), the first systematic theoretical approach to the 'new theatre' in the West, had a strong impact on the academic and art scene by 2004, and its English version (*Postdramatic Theatre*, 2006) entered the English-speaking world and the global South within a year of its publication. It is worth examining how a relatively new European theatre paradigm influenced regional theatre scenes and was in turn influenced by their aesthetic-political logic – in other words, how it went global and, at the same time, allowed itself to be localized by its critical reception outside of Europe and the US. Vlatko Ilić has this to say (about his own Serbian theatre context): 'The process of generating an art scene in a particular cultural space is a constant work in progress ... [and] it seems necessary to re-examine the *postdramatic* paradigm in regard to the current contextual circumstances (above all, domestic ones)' (Ilić 2011: 138). Interestingly, Lehmann himself wrote along this line elsewhere later, presumably looking at the changing course of the 'postdramatic' in locations beyond his own:

> Postdramatic Theatre could and can be (and is indeed) read very differently depending on the culture, the tradition, and the current 'scene' of the particular theater of the region: for example, as a critique of the dominant European theater model; or as a practice allied with performance experiments in visual art; or as a critique of a conservative theater practice that remains comfortably secured within the never-questioned frame of a theater of representation ... This concept includes now, for example, dance theater, or performance; installation works, or a walk through a city; theater presents itself as close to a rehearsal, as an exhibition, or as a public debate.
>
> Lehmann 2016: online

The flexibility and latitude of interpretation Lehmann awards to his concept of postdramatic in his post-2001 writings might have been caused partly by the shifting political scenario across the world and partly by his increasing exposure to the potential of a plethora of emerging theatre forms beyond Central Europe and the US to add variations to a still-developing performance form. This formal shift, on the whole, has changed theatre-making globally.

The reasons for Indian theatre-makers looking for a new theatre aesthetic, not necessarily postdramatic, are different from those that drove their European/American counterparts to seek out forms of theatre-making beyond the dramatic. Also significant is the fact that long before the publication of Lehmann's book, non-dramatic, hybrid theatre practices had emerged in India out of different social, political and cultural circumstances, feeding an anti-realist/modernist theatre movement. At the same time, there is no reason to deny that the post-Brechtian, postdramatic theatre –widely practised by contemporary theatre-makers since the 1970s and historically charted in Lehmann's book for the first time – has impressed Indian practitioners with a greater sense of contemporary relevance and helped them re-territorialize their own 'field of ... practice and theory' (Ilić 2011: 138). An equation of 'postdramatic' and 'post-Brechtian' is not implied here. The former does not organize 'historical reality' dialectically, as 'post-Brechtian' may be argued to still do, but instead flattens it to avoid specificity of referentiality and certitude of action. Nor is this to prioritize one paradigm over the other, or to draw a binary between the West and the East with a view to subjugating the local to the global, or even to imply that the postdramatic in India is an imitation of a Western performance idiom.

Formalistic and intermedial hybridity characterizes postdramatic theatre. Cross-pollination of cultural forms has been common in Indian theatre. Acknowledging his connectedness to Western dramatic theatre, Girish Karnad wrote in 1989: 'Oddly enough the play [*Yayati*] owed its form not to the innumerable mythological plays I had been brought up on ... but to Western playwrights whom until then I had only read in print' (Karnad 1994: 3). The task for Habib Tanvir, another stalwart in modern Indian theatre, was to accept all that can help make theatre of one's own times – from Western naturalistic theatre to Indian classical theatre to 'a greater amalgamation' in theatre of the various arts including music, dance, literature and painting (in Deshpande et al. 2009: 11). However, the basic point of difference my project has with their work is that heterogeneity now aids a sort of theatre-making that is hardly dramatic any more. In spite of the hybridity in the theme and structure of Karnad's theatre and its multiplicity of perspective, his *Hayavadana* (1970), for example, employs a text-driven linear narrative and the fourth wall. Tanvir's *Agra Bazar* (1955, 1989) leaves the proscenium setting, partly abandons the storyline and fills the space with bazaar noise, different types of speech and song, while his *Charandas Chor* (1974, 1977) makes use of the Nacha performance tradition to stage a Rajasthani folktale. Yet, in the ultimate analysis, his theatre shows an imposed 'proscenium discipline' (Tanvir's own phrase) and remains folkloric (depending on story and its scenic representation), albeit with a significant presence of non-dramatic elements in it.

In fact, the kind of theatre this book encompasses has the appearance of intercultural theatre but in a globalized space. This is not to identify postdrama with intercultural theatre but to point out the changed cultural space in which the postdramatic began a nuanced dialogue with Indian theatre after the 1980s. While the book recognizes that the cultural imperialist exploitation by Western theatre of traditional non-Western cultures is still a possibility, it also admits that contemporary non-Western cultures no less adapt Euro-American performance aesthetics into making *their* theatres that would simultaneously seek to preserve elements of indigenous practice. The book equally addresses the rethinking of the essentialist conception of culture, and thereby of intercultural theatre as well, following the weakening of the notions of 'national' and 'indigenous' in an atmosphere of cultural deterritorialization and a new cultural hybridization stemming from 'diasporic public spheres' (Appadurai 1996). This is different from our idea of 'globalized performance' (Pavis 2010) but relates considerably to a glocalized management of theatre in a porous world. Equally instructive in this context is Gerhard Steingress's observation that the concept of interculturality or transculturality has been surpassed by the contemporary concept of hybridization which 'in a multicultural contact situation ... creates a new meaning and a new subcultural community from transgression' (in Orosa-Roldán and López-López 2018: 40).

Contemporary theatre in India is neither naïvely imitative of the West nor enthusiastically nativist because the very presumption of reductivist essentialism about a particular culture, as mentioned above proves problematic in our times. Intercultural theatre (the term has not lost its usage yet) no longer worries about issues of legitimacy and 'representational authenticity' (Dalmia 2009: 290), as it did in the 1970s or 80s, because cultures are now 'intertwined' (Pavis 2010). More importantly, 'intercultural' adaptations and appropriations in contemporary theatre mostly remain restricted to what Vasudha Dalmia calls 'a preoccupation with technique' (2009: 285) or to what Lehmann describes as 'inter-artistic exchange'. '[W]e are dealing here more with an "iconophilia"', as he argues after Andrzej Wirth, 'than with interculturalism' as an anthropological postulate. 'Intercultural' today, even in Indian contexts, is 'not just "cultures" as such that meet but concrete artists, art forms, and theatre productions' (Lehmann 2006: 176). This ensures a different kind of exchange in times of mobile cultures existing in a double bind of particularity and mutual mediation: it is an inter-artistic exchange that must be distinguished from the representation of a culture per se (176). Theatre-as-performance in our times is driven more by hybridity at the formal level of production than by contextual relocation of an ethnoscape. Sociocultural 'reality' still has its context and specificity, but no longer immune from extraneous influences. Hence one has to reckon that the concept of intercultural theatre itself has undergone serious changes following the postmodern notion of culture and representation. Rustom Bharucha's long-standing attempt to disentangle Indian culture from its decontextualized use in the West's intercultural theatre does not seem much relevant today (see Dalmia 2009: 282–303) because no intercultural theatre in its mutated, or constantly mutating, form attempts to represent or imitate a 'foreign' culture that itself has not undergone mediation.

It is also important to remember that postdramatic theatre, when it emerged in Europe, was a practice in hybridity not in the realm of culture but in that of performance language. The question of inter-/transculturality enters into our discussion only when the practice is viewed in a location beyond its place and history of birth. The purpose of this book is to demonstrate how the contemporary theatre of India can participate in the larger debates on postdramatic practice and contribute significantly to the ongoing paradigm shift in theatre-making in general. In so doing, theatre in India performs a tightrope walk balancing between the changing notion of 'Indian' and the equally fluid understanding of 'Western', aligning with the traditional in an altered environment and adapting the global to reinvent itself. When it comes to practice, various cultural and aesthetic spaces appear more liminal and mutually negotiable now than they were until the 1990s, although no cultural or performance tradition can ever get totally erased in this new enterprise called 'glocal'.

Theatre-makers in (urban) India have not certainly built their works on the European 'post'. None of those interviewed, or whose works I discuss, said that it had a direct impact on their practice. But several of them have welcomed the postdramatic protocols of performative plurality and structural democracy and practised them in experimental, transnational ways. Their primary aim has been to invigorate and pluralize the language of Indian urban theatre that had turned stale under the stronghold of realism as a baggage of colonial stage practice and, at the same time, fairly prescriptive and homogeneous under the decolonizing drive of the 'theatre of roots' movement post-independence. Several of them abandoned linear narratives producing a 'fictive cosmos' via mimesis as imitation. They also broke with the postcolonial-nationalist tendency to institutionalize through theatre an 'Indian' culture in sync with the hegemonic state narrative of nationhood. The 'transnational' attempted by them means different things at once – going beyond a 'national' ideology performed through a 'national' aesthetic, adapting new Eurocentric performance language to a non-European theatre in a different historical setting, and adding new dimensions to the Western paradigm by cross-pollinating it with regional/traditional cultural and art forms. Indian theatre-makers experimented with their new forms not being conscious of Lehmann, but what they did in their own contexts fell much in line with some aspects of the kind of theatre that he highlights while theorizing his 'postdramatic'. Later, over the last two decades or so, their exposure to the postdramatic theatres outside of India, in conjunction with their training in the flexible and eclectic performance traditions of India, encouraged them to make their own version/s of postdramatic theatre around situations from home and the world. The conjunction 'and' in the (principal) title of my book, rather than a straight 'in', is a pointer to India's nuanced and layered relationship with the global postdramatic.

Predramatic and postdramatic

Deepa Punjani, in her lecture 'Initial Thoughts on the Curious Case of Postdramatic Theatre in the Indian Context', says: 'Lehmann's critical contribution to the discourse of theatre ... becomes very helpful ... in an upside-down manner to actually appreciate the dimensions of theatre in India that beat homogeneous descriptions. Here, "Postdramatic" can be construed as an overarching term that gives a historical insight into the multiplicity and diversity of Indian theatrical traditions that defy more conventional definitions of drama' (2018: online). There is no denying that the predramatic theatre in India was performance-centred – the reason why several European/Western theatre-makers or playwrights looked to India (and South East Asia) to radicalize their theatre which was predominantly representational. For example, Eugenio Barba visited India in 1963 to learn Kathakali and take it back to the Laboratory Theatre in Poland. Much of the predramatic theatre in India did employ multiple performance modalities including dance, music, movement and poetry. Indian performance traditions are also rooted in tribal/ethnic ritualistic practices. But one should not conflate (although many do) 'predramatic' with 'postdramatic' and commit the error of taking the 1990s performance trend as a continuation of unmediated traditional forms accommodating new themes. The 1990s mark the beginning of a *new* turn to performance. Let us first go to Lehmann's differentiation between pre- and postdramatic: 'Ancient tragedy, Racine's dramas and Robert Wilson's visual dramaturgy are all forms of theatre. Yet, assuming the modern understanding of drama, one can say that the former is "predramatic," that Racine's plays are undoubtedly dramatic theatre, and that Wilson's "operas" have to be called "postdramatic"' (Lehmann 2006: 34). For Peter Szondi, whom Lehmann directly draws on for his theory of postdrama, the third phase of what both broadly call the drama signalled a tentative solution of its crisis as a literary product that is reflected in the rupture between its content and form when put on stage. But Lehmann moves past this phase as represented by Erwin Piscator and Bertolt Brecht, among others, to look for a more definite sense of liberation from the literariness of drama and a move towards theatre-as-performance or theatre-as-theatre because, for him, 'epicizing distance' was not enough (34). As Neelam Mansingh Chowdhry from India observes in this context, one must take care to distinguish theatre from drama: 'Theatre is not an accessory to dramatic literature' (Chowdhry 2019: 50). Many forms of 'speech and action', banished from 'absolute drama' or 'true drama' during and after the Renaissance – or several performance elements in traditional Indian theatre, for that matter – returned to postdrama that emerged out of a complex of different historical and cultural factors. These contexts have received attention in the introduction and will now be discussed from Indian perspectives especially. But in no way does this mean for India that the postdramatic was already in its performance tradition when the West was struggling to get over what Szondi calls the historical 'crisis of drama'.

When it comes to India, the predramatic is also the precolonial. The advent of the colonial stage in the mid-nineteenth century posed a threat to indigenous performance traditions that include the Sanskrit plays, Kutiyattam, Kathakali, Yakshagana, Palas, puppetry and so on. These forms made a comeback to India's 'theatre of roots' during the 1970s but were in fact appropriated for the urban, (alternatively) modern stage that combined 'specific traditional Indian performance practices with Western [realist] theatrical conventions' (Mee 2008: 26). When some such traditional performance forms are used in some recent theatre productions that I have identified to be India's postdramatic, the context and purpose of their return appear strikingly different because, now within Indian/Western modernist/postmodernist frames, they bring in a different aesthetic that *makes* theatre in a political way. This never means that the 'pre' returns to the 'post' unmediated, or reappears to be redesignated as 'post', as if there were no changes and shifts for millennia in human and performance history. When traditional forms enter into Indian theatre post-1990s and interact with a set of contemporary performance protocols in response to changed social communication and cultural conditions, a new kind of theatre-making ensues. Moreover, the performative turn in Indian theatres since the 1990s involves many contemporary cultural forms that have no connection to traditional forms of performance – such as video art and theatre, immersive theatre, cinematographic theatre and performance installations. The postdramatic forms of twenty-first-century Indian theatre need to be seen in terms of broader social, political and cultural *form*ations during the late twentieth and early twenty-first centuries. But I would like to clarify further what I mean by 'India's postdramatic' before I call attention to those formations.

India's postdramatic

I have thought a great deal about the appropriateness of a 'postdramatic approach' to the study of Indian theatre since the 1990s and wondered, before settling for it, about other alternative approaches – such as 'modern', 'avant-garde', 'postmodern', 'contemporary', 'experimental' and so on. But considering the scope and scale of the present project, which aspires to bring into a flexible frame a wide range of theatre practice, I found each such alternative inadequate to hold the variety together. There are books on Indian theatre which individually focus on the 'theatre of roots', the 'politics of modern Indian theatre', gender in contemporary theatre, post-independence Indian theatre and the like. But they leave out, or had little scope to engage with, the modalities of practice over the last three decades that my project looks into under a label ('postdramatic') that has the plasticity to accommodate them together without subsuming their differences from one another. The book shall take on board the past scholarship on contemporary Indian theatre but, at the same time, seek to avoid the old East–West binary and argue that 'postdramatic theatre, though conceived and developed in the West', has – as Mary Mazzilli puts it in her book on Gao Xingjian – 'a transnational resonance' (2017: 5).

No discourse on postdramatic theatre's relationship with India is possible unless what happened between the 1950s and 1980s is glanced through. The debate on what constitutes '*Indian* theatre' took the first four decades since 1947, marginalizing in the process several theatre genres and subgenres, regional as well as Western. The first drama seminar organized by the Sangeet Natak Akademi (SNA) in independent India in 1956 promoted native performance forms that would enact an 'alternative modernity' (Mee 2008) on the urban proscenium stage. Despite the historical importance of the seminar which grew out of a strong postcolonial national consciousness, as noted above, it eventually erased the Parsi theatre and the political theatre of the Left-led Indian People's Theatre Association (IPTA), to pave the way for 'a totally new' theatre meant to retrieve a usable cultural past, to put it in Anita Cherian's words, and build a transhistorical 'nationalist narrativ[e]' (2012: online). In spite of the performative turn it provided to modern Indian theatre by emphasizing the element of physicality, troubling aesthetics of realism with a return to the *rasa* theory, and by creating an imaginative audience (all of which one finds in the theatre of Kavalam Narayana Panikkar), the 'roots' practice primarily built on the search for an exclusive national-cultural identity through a decontextualized use of indigenous performance forms on the urban stage. While the very aspiration to decolonize the stage by cleansing it of all Western influences looked unrealistic – the proscenium stage often used for roots productions is itself a Western performance space and 'Indian' cultural forms in general had long become palimpsestic – the agenda of a 'national' theatre to be developed on recommended guidelines inspired by elite, Sanskritic traditions seemed no less colonizing (see Prakash 2010). The arbitrary mixing of dialogue (whose predominance continued as the story did not go out of the roots theatre) with songs, dance and martial arts meant for many an exotic spectacle that masked the form–content dialectic. The 'theatre of roots' continued to elide experiments with forms and styles outside its prescriptive models that produced on stage an illusion of the progressive evolution of culture, history and ideology of the nation.

An exception in this regard is the 'roots' theatre of Ratan Thiyam, which with its 'formalized aesthetics' (Mitra 2014: 80) not only became 'globally legible' (Kapur 2010: 48) but challenged the state version of nationhood and cultural nationalism in the process. Hailing from Manipur, an erstwhile independent state merged with India in 1949 by an agreement whose legality is still perceived by many Manipuris to be suspect, Thiyam's hyperstylized appropriation of the regional folk during the 1980s 'challenged the SNA's construction' of national theatre. While showing a way out of the Western modern realist theatre practice, a parallel phenomenon since the 1960s, his performance-oriented theatre (for example, *Chakravyuha*) critiqued state oppression of Manipuri citizens for their demands for self-determination (see Mee 2008: 223–62). Thiyam's indigenous visual dramaturgy, open to 'inter-artistic exchange' globally, can definitely be considered as a forerunner of postdramatic scenography in contemporary Indian theatre. But long before Thiyam the plays of Mohan Rakesh had pushed the course of Indian theatre in a different direction of experimentation. An important modernist figure since he seriously experimented with the 'dramatic form itself' to engage with the 'fragmentation of "reality"' (Dalmia 2009: 136), Rakesh's theatre appeared remarkably different in his time for his characters without definite contours, his use of language as a failed medium of communication and his rejection of realism and naturalism in the absence of stable reality. Vasudha Dalmia's quotations from Rakesh's research notes on theatre are highly illuminating: 'Words as part of this multidirectional use of sound … may bid farewell to literature in the conventional sense and belong exclusively to theatre' (137). Dalmia maintains that Rakesh comes close to Peter Handke in separating movement from sound and often sound from words. While Thiyam took the 'folk' (public) route to Indian avant-garde, Rakesh preferred to experiment with (and problematize) subjectivity (137). However, we are not going to discuss further the theatres of Thiyam and Rakesh since their works, hallmarks of modernism in Indian theatre by different denominations, have been adequately discussed by theatre scholars.

What is found in the theatres of Thiyam and Rakesh – predominance of scenography, devising, undermining of textuality, narrative fragmentation, disintegration of character and experiment with sound – partly characterized India's theatre prior to the Nehru Theatre Festival of 1989. But the constellation of these elements around a plot in ruins brought forth stylistic moments only during the 1990s that can be considered nascently postdramatic in regional as well as transnational variations. The *new* turn in performance paradigms and protocols, often considered as having heralded the Indian 'avant-garde', initially came via 'the intimate, non-linear, non-naturalistic performances' of female directors of the 1990s (Mitra 2014: 80–1), which soon inspired their students, current or former, to experiment with form more vigorously in the following decades. Even as one may cautiously extrapolate the term 'avant-garde' from its Euro-American history to use it in Indian contexts (as Sudipto Chatterjee does), many of the strands and shades Indian theatre productions have acquired in recent times may refuse to be bracketed by that label – for example, the theatre solos of Maya Krishna Rao (*A Deeper Fried Jam*, 2002 and *Ravanama*, 2011); the documentary-type reality theatre of Anuradha Kapur and Ein Lall (*The Antigone Project*, 2003–4) and of Amitesh Grover (*Notes on Mourning*, 2016); Abhilash Pillai's theatre as media reportage (*The Island of Blood*, 2003); his cinematic theatre (*Midnight's Children*, 2005); and Deepan Sivaraman's scenographic theatre (*Peer Gynt*, 2010 and *The Legend of Khasak*, 2015). The list may also include Grover's theatre-as-event (*Downtime*, 2014), the performance installations of Zuleikha Chaudhari (*The Transparent Performer I, II and III*, 2011–14) and Anamika Haksar (*Composition on Water*, 2016). The (historical) 'avant-garde' is more an epochal term in Europe than 'postdramatic'. Spanning over the first decades of the twentieth century, it formulated and practised new, radical aesthetic forms with a view to bringing changes in society, politics and culture, but serving in the case of theatre the 'representation of textual worlds' on the whole (Lehmann 2006: 22). The neo-avant-garde of the 1960s not only institutionalized art and thus blunted the avant-garde's revolutionary newness but ultimately preserved in theatre the correspondence between the text and its performance (ibid.: 56). I would like to argue that 'postdramatic' as a paradigm emerged over a much longer period of time, especially following the mediatization of society, covering an explosion of experimental theatre forms in Europe and America (including the avant-gardes), and reinventing itself constantly in multiple 'foreign' locations after it left 'home' or in response to the changing sociopolitical situation across the globe. It is also applicable aesthetically for analysing the contemporary hybrid theatre-making practice in India which nevertheless grew out of its own glocal context. Postdramatic theatre can be both modernist and postmodernist – and so it is in India, too. India's postdramatic at once strives to create meaning through artistic autonomy, but with no 'internal logic' of a story (Lehmann 2006: 26), and also accepts an anti-representationalism that only celebrates a stylistic heterogeneity.

The paradox, if you will, of India's postdramatic is that it *began* as a sort of 'doing' within the theatre that was not, however, disconnected from activism in lived life. This is done in a manner that combined the dramatic with the non-dramatic, the signifying with the self-referential, and the pre-conceptual with the perceptual – which is to say, in a manner that is different from both Lehmann's standardization of 'postdramatic' and India's long-held colonial and postcolonial 'dramatic'. In fact, this 'double-diagnosis' is very much in the conception of the postdramatic itself. As Brandon Woolf (2013: 41) says, 'any move beyond the representational entails a deep engagement with representation itself'. And while 'the postdramatic critically questions the representational status of the dramatic, and foregrounds "real" elements, it also clings tightly to its [own] aesthetic (or representational) status' bringing in a process of signification that is nevertheless different from that in the dramatic type (ibid.). India's postdramatic, especially at its formative stage, consisted in the intersection of the 'social subject' and the 'aesthetic event' (Jackson 2013: 169) even though it primarily sought to expose contradictions in social gestures. A bulk of postdramatic theatre in India has made 'an attempt to dismantle the logic' by which a particular system of theatre practice, and 'behind that a whole system of political structures [and] ... social institutions', maintains its domination (Eagleton 2003: 128). This system involves the institution of dramatic theatre with its structural apparatus to subjugate the spectators to a preconceived narrative. The thoroughly depoliticized tribe of postdramatic performance where formal autonomy does not operate beyond the dynamics of the market in operation is another story altogether.

The forerunners of India's postdramatic, which may include non-dramatic performances such as *The Job*, *Sundari* (Kapur 1997–8), *Kitchen Katha*

(Chowdhry 1999) and *Antaryatra* (Haksar 1993), demonstrate a 'subtle interplay' of content with form, representation with presentation, thematization with physicality and sensuousness, and materiality with simulation rather than a sharp binary opposition between these coordinates. While Kapur's stage adaptation of Brecht's *The Job* tells through a hybrid language – traditional painting and music, installation of created objects and video projection – the story of a widow compelled to impersonate her husband to get his job posthumously, *Sundari* plays out the autobiography of an early twentieth-century Indian female impersonator by deconstructing gender through movements of the body and repeated changes of dress on a set spectacularly designed by famous Indian painters. Chowdhry's *Kitchen Katha* builds up a richly sensuous world on stage by making the performance a potpourri of folk dance and music, real-time action and self-reflexive telling of a love story. She has tried in her own Punjabi folk style to go beyond a theatre of dramatic representation. She is not interested in illustrating a text. Her plays are text-based, but she lets the text 'travel, change and evolve' on the stage (Chowdhry 2019: 51). Haksar's *Antaryatra* dismantles the stereotype of a woman from an Indian epic by projecting her inner journey through innovative spatial designs and by splitting the subject into diverse objects of landscape and drawings. Haksar's unique spatial designs, emphasis on poetry, use of body and its movement (including dance) and her visual dramaturgy redefined the theatre of India, bringing forth an experimental trail. 'Content has to *invent* a form when there's none readily available for it', she says (2019: 52). She subverts the existing forms to enable a transition of Indian theatre from authorship to collaboration, from text and dialogue to scenography.

India being a part of the so-called Third World arguably remains a historically dialectical, political society, and its theatre, despite its significant break with realism and shift to a non-realistic/non-dramatic language, sustains an endeavour to engage – but less by planting a preconceived meaning in a dialectically structured 'fictive cosmos' than by problematizing it through a layered story/telling. In response to the question if the story is important to her, Kapur says: 'I would say that the story is not a pre-given for me – it may be only a concern to begin from. If a story is already there, I devise it towards an adaptation' (2019c: 54). She does it in a manner to ensure active spectating that contains her political logic. 'Sometimes there may not be a story, just an idea or an image that instigates a performance. The process is important here', Kapur adds (54). Deepan Sivaraman's mode of storytelling is radically different from his predecessors', and so is his politics of engagement from many of his contemporaries'. When asked how he would describe his theatre, Sivaraman says: 'I don't want to make a dramatic plot development to make a statement. What makes theatre still exciting and socially meaningful is its ability to offer a multi-sensorial experience in a choreographed space and time. An object or a ritual act may deliver this experience better than the spoken text. Sivaraman appreciates the way '[t]heatre-makers of the West – such as Foreman, Kantor or Wilson and recently Ivo van Hove – have dealt with stories, but in a de-dramatized, fragmented manner. Plot is walking away from the theatre, and with it the whole dramatic structure' (Sivaraman 2019b: 61–2). Postdramatic theatre in India has also redeployed the element of story with a historical past in a way that makes allowances for discourse, but raising questions about the nature of the very discourse, as in Zuleikha Chaudhuri's *Rehearsing the Witness* (2015-18) and *Landscape as Evidence* (2017). This also challenges our 'assumptions regarding stable [and] consistent ... identities and the construction of credible narratives', whether in the theatre or in the court of law (Chaudhari 2019: 57).

Is there any dialectic in this process of engagement? The thematic dialectic, when present in such theatre, is expanded through scenography, music, multimedia and corporeality to the extent of being deprived of a closure, or pushed to the degree of an undecidability that culminates in the dilution, if not dissolution, of dialectic as such – the latter being more apparent in Pillai's *Island of Blood* (2002) and *Helen* (2009), and Sivaraman's *Spinal Cord* (2009) and *It's Cold in Here* (2014). *Island* is cast in the form of a seamless stream of television newsfeed that lacks linearity as well as veracity; and *Helen* presents reality as a symptom rather than a substance in theatricalizing the Iraq war of 2003 as a video game. Pillai makes his theatre by interlacing the mediums of film, video footage, text, music and movement: it presents his politics in the form he chooses for his work at hand that avoids plot development through dramatic collision. He uses the new media (especially recorded video material) to 'introduce other ways of looking at the stage and the self-reality it seeks to create' (Pillai 2019: 60). Both of Sivaraman's productions, as mentioned above, are developed scenographically, fragments of text merging with visual dramaturgy instead of visuals illustrating the text dialectically. This variety of postdramatic theatre 'enables reflection' on norms and conventions (Jürs-Munby, Carroll and Giles 2013: 25) without organizing the 'real' ideologically and, therefore, bearing no clear blueprint for social change. None of the productions cited above, are, however, detached from society. While Pillai's show the devastating effects of war (including civil wars), Sivaraman's offer fractured pictures of human atrocities within the family and outside.

This does not evidently mean a total separation of stage and external reality. The interrogation of an integral and determinate reality, different as it is from the earlier interrogation of 'the conceptual possibility of the real' (Tomlin 2016: 117), complicated the already-existing 'crisis of representation'

(Alcoff, in ibid.) at the close of the last century. Onstage action, nevertheless, may 'partake of referentiality', Jerome Carroll notes, since it is seldom separable from 'a web of attitudes and assumptions . . . beyond the confines of theatre'. Only this in postdramatic theatre is 'characterized by connotations that do not translate into clear, discursive meaning' but function as 'vestigial' references (Carroll 2013: 252–3), as several recent productions in India will show. Deepan Sivaraman, for instance, prefers delineating the narrative without structuring it *dramatically*. He would like to explore its experiential potential for spectators, irrespective of their backgrounds, by bolstering the reality status of the performance. Indian audiences are fairly acquainted with theatre's physical/material form and its self-reality that are often evoked (for self-definition) against the Western realist mode of representation, Sivaraman maintains. India's new theatre, according to him, has exploited this advantage by 'making objects/signs work well within their specific contexts' and thus engendering a relatively fluid semiology, one without any stable relations of signification. This may, however, still 'share some dramatic positioning or possibilities but definitely seeks to avoid direct dramatic representation' (Sivaraman 2016). In such theatre situations, the 'aesthetic of responsibility' (Lehmann 2006: 185) rests as much with the spectator as with the theatre-maker. This responsibility comes not from an unproblematic affirmation but from a contemplated reaction processed both perceptually and cognitively.

The postdramatic in India has remobilized itself over time, coming far away from mimetic representation on one hand and striving, on the other, for the experiential through new forms and performance strategies. In place of narrativization of external reality, now we have in theatre its self-referential construction or dispersal, use of parallel performance languages to break the tubular viewing of a happening onstage, devising to layer the 'fictive cosmos' or shatter it, video projections exposing certain conditions of 'reality' without any claims to authenticity. Most productions of the present century include real-time activities and events inserting the spectator into the performance, solos where the body speaks without being subservient to text, if any, and multimedia applications. Experimental theatre in India today lends performance a sense of presence that has no metaphysics about it or pride in its purity, but grows out of the materiality of art, physicality of performance, reflexivity of form, and with a readiness to accept any possible leakage of that presence.

Recent productions such as Maya Krishna Rao's *Heads are Meant for Walking Into* (2005); the multi-artist project *409 Ramkinkars* (2015); Chaudhari's *Propositions: On Text and Space* series (2010–12); Grover's *Encounter* (2014) and *Leaky Folds* (2017); Kapur and Sivaraman's *Dark Things* (2018); and Sivaraman's *Work in Progress: A Nationalism Project* (2018) should substantiate this claim. First, the variety of form is impressive: theatre as cross-media performance treating both humans and materials as agential, theatre as promenade work and spatial experience, theatre as performance-installation, theatre as performative exchange of information, theatre as digital intervention in the job market, theatre as plurimedial experiment, and theatre as 'public artefact', respectively. What characterizes these shows taken together is the use of non-conventional space, everydayness of life, prominence of onstage labour, processuality, durationality and technological reproduction of the 'live' with a kind of 'presence' about it that teases the sensorium and generates a participatory, immersive experience alongside 'flashlike cognition' (Weigel 2015: 361). Experiencing this postdramatic 'real' is not possible by way of seeking an imitative relationship between the world and its stage image; it happens, according to Hal Foster, 'between the perception and consciousness of a subject *touched* by an image'. The spectator becomes of supreme importance in this new conception of re/presentation that thrives on the skilful 'shifting of the borderline between fictionality and reality' (in Borowski and Sugiera 2007: xxv–xxvi) and making the spectator aware of the process of this shifting.

In India's postdramatic, fictionality keeps returning by different routes to reinstate the political – but now via a parallax view produced of the performance, through 'a series of more complex and tenuous mediations between seeming binaries' of theatre and event (Woolf 2013: 39). The performed real 'within a situation that is somehow real' (Jürs-Munby et al. 2013: 15) enables the 'politics of perception' through such theatre's different sign usage (Lehmann 2006: 185). It is a negotiation between theatre's aestheticity and an event's externality that is more complex than ever before because of the double bind of knowledge that theatre must go beyond representation and, at the same time, cannot be a social situation on stage without being a performative reality. It is not that this knowledge was not available before, but it was not self-consciously worked into the very act of theatre-making. Kapur and Lall's *The Antigone Project* (theatre as text, movement and film footage), Sivaraman's *The Cabinet of Dr Caligari* (an interplay of performance design with a play of shadows and visuals, 2015), and Pillai's *Talatum* (theatre-as-circus, 2016) may serve as illustrations: innovative theatrical forms engaging with and again refracting from referentiality. The self-evident play between this engagement and that refraction is a '"process" of creating performance itself' (Grover 2012: online) and thus of its eventness, which has given the theatre in India a distinctive postdramatic turn in the twenty-first century. Zuleikha Chaudhari, for one, investigates the nature of performance by developing a series of questions to interrupt the narrative structure and probes the formation of images and the process of experience or its production. Her work explores the relationship of text and performer, text and visual, performer and spectator, and 'the tension between looking or watching and doing or acting' (Chaudhari 2019: 56).

Occasions and contexts

The factors that count for the new pattern of hybridization in Indian theatre and performance include the emergence of women directors who were experimenting with a plural language to free their work from the long-held realist-naturalist (male) tradition, the opening of the world market in India in 1991 leading to an encounter of cultures within a frame of consumerism, artistic exchanges through international theatre festivals, pedagogic changes in theatre training schools with an accent on cultural inclusiveness, the availability of foreign sponsorships to contemporary theatre-makers to take their productions abroad and the search for a theatre idiom for 'Indian' material that would be legible to the audience at home and abroad. Most importantly, the fast spread of multimedia and digital technology gives dramatic theatre a chase while providing the new generation of theatre practitioners with hitherto inaccessible resources to contemporize their art on a global competitive basis. The contextual analysis below is, therefore, vital to understanding the postdramatic turn in Indian theatre and performance.

I Autonomous women's movement

The autonomous women's movement beginning in 1970s India around issues of rape, dowry, domestic violence and other forms of gender discrimination outside the family had its effect felt on a whole society and its art forms. Women's literature, theatre and performance were directly affected by it. The generation of women directors who emerged in the 1970s and 1980s, as theatre-maker Kirti Jain (2001: 23) observes, gradually started building their work on women's issues and experience. But it was not until the 1990s that several women directors stormed into the theatre scene with a different approach to *practice* – often to the chagrin of their male counterparts who had long dominated the world of playwriting and directing. These female directors questioned and subverted the existing 'orthodox theorism' of realist Hindi theatre, Anuradha Kapur tells the author (2016), purposely bringing in an excess of colour and objects, interrogating the primacy of text and indulging in concrete imagery. Aware of the essentialist tendency of feminism of those times and of its copiousness, Kapur maintains (2001: 5) that 'feminist theatre' in India is 'a tentative designation' for working on the 'sort of experience that may not have found visibility until now' and for proposing 'the idea of a "woman's language" in theatre'. The issues came from lived life, but found freedom from the existing theatre practice rooted in privileges of gender, language and performance aesthetics. As Heiner Müller notes, as long as the practice of art is rooted 'in privileges, works of art will tend to be prisons' (in Case 1983: 101). The major productions of Indian women directors were attempts to challenge the power structure within the theatre institutions and work towards liquidation of the hierarchy of director, playwright and the star actor. This rendered irrelevant many earlier debates over the Indianness of India's theatre. Rather, the focus now shifted from decolonization to an interweaving of traditional Indian aesthetics with (Western) modernism and postmodernism in theatre and performance arts. The pursuit of a single India was abandoned for 'a far more contingent and contestatory approach, a tactic of surviving in an increasingly ... globalizing cultural landscape' (Mitra 2014: 65). Contextually, the moment does not parallel the postdramatic moment in Europe, but the trappings of contemporary global practice (arguably) helped women directors better articulate their sense of autonomy and collaborative spirit in art and culture.

The result was a *new* 'turn to performance' in Indian theatre, from the dominance of the playscript to the rethinking of theatre's aesthetics. Plot and character remained important elements of theatre for some time to come, but the 'plot/character configuration [now moved] towards a new set of subjectivities where change in the way of drawing character [resulted] in redrawing the parameters of plot' (Kapur 2001: 6). Character becomes a field of indeterminate possibilities, no longer an entity in need of psychological realism or linear development (7). Realist characterization is replaced by 'performing soliloquies and monologues, stylized gesture' and 'ceremonial procedures' (Lehmann 2006: 21), by 'posture employed in order to bring to mind figuration as in paintings' and direct address demanding a dialogue with the audience (Kapur 2001: 8). Consequently, plot meant no conventional development of action, with character changing status, objects redefining social relationships, and dialogic communication losing its relevance in most cases. The element of story did not leave the stage so early, but it came in fragments, integrated, if at all, only by chance procedures or in the spectator's reflective intelligence. Making 'room for interjections, lapses in concentration and focus', accompanied by 'stylization and [hyper]naturalism', or collapsing the 'incommensurable worlds' within a spatial structure, as seen in Anamika Haksar's work, became the new rule of theatre (Kapur 2001: 10). The devising of plays and improvisation became a norm, as with Kirti Jain and Neelam Mansingh Chowdhry.

Visual dramaturgy gave women directors the freedom to see the world as they wished to. They ventured into 'areas that we were not specialists in', says Kapur (2019c: 54). Yet they made an attempt to move 'beyond a closed discipline', beyond 'one way of looking at things' into the 'porous aspects of the discipline called theatre' (Kapur 2016). The stage, sometimes decked with installations and paintings, generated a multi-layered experience that could never be expected from a realist dramatic world of cardboard characters in a 'set of architectural quotations like sofas and door frames and curtains' (ibid.). By using visual aesthetics, women theatre-makers wanted to visibilize the process of gendering, as in Kapur's *Nayika Bhed* (1990) and *Sundari* (1997): 'the *process of showing* ... how bodies are "materialized as sexed"' (my italics; Kapur 2001: 10). They built their work on visual and musical narratives that run parallel to text and action. In this straying, elliptical style of storytelling, even 'words and actions are made to detach themselves from the biography of the main character' and 'the presence of many "hands" as it were [read: as it actually was] in the making of the theatre pieces' is felt as a consequence of collaborations that strove to avoid the tendencies of a single authorial signature' (11). New texts for the theatre started emerging out of long dialogues between the playwright, the director, the designer, actors and visual artists. The storyline, when present, no longer remained a pre-given but evolved out of such collaboration (Kapur 2016) and research-based improvisation.

The relationship between postdramatic theatre and feminist practice is arguably problematic. Many scholars favour the political style of Brechtian theatre in dealing with women's issues over postdramatic theatre's 'elliptical, affective' style which, according to Janelle Reinelt, abandons direct engagement with or representation of a political sphere outside of the stage. While Reinelt thinks that the postdramatic in general is 'incompatible with serious politics' (in Boyle, Cornish and Woolf 2019: 6), Birgit Haas goes further to say that postdramatic theatre 'is "postpolitical" and politically dispiriting for activists' (ibid.). Although Lehmann admired She She Pop's postdramatic work, and even Sarah Kane's new texts, he does not include feminist productions in his panorama of postdramatic theatre possibly because of their usual activist bias. He is in favour of 'the energetic properties of the signifier' on stage (Berger 2016: 39) rather than theatre's socially productive potential since it is, to him, seldom supported by history. Both Lehmann's and the above two critics' positions are, however, subject to interrogation in this respect. Lehmann first. He distinguishes, citing Judith Butler, the productive aspect of 'performative' from the habitual or obligatory tendency of 'performance'. 'Performance has become', he argues, 'the new paradigm of disciplinary [and regulatory] society' (Lehmann 2011: 44). The performative, on the other hand, 'cannot be completely separated from the idea of ... a positive doing, an achievement of a goal' (44). Then how does Lehmann dismiss the *performative* when it enjoys an artistic status of its own in theatre or when it even disrupts performance as normative practice but by presenting politics as a formal category? The 'performative', moreover, does not necessarily project a journey towards a goal but may be viewed as an ambiguous possibility stuck between its extra-aesthetic position and its 'staged' construct. Lehmann makes better sense when he observes later that the postdramatic today resides in the liminality of activism and aesthetic imperatives.

On the other hand, Cara Berger's understanding of the relationship between politics and contemporary feminist theatre may be considered as a way out of Reinelt's and Haas's approaches to the political in postdramatic theatre. Berger says that feminist theatre may not *represent* politics and yet it *performs* an aesthetic that can potentially accommodate politics in other ways. Drawing on Hélène Cixous' *écriture féminine* via Heideggerian phenomenology, she observes that feminist theatre can go beyond 'human cognition' and any compulsion towards interpretation. It can instead encourage appreciating 'thingness' or 'the thing's worldling being' by overthrowing the traditional structuring of the world into subject (knowing) and object (knowable) and thus bringing in 'a form of more-than-human performance' (Berger 2016: 43, 48, 53). Kapur's *Navalakha* (2001) serves as a good example from India. It takes the human body as well as other objects on stage with equal agential potency. It is new materialism in theatre, which experiments with an unconventional mode of meaning-making, one beyond the humanist as well as the 'linguistic turn'.

Feminist theatre as such does not form any chapter of my book. But its relationship with postdramatic theatre is important to me since theatre in India, in fact, started turning postdramatic through the devised, collaborative, non-realistic and visually powerful theatre of women directors in the 1990s who, however, shied away from calling themselves 'feminists' lest the label sound 'Western' or exclusionary, in local contexts anyway. Their journey was largely to mount a multi-pronged assault on the Freudian symbolic and bring out new dimensions of theatre in ways more than the one suggested by Berger – new spatial formation, as in Haksar; creation of a new sensory experience that destabilizes, as in Chowdhry, traditional sensory associations; cohabitation of humans and non-humans, as in Kapur; a *'parallel (inter-) textuality'* (Jürs-Munby 2013: 214) that consists in the simultaneous run of two or more texts, as in Kapur and Jain; and 'female-coded images' of the world that create in theatre 'an "experience of potentiality" ... beyond the current system of hierarchies' (Berger 2016: 57).

II Cold War, globalization, theatre practice

The Cold War divided the whole world. The Berlin Wall raised in 1961 served as a historic symbol of the divide for decades to come. Heiner Müller, 'a transitional figure' in European theatre usually associated with the emergence of the postdramatic, became critical of both the repressive Soviet experiment in the GDR and the consumerist 'feel-good', expansionist politics of the US/West (Friedman 2007: 4). This moment of stagnation in European politics takes the form of 'constructive defeatism' in Müller – a moment which India never encountered. Post-independence India's non-alignment neutrality, a condition very different from the divided Germany, was, however, destabilized domestically by the Leftist movements of various denominations under the banners of the Communist Party of India (CPI), the Communist Party of India (Marxist) (CPI(M)), and the Communist Party of India (Marxist–Leninist), (CPI(ML)). Not only did these movements gradually lose their mass appeal about the mid-seventies or later, but the dialectical structure of Indian society, both in political and economic senses, started weakening after the fall of the USSR.

In a 1990 lecture, titled 'Some Thoughts on the Soviet Collapse', I. K. Gujral, then external affairs minister of India, expressed the anguish and moral frustration of the majority of Indians in the following words: 'And then, suddenly, that mighty state [USSR] lay prostrate. Its creed and doctrine, communism, was in disgrace'. On the other hand, he admired Gorbachev's determination to transform 'a seventy-year-old rugged dictatorship into [a] social democracy' (in Chand 2011: online). This ambivalent feeling continued in India long after 1991, but gradually started fading out with successive governments 'usher[ing] in much more openness towards foreign capital, imports, currency and industrial licensing' with a view to increasing productivity and wages in the economy (Ojha and Bhattacharya 2016: online). Indian economy had a steady growth during the first decade of the new millennium, protecting itself considerably against the 2008 meltdown. The United Progressive Alliance government (UPA I and II), led by Manmohan Singh who as finance minister liberalized the Indian market in 1991, ensured a steady GDP growth through the 2000s. The aspirations of the people, especially of the literate/educated youth, to live a comfortable life, and the emergence of a robust middle class changed the ideological landscape of India as well as its theatre, which was previously dominated by class issues.

India under Prime Minister Narendra Modi (since 2014) has asserted 'the need to support and sustain a "regime of openness"' and rise above the current trend of protectionism that 'threatens to take away the gains from globalisation' (PTI 2017: online). His campaign 'Make in India' was geared to invite foreign investment and private capital in manufacturing. But the economy has steadily plummeted since the demonetization drive in 2016 that has by now proved to be ineffectual, if not detrimental to development. On the political front, the uneven India story of economic liberalism, which had earlier brought many out of poverty as in other developing countries, is now deeply fraught with contradictions. The economy has not only touched a new low but the 'ideology' of the ruling regime is to end all other ideologies and address issues on a hypernationalist (read: politically illiberal) basis, thus naturalizing 'the dominance of the [political] right', marginalizing the religious and ethnic Other and erasing 'the rationale for debate' (Glaser 2014: online). In Modi-fied India, 'politics is a matter of technocratic optimisation' (ibid.) of resources to retain power and rhetoric (which in itself is an interesting subject of performance studies), creating for many a post-truth India. While claims about secularism and development are untruly made to impress the domestic electoral base, they also symbolically garner for India the support of the West (which at the moment is considerably bigoted) in larger strategic matters. Sporadic protests against the NDA government's divisive agenda currently influence the theatres in India, but no longer in the manner of political theatre of the past that would thematically make an empiricist/didactic approach to social relations and subaltern realities or use them naturalistically for 'pathetic emotionalism' or project a future based on the Marxist–Leninist ideology (Bannerji 1984: 137). This is because of a complex of factors: the artist's self-censorship or compromise on directness of telling and showing in a repressive regime, the weakening of the revolutionary spirit in post-1991 politics, the indeterminacy of the status of reality in a society saturated with media hype, and theatre's increasing separation from drama to realize its fuller performance potential since the late twentieth century. Activism in Indian theatre has of late taken a new *form*al turn marked by a tension between ideological imperatives and the autonomy of aesthetic practice. Paradoxically enough, this activism is no less facilitated by the pervasive presence of the new media, the mover of the late capitalist/neoliberal market economy. Technology has brought significant changes into theatre aesthetics, radicalizing the modes of re/presentation.

III Mediatization of society and the use of technology in theatre

Lehmann thinks that postdramatic theatre is 'a caesura of the mediatized society' (2006: 22). In *The End of History and the Last Man*, Fukuyama also writes that the advancing technology has a 'tremendous homogenising power' – power that can bring people together in a post-ideological landscape (Glaser 2014: online). Postdramatic theatre is an aesthetic response to the thoroughly changed social communication in a world that operates through information/digital technologies. In India, as in the rest of the world today, power is 'increasingly organized as a micro-physics', depriving all, including the political opposition, of any real sense of economic and political processes. Political conflicts steadily evade 'intuitive perception and cognition', as a result of which contemporary theatre lacks the scenic representation of the earlier/dramatic type of (political) theatre (Lehmann 2006: 23, 175). The new media entered India as recently as the late 1990s, but ever since its foray into every nook and corner of the country, it has pervasively dominated the public as well as the private sphere. As the reality is not graspable, slipping off into a deluge of images (whether it is Guy Debord's 'society of the spectacle' or Baudrillard's simulacrum), the world is not a 'surveyable public sphere' any longer (Habermas). The building of a collective political opinion, and the advocacy of correct (political) action, becomes difficult in the absence of truth's lack of transparency, whether in life or on stage.

This in contexts of postdramatic theatre signals the gradual fading away of dramatic theatre's 'ideology of a unique and well-ordered micro-system as the only legitimate one' (Ilić 2011: 138) and of its dominant 'principle of *coherence* (or a well-ordered unity)' which now had to be rethought in terms of 'categories such as event, communicational exchange, active participation of the audience and others'. It is a marked shift from the realistic representation of political reality, or the 'realism of representation', to a 'realism of experience' in theatre. As Amitesh Grover says, 'I take the liveness of an event to be its fundamental inquiry, one that problematizes its ontology' (2019: 58). Reality is now also 'a crisis of simultaneity. The politics of performance is in staging this multiplicity ... of events and of ways of experiencing them' (ibid.). Life is now largely conducted by an intimate use of technology which in turn mostly constitutes experiential reality on or off the stage. The 'emerging techno-sensorium', Grover notes, 'has affected our conceptions of sociality' and modes of theatre-making. Many Indian theatre-makers of his generation 'try to enframe this changing experience' by inserting it into 'the fold of performance' (ibid.).

Information technology and media, generators of globalization, have altered Indian theatre structurally, as just noted. They have widened the gamut and texture of theatre cultures, changed the theatre-maker's approach to social 'reality' and their making process to the extent of becoming theatre's current language. For example, Abhilash Pillai's *Midnight's Children* divides the stage into three parts: the lower and the middle for live action while a

Figure 1 *Midnight's Children* (2005), directed by Abhilash Pillai, presented by National School of Drama (NSD), New Delhi. Photo credit: S. Thyagarajan.

raised part from the middle functions as the movie screen on which are projected historical footages of post-independence projects and plants, movements and marches from colonial and postcolonial India. His *Island of Blood* is another response to the splurge of the media in daily life. It leaves little distinction in form between television broadcasting of news, screening of recorded interviews and staged action. There are other types of responses, too. Maya Krishna Rao's use of video feeds, for instance, enters into an interactive relationship with her live movement in improvising scenes in *The Loose Woman* (2019).

At another level, the popularity of the television in the late 1980s and the invasion of the internet in the 1990s, as Santanu Bose points out, brought home new images from all over the world. Indian theatre directors and artists, who wanted to test their work beyond national boundaries or reinvent it subsequently for domestic audiences, found these images beneficial to the making of a new language for their theatre. They not only had traditional performance material in dialogue with urban modern practices but also put it occasionally into Euro-American forms keeping in view the global spectatorship. Bose (2016) cites Roysten Abel's multi-sensory *Kitchen* (2014) as a quick example – cooking (*payasam*), a metaphor of life, is performed before the audience and the *mizhavu* players drum through the entire cooking time, seated in niches in a three-tier structure that resembles the facade of buildings in Amsterdam's sex workers' district. The works of such theatre-makers became hybrid in a way that helped them transcend their postcolonial anxiety for articulating their specific 'location of culture' and turn rhizomatic in approach by drawing on cultural and artistic resources from other parts of the globe besides their own.

If all this is formalism, it is not 'a bad object ... plagued by ... political indifference', as alleged by Alan Ruiz, or which solely feeds on 'medium specificity' as distinguished from the centrality of social text (Boyle et al. 2019: 7). On the contrary, it signals a shift in our perception of and approach to political reality in theatre (ibid.: 10). Nor does an artist's use of technology, as often perceived by some theatre-makers in India, mean selling one's soul to the neoliberal market. The aesthetic, often partly technology-based, is not divorced from the social or the political here; contemporary theatre actually goes past the predominantly textual, realistic approach to the sociopolitical in art, pointing to a kind of 'historical rematerialization' (Kapur 2019a: 19) arising from 'structural transformations in society itself' (Boyle et al. 2019: 16).

IV Intercultural/inter-artistic engagements, training, influences

Amitesh Grover, himself a Charles Wallace fellow and winner of Artist Residency (Switzerland), writes that with the founding of foreign art and culture councils in India between the 1970s and 1990s, including the Japanese Foundation, the British Council and Goethe-Institut/Max Mueller Bhavan, the performance horizon in India began to widen intercultural and inter-artistic dialogues between artists. Those organizations flew foreign troupes into Delhi to have them perform and interact with the city's vibrant theatre communities, and also awarded grants/fellowships to Indian theatre artists to visit abroad. 'This exposure left an indelible impression on [India's] performance scene', says Grover, 'sparking fresh debates about the nature of performance and experimentation in a country, then faced with ethnic/subnationalist movements, insurgency, class struggle and abrupt economic (and ideological) re-organisation' (Grover 2014: online). Santanu Bose sounds critical of the intervention of those funding bodies in the theatre-making process in India. Following the signing of WTO in 1995 and the advent of cultural funding, many aspiring urban middle-class theatre-makers, he thinks, tried to obtain such funds for making theatre that would be visible internationally. 'It created a neocolonial situation where the funders could execute a cultural hegemony through these "mediators of culture"'.

'Moreover, some such funding organizations', he continues, 'set up corporate bodies as their sources of finance – as a result of which India became a new market for international products' (Bose 2019). But irrespective of all such criticism, the wide exposure and mobility of theatre artists in this respect remarkably contributed to the experimentation in, and contemporization of, Indian theatre and performance.

The cultural exchange happened in other ways, too – which is to say, beyond the foreign culture councils' sponsorships. Formal education in theatre arts at schools in Europe and invitations extended by foreign art and performance organizations (public or private) to Indian theatre-makers to work with them at their festivals or on their projects also 'redrew the profile of [theatre/performance] conventions, which had firmly been in place in India for more than half a century' (Grover 2014: online). Anuradha Kapur, for one, obtained her master's from the University of Leeds in 1977 and wrote her doctoral thesis with Martin Banham as her supervisor, a specialist in African theatre. This exposed her to a broad spectrum of cultural diversity and led to cross-fertilization of theatre forms in her work. 'My years at the workshop theatre gave me the opportunity of interacting with colleagues ... with diverse performing backgrounds and histories: *something that has greatly shaped my theatre work ever since*' (my emphasis), Kapur says (n.d.: online). Having studied and worked at Leeds, she could look beyond the hierarchical structure of dramatic theatre, dominated by word and story, and think of newer performance forms that included non-dramatic native theatre traditions.

Kapur's participation in international theatre/art events, such as the 'In Transit' project hosted by the BHWC (Berlin House of World Cultures), a performance laboratory focused not on 'finished products but on encounters between ... performance artists, musicians, theatre and video artists' (In Transit 2002: online) from around the world, also seems to have contributed towards the pluralization of form in her theatre far beyond the traditions of precolonial performance and colonial dramatic theatre. Her *Makeup* (2003), a totally devised piece on female impersonation comprising text, video work and Hindustani classical music, asked significant questions without politicizing issues directly: what does external material do to the body and how do fiction and reality appear inseparable in the defining of (gender or cultural) identity? Kapur's recent fellowship at the International Research Center, University of Berlin, should again validate my claim. She writes about her project there: 'While site and material have been part of traditional practices, contemporary approaches seek to disalign these as well as converse with them. I want to reflect on what these dialogues are and how they have intervened in the expanded field of theatre-making in India today' (Kapur

2016/17: online). Such intercultural, intermedial conversations have played a vital role in bringing a new (often postdramatic) turn to Indian theatre. This does not in any way idealize the West as an agent of change or feed into the East–West binary. The exchange of knowledge and craft has been more on an equal footing in the recent past than ever before.

Invited by foreign embassies, international theatre festivals and universities, Neelam Mansingh Chowdhry also directed a number of her plays abroad. Her work with directors and actors in Greece, London and Avignon was 'all a part of growing, picking up, absorbing', says Chowdhry, although 'one didn't really know where that got embedded and how it is going to express itself and when' (1998: 14). Chowdhry's wider exposure to theatre craft abroad, mixed with her old interest in sensuous images and non-realistic dramaturgy, has contributed enough to bringing about a shift in Indian theatre from 'sense to sensuality', as in *Yerma* (2002). *Yerma* shows the pervasive presence of 'the sensual *within* sense' – a presence that Lehmann (2006: 148) would identify as an aspect of postdramatic theatre. The lyricism of images, heightened by an understanding of visual aesthetic ('I do live in a visual world', she says), the slowing down of the text, or the collage of scenes in her theatre certainly made her work globally popular (in Singh 2010: online). She was commissioned by the Opera Circus Company, London, in 2013 to direct her maiden opera *Naciketa*, based on *Kathaponishad* and rewritten by Chilean-American novelist-playwright, Ariel Dorfman. Chowdhry improvises her performance, ignoring the importance of the dramatic mode of meaning-making. For most of the play, it is a collage that she loves. 'Anyway, "purity" is something that scares me', says the director (in Sukant 2013). The hybridity and sensuousness of Chowdhry's theatre, which can be traced to a complex of factors including her training under B. V. Karanth in folk performance traditions and her rewarding experience of working with international theatre-makers, seems to have heralded a style that was clearly non-dramatic before it indirectly influenced the making of India's postdramatic a decade later.

The training of a new generation of theatre-makers in both Indian performance traditions and contemporary European theatre practices has given a unique and decidedly postdramatic turn to recent theatre productions in India. The intercultural, inter-artistic factor worked in an intriguing manner with Abhilash Pillai, resulting in a remarkable change of India's theatre language in the new millennium. While working with his teacher Anamika Haksar, Pillai discovered that 'my identity isn't only my folk art but also the machines I use and the gadgets I collect' (Pillai 2017b: online). This realization has always inspired him to present post-independence India through a collage of pop visuals, video footage, music and soundscape, changing the definition of theatre for a whole generation. An NSD graduate, Pillai obtained a diploma in theatre production and stage management from RADA, London. His training there was discernible in his conceptualization of *Verdigris* (2000), 'a play on the history of cleaning toilets'. The sets were designed by scenographer Deepan Sivaraman, 'with plants and flowers and props made from drainage pipes' (Pillai 2017b: online). The fifteen-minute short film, made about the history of toilet-cleaning in India, was screened on the painted curtains. And by the end of the play, 'the stage would be full of water and *keechar* [filth]', says Pillai (ibid.). The play, very unusual and also disturbing to many who walked out of the theatre, 'was a political statement on art and culture', he adds. Pillai was also exposed to 'New Circus' during his stay in London, 'a new stream in which circus' – as he puts it – 'is successfully blended with theatre, cinema, puppetry and so on' (Pillai 2011: online). This left a deep imprint on two of his later works – *Clouds and Clowns* (an unfinished project) and *Talātum*, a fully developed one for the Serendipity Arts Festival in Goa, in 2016. Curated by Anuradha Kapur and Lillete Dubey, Pillai's *Talātum* (an adaptation of Shakespeare's *The Tempest*) is set in a circus tent, using circus acrobatics, gypsy art, puppetry, pre-recorded video material, dance, gestures, music and minimal dialogue to tell a story that does not obviously unfold dramatically but mixes orality with the predominantly visual poetry. Much of what happens in the show is real, judged by its performance status, even as it may remotely relate to a narrative. Spectating is not only horizontal but vertical (the latter being rare in theatre) because of the feats performed by the trapeze artists of a circus company.

With a vast exposure to global performance cultures, Deepan Sivaraman, founder of theatre company Oxygen, claims to be constantly trying to 'break down the hegemony of the word to lead us to ... different, deeper and more provocative [theatre] experiences' (Sivaraman 2019a: online). A Charles Wallace fellow, he wrote his doctoral thesis at Wimbledon College of Arts in London, and then taught scenography there until he returned to India in 2012. His visits to Poland provided him with access to a wide variety of Eastern European theatre, which he describes as 'an important turning point' in his theatre career (Sivaraman 2017b: online). He has increasingly dismissed text/narrative-dominated theatre for more visceral and visual performances. While Sivaraman admits that his work is a continuation of experiments introduced by directors like Anuradha Kapur and Anamika Haksar, he also traces the visuality, the sensory experience and the structuring logic of his productions to influences from Polish avant-gardists such as Tadeusz Kantor and Jerzy Grotowski (Sivaraman 2016). Imprints of Kantor's treatment of 'animated objects' are fairly discernible in Sivaraman's theatre (*Peer Gynt*), and with it Heiner Müller's uses of historical ghosts, too. Theatre, for

Sivaraman, is a ceremony, a ritual. It builds up scenes not in a causal, logical manner but by 'associations' that trigger them. It valorizes, as in *The Legend of Khasak*, 'the objects and materials of the scenic action' the way Kantor's work would (Lehmann 2006: 71-2). Like Grotowski's, again, Sivaraman's theatre often brings out the irrational and the unconscious recesses of the mind and presents them in a Surreal mode (*Ubu Roi*).

Sivaraman, on his own admission, has been equally influenced by Romeo Castellucci's work. His aestheticized damaged characters on stage can be read, as Katrien Vuylsteke Vanfleteren would say, as a postdramatic presentation of psychopathology (2008: online). Sivaraman also seems to have drawn on the works of theatre companies like the Wooster Group so far as the 'happening-like' form of his theatre is concerned. He, like the Group, hardly ever used the media unless it was constitutive of the production. Again, in several of his performances, as in his *Ubu Roi*, the visual dramaturgy is complemented by an auditory language comprised of 'all manner of sounds, music, voices and noise structures', reminding one of the performances by Societas Raffaello Sanzio, such as *Oresteia* (Lehmann 2006: 88). Sivaraman has taken the best from both the scenographic theatre of the West and the spatiality and visual language of traditional Indian theatre (especially from Kerala). He is not exactly averse to text. 'During the playmaking process', he believes, 'the scenography and the written text should evolve together' (2013: online).

For space constraints I have had to leave out many such examples, of which Zuleikha Chaudhari's training and inter-artistic engagements form an important part. Her diploma in Theatre Directing and Light Design from Bennington College Vermont and her association with the works of Richard Serra (involved in the Process Art movement), Mark Rothko (abstract painter), Padmini Chettur (dancer-choreographer), Tim Etchells (artistic director of Forced Entertainment), Christoph Marthaler (musician working in the avant-garde style theatre) and Sumedh Rajendran (sculptor working on industrial material) deserved detailed discussion since all of this has an interface with her productions, adding a postdramatic edge to Indian theatre and performance in general.

V Theatre festivals, pedagogy, entrepreneurship

This section is somewhat an extension of the previous one, but focuses more particularly on the interrelatedness of festivals, state funding, drama school syllabuses and entrepreneurship that took (urban) Indian theatre beyond the 'dramatic' mould and even, at times, beyond early modernist tropes, 'preferring interdisciplinarity and indeterminacy to orthodoxy' (Hadley et al. 2013: 96). Here I restrict my discussion on festivals only to those held at home. Until quite recently theatre fests in India led to a staging of national identity in terms of issues and were not very welcoming of theatre's intersection with other contemporary art or cultural forms. But the contested ideas of and contestatory approaches to theatre-making that saw the National School of Drama through the times of Kirti Jain, Ratan Thiyam and Anuradha Kapur 'have come to be more explicitly acknowledged over the years as its directors have ... carried the School from modernity to postmodernity' (ibid. 2013: 96). The institution steadily moved from 'traditional learning systems' to initiating sustained dialogues with other parts of Asia, Africa and Europe, inserting in the process regional art forms, new readings of classical works, transnational/cross-cultural aesthetics and new media technology into the curriculum. In so doing and by organizing annual theatre festivals more imaginatively, the National School of Drama considerably helped Indian theatre realize its potential to radicalize performance language away from its early emphasis on 'a didactic performativity' (ibid.) based on the Nehruvian vision of a modern India with 'a clear cultural identity' (Kapur in Hadley et al.: 2013: 96). Kapur strongly believes that apart from feminism, 'internationalization' of the curriculum and frequent interactions with international theatre communities from abroad have helped Indian practitioners (as well as their foreign counterparts) to discover connections through differences between multiple theatre cultures for mutual benefit (Kapur 2016). Kirti Jain thinks that the democratization of theatre language, effected by such exchange, has led to 'transformation in theatre practices' and that the 'shift in pedagogy', 'a collective venture in response to world trends in various disciplines of theatre', has eventually encouraged postdramatic theatre practice in India (Jain 2019a: 29, 31). The notion of purity and authenticity about tradition, once left behind, helped the young generation of theatre-makers to think outside the box.

Theatre festivals 'are constructing various sorts of arenas into which performances are inserted – often leading to a sort of global legibility; which is equally adaptable for India's multilingual cultural spaces', Kapur writes (in Hadley et al. 2013: 99). The theatre festival is one of the influential institutions that postdramatic performance practices engage with and, at the same time, are constrained by (Boyle et al. 2019: 17). Festivals have a tendency to become 'a marketplace for experimental performance, defanging the avant-garde impulses of postdramatic artists' (ibid.). But the festival as a new institution has also lent visibility to the radically innovative theatres in India that are at once, to quote Andrew Friedman, 'cutting edge' and market friendly (in Boyle et al. 2019: 18). Kirti Jain acknowledges this indirectly in her observation that 'an increasing exchange of artists across continents' centring on festivals has helped Indian theatre artists keep up with the fast-changing trends in global theatre (2019a: 32). Of the festivals in India, the first that comes to mind is NSD's annual Bharat Rang Mahotsav (BRM), which began in 1999 to stimulate the growth and development of theatre across the country. Some creative/experimental theatre artists, however, are sceptical about the format and quality of the festival. They are critical of the drama school's 'centralised approach, and its token engagement with the contemporary' (Ray 2016: online). Nevertheless, a number of BRM editions have featured productions from India that clearly demonstrate the festival's power to bring out the creativity of Indian artists, mostly young (such as Grover and Sivaraman), known for their close partnership with theatre-makers around the world. On the other hand, international works at BRM events – such as *Mephisto Waltz* from Germany in 2013; *The Complete & Condensed Stage Directions of Eugene O'Neill, Volume 2* from the US in 2016; and *Rags of Memory* from Italy in 2016 – might have also impacted the imagination of Indian theatre-makers and their attitude towards the use or non-use of technology in theatre.

The Ibsen Theatre festival, inaugurated in Delhi by the Dramatic Art and Design Academy (DADA, a private academy) in 2008 and held in the national capital for five consecutive years before moving out to other cities, has proved to be a stronger platform for an exchange of ideas that has significantly influenced the works of theatre-makers in India who are looking for ways out of the dramatic structuring of plot. The festival has always brought 'together possibilities for international collaboration between theatre directors from abroad, and actors, designers and technicians from India', says the 2012 festival director Nissar Allana (2012a: 7). A quick look through the festival's video session in 2012 with Shuddhabrata Sengupta of Raqs Media Collective, New Delhi, sums up my contention that such festivals moved Indian theatre towards a new performance language that shares many grounds with the postdramatic. Sengupta encourages the crossing of borders between different cultures and cultural forms, between theatre and other art practices, or between aesthetic methodologies within the same geocultural space, since such transgressions bring forth new theatre (or) art forms. He compares the purity of form to a kind of 'patriotism' that stagnates the growth of performance and performing arts. Postdramatic theatre's 'between the arts' line is highlighted with special reference to theatre's relationship with visual and media arts (Sengupta 2012b: 46). This does not recommend discarding text, but favours meddling with it, if you will, by putting the text (not necessarily dialogue) in a performative relationship with other forms of communication. Zuleikha Chaudhari's *Some Stage Directions for Henrik Ibsen's John Gabriel Borkman* (presented in the fest's 2009 season) serves as an apt example here (discussed in Chapter 5). Ratan Thiyam's *When We Dead Awaken* (2008) from India also opened new vistas for Indian theatre, demonstrating how to combine architecture, movement and scenography even as the story may not be totally dismantled. There are other theatre festivals, government-sponsored or not, which contribute to the making of theatre-as-performance in similar ways by experimenting with space, scenography, text, acting, materiality, movement and presentation – the International Theatre Festival of Kerala (ITFoK), Kochi Biennale and Serendipity Arts Festival being the most influential of them. But I am not going to discuss them here because I think I have already made my point about such events.

Many of the theatre-makers/performers whose works are discussed in this book are either graduates from NSD or connected to it in different ways and capacities, while others are teaching in universities or are independent artists who are nevertheless often dependent on grants from public and private bodies. Most of them work within some sort of a political structure of the state or institution; yet their ground-breaking productions are also marked by their desire for what Jennifer Craik calls 'destatisation' of performance practices (in Hadley et al. 2013: 96). They have redrawn the maps of theatre by working intimately across communities of artists and performance-makers in India and abroad. This has no less resulted in a shift in 'practices and the ecologies in which practices sit', in 'the systems of production, distribution and reception' (Hadley et al. 2013: 96). These theatre artists, veteran as well as young, have made possible remarkable creative dialogues and transactions between 'the traditional and the modern, the global and the local, the generic and the particular, the central and the regional, and perhaps most importantly the passive and the participatory' – giving birth to a culture of entrepreneurialism that 'broker[s] useful relationships between artists, art organizations, infrastructures, sponsors and audiences' (ibid.: 98). Mutual sponsorship, cultural exchange and inter- and transcultural endeavours are fast collapsing previous formal binaries, generating a multiplicity of performance perspectives and practices that feed the postdramatic globally.

Endnote

Space has played an important role in the designing of India's postdramatic. Productions have sometimes been held in the proscenium theatre, but the stage in that case is innovatively set for an intimate as well as critical spectating. The set in Sivaraman's *Peer Gynt* (discussed in Chapter 4) may be cited as an example. A four-sided gallery was built on the stage and the audience was seated around the square performance space. The aim was to create an interactive relationship between material, space and the audience. Unconventional spaces have also served as venues for a variety of experimental productions: the sprawling lawns of theatre schools (Bhawani's *Active Space*, an installation of broken glass with fragments of texts fitted into frames resembling window panels, and Sivaraman's *Ubu Roi*, a story performed in a rectangular paved space, enclosed by waist-high iron barricades and barbed wire to create an environment of terror); streets (Rao's *Walk*, an improvised performance in protest of a rape victim); libraries (Chaudhari's *Propositions: Text and Space III*, a performance-interface of a book, a tube-light structure and an audio text); art studios (Chaudhari's *Rehearsing the Witness*, theatre-as-rehearsal, rehearsal-as-exhibition, and exhibition-as-installation); and university premises (Sivaraman's *Work in Progress*, a combination of a brick-and-cement construction and readings/lectures).

The postdramatic in India moves on, defying criticisms of being imitative of the West at the expense of 'native' performance traditions. The criticism comes as much from some of the veteran theatre-makers in India as from a section of the audience, who appear fairly conservative in their notions of India and its culture/cultural forms. Their concerns over experiments with the new (visual) language in theatre, the 'reduction' of text to performance, 'marginalization' of actors, the 'conflation' of theatre and performance, and the use of the new media in theatre have been answered in the conclusion and hence are not elaborated here. I would only note at this point that there are also theatre-makers whose works decades ago had in fact brought a non-dramatic idiom into Indian theatre, paving the way for what in contemporary performance parlance can very well be called postdramatic theatre, and a few of whom continue to make theatre far beyond dramatic frames. There is a whole host of young theatre-makers (Sivaraman and Pillai, for instance) who, initially inspired by their teachers or seniors, have subsequently created their postdramatic works with theatre and performance artists across geocultural boundaries. Audiences are also becoming increasingly interested in the new forms of urban theatres in India, caring little for labels, though. It is equally important to mention that the postdramatic is not dated, as some performance studies scholars in the West think, but has expanded its scope and redefined itself depending on varied social, political and cultural contexts and contours. The next five chapters discuss at length the long, uneven trajectory of India's relationship with postdrama with close analyses of a number of productions since the 1990s, but more particularly over the last two decades.

2

The Non-Dramatic Turn in Indian Theatre: Early Adaptations and Devised Plays

This chapter probes into the works in Indian theatre from the late 1980s through the 1990s where, as Lehmann would say, '[t]he newly developed aesthetic forms allow both the older forms of theatre *and* the theoretical concepts used to analyse them to appear in a changed light'. While he warns against overestimating the extent of the break with 'the foundations of dramatic theatre', he also points to 'the obverse danger (especially in academia) of perceiving the new always as only a variant of the well known' (Lehmann 2006: 23). The objective of this chapter is to examine how theatrical means that have been used before can have their meaning radically change in different contexts and how they can simultaneously engender new forms as theatre's response to changed cultural conditions and social modes of communication (23). It is interesting to observe the varying ways of emergence of such means and forms in culturally diverse regions. This happens in Indian theatre through the transformation of the dramatic into the non-dramatic under an imperative felt by women directors to change the protocols of practice long dominated by representational realism or, alternatively, by classical traditions.

The chapter deals with early adaptations and devised plays (the distinctions made between them are more fluid than fixed), which dwell between the dramatic and the non-dramatic on one hand and between the non-dramatic and the postdramatic on the other. Taking up 'the many strands that had evolved through the post-Independence decades' – non-modern Indian, modern Western, 'the feminist and the cinematic' (Dalmia 2009: 314) – these productions show a distinctive tilt towards non-textual elements in performance like visual dramaturgy, dance and music, materials that bracket the animate with the inanimate, spatial experiments and use of technology. The works of the 1990s, mostly directed by women, are adapted and devised from dramatic, literary and non-literary texts. While the adaptations discussed here have a storyline somewhere to begin from, the devised production I have chosen for this chapter derived from no existing stories. The latter was made out of anecdotes and interviews, blogs and news clips, although it reached the stage almost as a ready product. Both of the adaptations and the devised production are collaborative works between directors, actors, performers, scenographers, painters, dancers, singers and musicians.

Early adaptations

Jozefina Komporaly defines adaptations as 'active and risk-taking interventions on pre-existing sources' ranging from 'single-authored plays to collaborative creations and devising projects'. Radical adaptations can operate 'at the intersection between experimental practice and multiple creative transpositions and crossovers among genres and media', Komporaly adds (2017: online). Frances Babbage, on the other hand, asks in her book on adaptation why contemporary practitioners usually prefer non-dramatic texts for their works. She thinks that it is to explore the impact and power of books as physical objects within productions and to see what 'becomes' of prose literature when adapted as 'found text' in contemporary theatre and performance. Babbage contends that given the current trend of doing experimental theatre with 'a pluralist perspective' and the audience's informed understanding of intermedial performance, it is but natural to bring non-dramatic texts and non-conventional theatrical forms to the stage (Babbage 2018: 1–6). Kara Reilly perhaps strikes the most balanced note in her introduction to *Contemporary Approaches to Adaptations in Theatre* by calling 'adaptation' a 'slippery term' since it is primarily 'context-specific' (2018: xxi–xxix).

Adaptation is 'rewriting', which has often been interpreted as intertextuality. Roland Barthes calls 'any text . . . intertext' (in Sanders 2006: 2). J. Hillis Miller also considers a text as 'inhabited . . . by a long chain of parasitical presences, echoes, allusions, guests, ghosts of previous texts' (ibid.: 3–4). Adaptation may again come, as Sanders thinks, out of a writer's or director's ethical, political and aesthetic commitment 'to reinterpret a source text' (2006: 2). All these understandings of text as rewriting should help us engage with the methods of theatre-making in non-dramatic ways because many of the productions in the 1990s are adaptations beyond the dramatic structure by being intertextual, intermedial and improvisational. Henry Louis Gates's *Signifying Monkey* is a good example to show how literary texts may contain tropes of the non-literary that have a great possibility of transforming themselves into various forms of performance in the theatre. Non-literary, non-fictional texts have also been adapted to the stage. The 'interleaving of different [kinds of] texts and textual traditions' is connected to the notion of hybridity, and the precursors of postdramatic theatre in India took intertextuality in its broader sense as a salient condition of their works. Lehmann identifies 'palimpsestuous intertextuality and intratextuality' as 'a significant quality of much postdramatic theatre' (Lehmann 2006: 8). He draws on Gérard Genette's *Palimpsests* (1997) to pronounce in his performance context the quality of palimpsest as a 'product of the devising and rehearsal process, of companies using and reusing the materials left on stage or found in the rehearsal room or recycling material from previous shows in new contexts' (Lehmann 2006: 8). Lehmann's notion of intertext as a form of palimpsest also includes other 'textscapes', such as 'audio landscape' (Wilson's term), visual material and 'musical motifs of sound or "concrete" noise' (148). Hybridity as inherent in such intertextuality has a greater presence in postcolonial cultures in the form of constant negotiation between intra- as well as intercultural differences, but with a rider that the essentialist notion of culture does not work any longer. Non-dramatic theatre in 1990s India, leading to the postdramatic (turn) a decade later with its own combination of aesthetic and social texts, serves as a site of liberation from the dominance of word and mimetic representation that had defined Indian theatre for a long time. The entry of the electronic or digital media into performance since the late 1980s has made adaptations increasingly intermedial, expanding the meaning and scope of intertextuality and hybridity in the theatre.

This chapter probes into the non-dramatic works in Indian theatre during the 1990s, where material in one artistic or non-artistic medium (short story or novella or non-fiction) passes to the medium of theatre with changes (additions or omissions) in content and/or style. However, this is not all about the transformation of non-dramatic texts into non-dramatic theatre. The works under study are a dialogue between the past and the present, between two historical phases in theatre-making: adapted or devised, they are developed to define the contemporary by highlighting the 'non-dramatic' properties of Indian theatre after the 1980s (Lehmann 2006: 23). They may be considered as 'anticipations', if not beginnings, of India's postdramatic theatre. I call this a non-dramatic turn because the making of theatre is neither postdramatic yet nor any longer dramatic but bears symptoms of a new paradigm owing to the changing politics of gender and general reactions against the prevalent idiom of theatre long dominated by men. The works discussed in this chapter de-privilege dramatic texts, as Melissa Poll would have it, and thrive on 'evocative, visual [and physical] performance', putting on stage material that is aesthetically and politically provocative by being perceptual and reflexive (Poll 2018: online). They break free from theatre's tendency towards cultural homogenization and from the dominance of text, as already noted, over the other elements of performance. Physicality and self-referentiality of action characterized India's predramatic theatre too, but now their presence has a different political and aesthetic purpose to achieve.

Although in this section I discuss the works of Anuradha Kapur, Neelam Mansingh Chowdhry and Kirti Jain only, their contemporary Anamika Haksar must be credited as one of the pioneer female theatre-makers to have brought Indian theatre out of the conventional dramatic structuring with her radical work *Antaryatra* (1993), among others. From the prevalent realist practice of performance-making or, alternatively, the decolonizing motif of the 'theatre of roots', Haksar's *Antaryatra* was a remarkable departure. For many playwrights and directors (mostly male), who were guardians of the two parallel performance traditions, it was an almost shocking experiment. Based on a Tamil epic, *Silappatikaram*, it signals a transition from authorship to collaboration, dramatic text to lyrical adaptation or devising, dialogic communication to a new scenography and choreography, and from mimetic representation to fluidity of performance. The circular and often meandering manner in which the story of a woman is told also demonstrates a remarkable move away from linear progression of action in the theatre. The dome-like structure of the performance area opening into a seventy-foot-deep field, thus creating a sense of a panoramic vista, seeks to capture the expanse of the epic. The performance gains its flexibility from the continuous movement of a woman (Kannagi) in her quest for the 'self'. The landscape and the mindscape interact with each other, and the once unified subject is distributed (Kapur 2001: 10) into a plethora of diverse objects, props, movements and drawings (*kolam*) – thus bringing into the theatre in India a whole new dramaturgy. *Antaryatra* dismantles in a radically performative way the stereotype of the 'Indian' woman either as a devoted, docile wife or as a tempting, fallen woman. Haksar's directorial oeuvre demands a full-length study that I plan to undertake in the near future.

The Job (1996/1997)

Anuradha Kapur's stage adaptation of Brecht's short story of the same name is a ground-breaking production that brought together in Indian theatre painting, installation, video projection, narration, physical movement, film and music. The performance my analysis is based on was held at Max Mueller Bhavan, Mumbai in 1996. There was also a show in Delhi the next year. Kapur's *The Job* is a fine example of collaborative work: the story is told in three different modes – the (recorded) voiceover of a narrator, the silent action of a solo actor and the artworks of visual artist Nalini Malani that created the environment for the performance. The Indian stage witnessed de-hierarchization of theatrical structure and language, and artists collaborated to create a different level of communication in theatre: text is accompanied by a strong evocative quality of light; soundscape overtakes the body in motion; and painting complements silence on stage. These are the features, among others, which influenced the theatre of the next decade/century, bringing forth a postdramatic turn in performance. There are no laboured attempts to integrate the three mediums in *The Job*; rather these mediums are meant to run parallel to one another, producing a modern hybrid language that even urban Indian audiences were not so familiar with when the production premiered. Malani's installations (the 'memory membrane' on the screen, the moving pistons, food jars, plastic foetuses, gloves) are more than part of the play's set; they also perform the action, giving it a fluidity and depth required for the story of a woman impersonating her dead husband for mere subsistence. They were 'conceived separately from the play', Kapur tells the author in an interview, introducing the autonomy of other art forms in theatre and pronouncing parataxis and simultaneity as stylistic traits of the performance (Kapur 2016).

The performance begins with the projection of a newspaper clipping whose headline reads: 'Accident in Factory reveals Chowkidar to be Male Impersonator'. The whole play (we are dealing with works in this chapter that can be described as 'plays' after all) is about gendering, about performing male identity within a female body, the obverse of what happens in Kapur's *Sundari* (1998). Female impersonation has a long tradition in Indian performance, but the male impersonation in *The Job* lacked history. The repeated changing of dresses, from a woman's sari to a man's trousers and shirts, theatricalizes the fluidity of gender – a deconstructive approach to identity that is returned to its 'natural origin' at the end only to mock the essentialist assumptions of society about gender. Gender is *made* to look natural through repeated but unconscious doings of its norms, as the illusion of presence is achieved in dramatic theatre through 'repetition and representation' (Artaud) – both concealing the very process of construction and thus passing off the fictive as true and the construct as natural. The story has already been told, we are reminded by the voiceover on the soundtrack. Moreover, the report on the exposé of Chowkidar's identity deliberately takes away all the suspense that is an important aspect of storytelling in dramatic theatre. What is then left for the theatre-maker is the challenge of an aesthetic retelling that will not be representational as such but aim to be presentational by playing with the density of signs in the play and thus keeping the form flexible.

The entire performance is conceived by Kapur and Malani in an intermedial format, where the female body and mind (neither essentialized) dictate terms. The newspaper report on the screen dissolves into a film that may be taken as the play's subtext, ferreting out the woman's mindscape. 'The sepia on the screen deepens', says Yashodhra Dalmia, 'then becomes bound by black, then erased like a continuous flux of emotions and identity' (in Dalmia 2009: 320). As the fluid lines on the screen acquire prominence, gradually facial contours of women emerge, surfacing as if from a pool of liquid industrial rust – sometimes only to drown therein again, pushing up more lines that take the shape of hands, the prerequisite for labour. The 'extensive installation' that follows is a collection of objects, mostly inverted, implying subversion of social expectations around femininity that has become culturally synonymous with nurturing – food jars, plastic foetuses, grains and other foodstuffs. The interplay of the 'natural' and the Derridean 'supplement', in the form of a sleeping woman's artificial breast that meets her natural upper chest, interrogates the self-sufficiency of nature by extending the subject and the object into each other and creating a reality on stage that is neither representation nor pure presence but performatively creates a sense of a presence that did not exist prior to its formal presentation. The borderline between the live (or the thing itself) and the reproduced (or the performed) is kept porous 'to work a presence into various objects' that Malani has assembled there, 'including the sets and costumes'. 'In fact, many of the things I've planned', Malani adds, 'will come alive only because of the performance' (in Dalmia 2009: 320). In such performative turn began the non-dramatic journey of Indian theatre.

The Job builds on the productive tension between presentation and representation, putting text, narration, movement and image in an unprecedented relationship. The materiality of labour and rawness of hunger meet in the interstices of installations and pre-recorded narration (mostly in English), the 'narrator' being neither the Sutradhar of the traditional Indian theatre nor the choric figure of classical Greek theatre but more akin to a modern-day text-bearer. The dialogue between character and objects becomes a new way of replacing the conversation between characters that develops a dramatic plot, while character forms tentatively at multiple artistic levels. As the woman turns back and goes past the jars overhead, more lines appear on the film, gradually taking the shape of a woman's drooping face. 'On the screen she-he is already a memory, scarred, eroded ... marked, burnt, and still alive', the 'narrator' offstage reads. We see an opaque bodyline dissolving gradually, as the music plays, into a mass of unrelieved rust colour. The to-and-fro movement between the live body and its associative images on the film reinforces the complexity of negotiating the space between the presentational and the representational. When representation becomes problematic with the knowledge of an always-already marked, and therefore mediated, presence, presence can register itself only in the form of presentation (whether of the body or of a thing). The dramatic theatre refuses to recognize it even as it may show the fragmentation of the 'real' because it stubbornly seeks authenticity in 'truthful' representation.

The narrative thus clearly shows the drifting of theatre from drama. The inverted words from the Bible, 'By the sweat of thy brow thou shalt fail to earn thy bread', are recited para-ritualistically as the six-feet-long glass pistons come down on her, with images painted around them evoking an early twentieth-century industrial landscape, and then go up again. The non-textual elements had played an important role in Indian theatre before; but a well-made plot, psychologically developed character and a moving story told in dialogue always dominated the 'structuring components' (Lehmann 2006: 31). In the centre of the warehouse filled with cardboard cartons is a painted picture on the floor. Image as mere appearance, which is more or less common to postdramatic theatre, pervades the play. Simultaneously, this concept of image is made to interact with the body in motion. The image of rest, marked in her relaxed postures from the beginning, is now set against the acts of actual labour that follow. The woman wakes up and begins to pull the cart with loads of goods on it. She comes back and mops the floor of the warehouse. Through such hard acts appearances acquire tangibility, making impersonation a self-referential performance. Besides, the narration played on the track, a 'voic[e] in space' (Lehmann 2006: 68), and the woman's

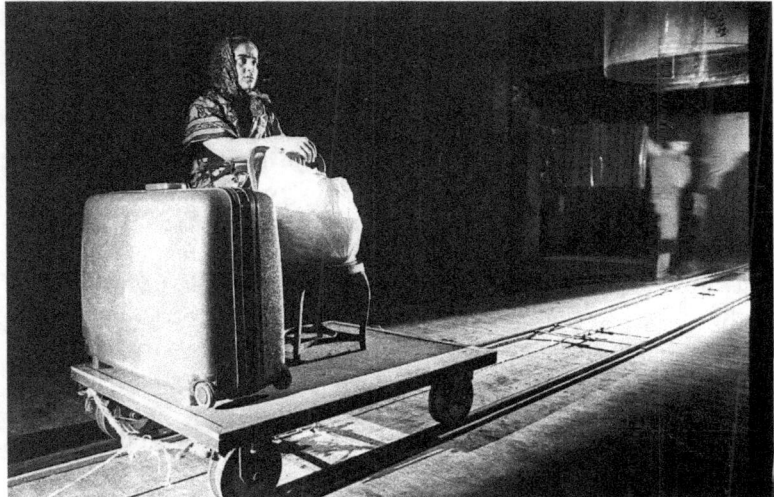

Figure 2 *The Job* (1996), directed by Anuradha Kapur, presented at Max Mueller Bhavan, Mumbai. Photo credit: Prakash Rao.

occasional silent lip movement create a distance between plot and character, voice and embodied action. This obviously upsets the mimetic theory of representation that has characterized dramatic theatre all along, including drama's outreach to performance. The play tells a story and yet reflexively shows its artistic reluctance to develop it as a dramatic narrative by leaving 'associations' between voice and text, action and 'states' disjunctive.

The process of gendering continues through dressing, undressing and re-dressing. The next part is narrated in Hindi, which in the English translation of Brecht reads: 'No sooner had she settled this in her own mind than she tore the black rags from her body, undid the cord of the suitcase, pulled out her husband's Sunday suit and clumsily put it on before her children's eyes, with the help of her new-found friend who had almost instantaneously understood what she was up to' (Brecht 2015: 158). But in all of this the woman was not merely translating the narrator's words into action. She was playing with and within a suitcase, creating sculptural patterns with her moving body against the background of painted images on the underside of the suitcase cover. She also rolls up the paintings, including the one lying spread out on the floor, and then comes out of the suitcase, locks it and sets out for the job. The immobilization or freezing of the figures in the paintings, which partly de-dramatizes the scene, comingles here with 'kinetic sculptures through slow motion' of the performing body (Lehmann 2006: 87, 156). The colourful paintings have a special effect on spectators when they are invited to walk around them lying on the stage floor – thus radicalizing the art of spectating, too. The relationship between theatre and painting is old enough insofar as the latter has been mostly used to prepare the set on stage. But painting acquires an autonomous role here, which is more than its complementary relationship with the textual narrative. Consider this series of painted images that are complete in themselves: a girl seated with her chin close to her knees folded up; a woman lying down; a house held by two hands; a watchman with a stick in his hand. But they also open up a horizon of conjectures bearing on the story: girlhood is left behind, and all the pleasant memories with it; the house is now the woman's responsibility to hold together; the treacherous world of labour awaiting her. Moreover, while painting is occasionally made to interact with technology, especially the film (the 'memory membrane' here) which had long posed a serious threat to the future of the theatre, the art of showing takes a new turn in Indian performance.

The 'telling' quickly shifts from paintings back to repetitive acts of gendering in a bid to further visibilize the process of *wearing* a gender. Performing gender, or 'materializing' it on stage, is a recurring motif in Kapur's work. In *Makeup* (2003), she even used prosthetics to underscore such materialization. The woman now alters her physical appearance with face make-up, notes Kapur, wearing men's clothes, putting 'felt shoes in her chest to make it appear flat' (in Subramanyam 2002: 244). She looks at herself in a small mirror to scrutinize any possible rupture in appearance between her anatomical and worn body. She picks up a stick and wields it as a Chowkidar, mastering (pun intended) a body language that suits a watchman. The undoing and redoing of gender continues: she breaks eggs in a bowl, applies them all over her face as a man would apply lather, and starts 'shaving' with a spoon – a brilliant mixture of things to lay bare the 'process of production' of maleness that is synonymous with 'courage' and 'power'. Repetition is typical of postdramatic theatre – so much so that a new '*aesthetic of repetition*' has developed around it (Lehmann 2006: 156). This repetition is different from that in dramatic theatre which consolidates its formal wholeness through it. In this play, it is employed to hollow out the unity and consistency of an act, thus contributing to the de-structuring of the dramatic form itself. This repetition again is not a copy of the 'original' that constitutes the norm, but a reflexive doing of it that shows the chasm between the attempts-to-hold and the constant-falling-apart.

The insertion of other materials into the performance, which do not aid the storytelling directly but have evocative associations with it, is noteworthy. The woman draws a quilt over her body, with a number of gloves stitched onto it. Rest at night is not without the gnawing thoughts of work the next morning. She rolls over and out of the quilt and spreads it upside down, with the gloves now invisible. These figurations are not symbolic signs but refer to themselves as part of an environment. The woman falls asleep and sees in her dream images that coalesce with those painted on the rotating glass pistons descending on her from the flyer, refracting light all over the body and adding an opaque quality to the entire scene. Such '[d]ream thoughts' – as Lehmann calls them – 'form a texture that resembles collage, montage and fragment rather than a logically structured course of events' (2006: 84). The turn to performance is paramount in the conception of *The Job*. The last example could be the presentation of the post-accident scene mainly through the woman's acrobatic movement over, under and around a hospital stretcher, accompanied by brief citations from Sofia Gubaidulina, Steve Rife and Laurie Anderson.

Kitchen Katha (1999/2000)

Neelam Mansingh Chowdhry's *Kitchen Katha*, performed by The Company at Chandigarh's famed Rock Garden, is a play with many non-dramatic elements in it, which brought onto the Indian stage a new genre of theatre that is at once different from most of India's folk and dramatic traditions. It builds a rich sensorium and introduces an art of storytelling in theatre that combines food and memory at one level; touch, taste, smell and sight at another; and narration and real-time action at yet another level. With postdrama narration does not go out of the theatre; instead the theatre often becomes what Lehmann calls 'the site of a narrative act' (2006: 109). The storytelling in *Kitchen Katha* (the telling being more important than the story told) through an assemblage of diverse performance forms in fact births the play onstage. The play has used folk performance elements but within an artistically hybrid form. The 'folk' does not return to this production unmediated by the 'dramatic' intervention, but is re-employed as part of a play that is structurally non-dramatic. In *Kitchen Katha*, telling and embodying happen at once; and the narrator does not fully become a character. This is achieved through a simultaneous process of narration and gesticulation at the crossroads of real-time and symbolic acts. The materiality of objects and physicality of action occupy the foreground of the production, underscoring the process of fiction-making in a theatre that is not beyond representation. What might have been a conventional dramatic text has been turned into a monologue, paradoxically polyphonic in texture in that several characters from the past 'speak' through the narrator. What Cormac Power says of 'presence in the theatre' would explain in our case the relationship between the stage and the audience. Rather than using 'the stage as a privileged site' which the audience experiences 'in terms of presence', *Kitchen Katha* examines 'the potential of theatre to put presence into play'. The audience experience derives from a set of doings where fictional reality (illusion parading as real) and real fiction ('the process of world-making') intersect (Power 2006: ii, 2).

Adapted from Laura Esquivel's *Like Water for Chocolate* and Isabel Allende's *Aphrodite*, *Kitchen Katha* is 'a deliciously intimate tale of love' (Company 2007: online). It has a community kitchen set, decked with fresh colourful vegetables that are being peeled and chopped for making *sabji* (cooked veggies) and *pakoras* (veg fritters), *atta* (flour) that is being chaffed from the husk and then kneaded for making *rotis* (homemade unleavened bread), oil that is being heated in large pans to fry *jalebis* (a type of Indian sweet), and various sorts of utensil that are being washed for fresh use (ibid.). The story is performed by a young woman (Tara in the play) in a vigorous and celebratory manner to narrate how her (Tara's) grandmother Chand learnt to sustain and nurture a man's (Mangal's) love for her by cooking delicious cuisines for him. A series of recipes in fact fill the narrative from the beginning to the end, some of which materialize into cooking on stage and others are recited or sung by chefs and musicians who are not characters per se but aid the storytelling by performing various tasks. The legend '*dabta woi dabta*' ('invitation to a feast') looms out of the rich assembly of names of Punjabi/ Indian cuisines printed on the cyclorama and stage wings. The play becomes a 'sensual odyssey', a 'mapless journey through the realms of sensual memories in which the boundaries between love and appetite become diffused' (Rang Swarn Festival 2003: online). The fictional time often cannot be separated from the time of the audience even as the story takes us back to the time past.

Kitchen Katha theatricalizes the scripting of a play rather than playing a script, although it has a script of its own (by Surjit Patar) in verse. The Writer in the play is the figure of the 'theological' playwright of dramatic theatre in search of a story, a perfect contrast to the narrator-performer who makes her theatre out of her simultaneous acts of telling, cooking and dancing. Tara reads out various recipes from her aunt's kitchen notebook. Whether or not this can be called performance reading, here is an example of spoken text, distinguishable as it is from dialogue, where the scope for improvisation and interface with other elements of performance is greater. Tara offers to cook for the whole theatre troupe, which she does through a choreography of movement elaborate with culinary rituals. While the dramatic theatre conceals the 'process of the body' in the making of a role, as Lehmann observes, postdramatic theatre aims at exhibiting the body itself that makes no clear distinction between art and reality (2006: 166). Apart from Tara's movements, which no less make the play a 'theatre of the body', her constant alternation between role-playing and real-time performance mixes art and reality in a manner that was unconventional in Indian theatre. She picks up vegetables of different sizes, shapes and colours, dances holding them in her hands and between her fingers, and then leaves them in pans on the gas stoves where real cooking is being done. She feeds *pakoras* to the co-performers as well as the audience. As she puts some into her own mouth, the choreography changes to a form and tempo that demonstrates the magic that food can perform on one.

There is a scene in *Kitchen Katha* where the narrator, by a veritable rite of passage performed through telling and stylized acting, changes into the character of her aunt. Tara drapes her body in a long cloth before a mirror and looks at her image, taking it as the full-blooded Chand. The mirror is not a device here to stage Charles Cooley's 'looking-glass self' (1902), but a medium for the actor to impersonate a character-within-a-character and, at the same time, remain her own person to assess and scrutinize the double-edged transformation-in-progress. The actor-as-double-agent (Brecht) is put on stage as an open-ended, self-referential identity. The double agency between oneself and another person, between one body and another is a playful blend that as a 'paradoxical logic of expression' (to use a Merleau-Ponty concept) creates a sense of 'defamiliarization' in spectatorship as well as allowing the actor the freedom to experience consciously the process of character-making (see Landes 2013). Unlike in method acting, the actor can 'play into character while occasionally playing out of' it, thus making fictional reality and breaking it down for spectators to involve them in the process of its making (Ambrose 2015: 2). In *Kitchen Katha*, Brecht's *Verfremdungseffekt*, if you will, is used not to build criticism from 'a social point of view'; nor does it interfere with the production's indulgence in 'improvisatory, impulsive activities' that Brecht warns against (ibid.). The role of the mirror quickly changes as Tara, back to her role as narrator, theatricalizes the love–hate relationship between the beautiful Chand and the inadequate mirror that always reflects a poorer image of her, thus raising more questions about the adequacy of mimetic representation and introducing a new aesthetic to the Indian stage for making theatre more presentational.

The disintegration, if not absence, of dialogue brings about a new idiom in modern Indian theatre that seeks to transcend what Wirth calls the 'dramatic discourse' (in Lehmann 2006: 31) and character as the vehicle of a play's content. Chand's pangs of love, as her lover is whisked away by her aunt for the latter's own daughter, are exteriorized through a performative feat. Tara sits on a large bowl used for kneading *atta* – and a co-performer begins to sieve the flour over her, symbolizing Chand's ageing in grief. The showering of the flour is also an initiation ritual for Chand: here begins her venture to keep her lover close to her, and her own love alive, through food whose irresistible taste and smell grows out of her desire and sensuality. The performative act creates a ceremonial environment that dismisses the mimetic referencing of the real that dominated the theatres of India for decades pre- and post-independence. The Writer now participates in the ceremony by closely following the performing narrator who is at once telling the story and playing the lead character. A new kind of movement ensues, which is less signifying than self-indulgent. Tara climbs atop a ladder and reads out the recipes to the 'congregation' beneath, interspersing them with comments that may be read as leads for the Writer to work on for her play and giving the kneaded dough a sensual shape. She also makes an aromatically rich sherbet for the lover, into which goes the rose water she washes her hands and breast with. Such performative acts, which do not correspond to anything existing in reality and hence are anti-representational, add a 'lyrical-ceremonial' dimension to the play. Performance as presentation is privileged over representation qua text, the latter experienced in its processual status only.

The play's focus is not on 'the (epic) attention [to] the course of actions' but mostly 'on the presence of the performers' (Lehmann 2006: 111). The dance with which it comes to an end has an 'unorganized' appearance that accentuates visceral sensuality and 'corporeal experience' (171). The free play of the body, the abundance of colour, sound and smell – all together turn the stage into a space and a moment that do not look for any correspondence between what happens on the stage and what had occurred in the fictitious past of a narrative. Fiction enters the performing space without any truth claims and becomes in its self-reflexive presentation an event where the actors as performers enact in a demonstrative, stylized manner a story while simultaneously doing real things in the presentness of theatre. The show is obviously not devoid of the element of representation, but representation does not have its continuity and linearity even in the overall sequential narration of Chand's life. Broken into fragments that are performed through a system of signs that often speak for themselves and demand the spectator's imaginative power to piece the parts together, the performing of Chand's life story exposes the spectator to a rich world of sense and perception. As a result, in spite of building on a story (pure fiction), the production is not illusionist theatre per se.

The doing in *Kitchen Katha* is in the playful performativity of things onstage without an activist bias of feminist theatre. By situating a woman's story entirely in the kitchen, traditionally a confined space for females, Chowdhry's work may, nevertheless, be accused of returning the female subject to the trivialities of domesticity. Critiquing such marginalization, seldom experienced by males in an androcentric society, there are productions by other theatre-makers that have the audience experience the risk and toil of the women who work there life-long to feed the family. That said, *Kitchen Katha* not only takes place in a large community kitchen where people irrespective of gender and sexuality work together but the woman whose story begins and ends in a kitchen also accepts her place only to turn it into a space where 'one can practise what is prohibited'. What Josefina Ludmer says of a woman's relationship with domestic spheres in reference to *Like Water for Chocolate* applies no less to Chowdhry's work which looks somewhat similar to Esquivel's in its narrative outline. The challenge in such a context consists in changing the meaning of a place, and 'this practice of movement and transformation reorganizes the given social and cultural structure' (Spanos 1995).

Further, the director's note is of equal importance here:

> My favourite haunt has always been the vegetable mundi (market). The array of colours, textures, and the shape and feel of different vegetables has always fascinated my tactile and olfactory sensibility. The chopping, cutting and cooking of vegetables has always played a therapeutic role as it involves discipline, precision and imagination. My early childhood had

me spending a lot of time cooking in our family gurdwara's *langar*. The flying atta, the hundreds of little dough balls, the sound of hands while making *chappatis*, the slapping of the *rotis* on the *tawa* bound by the spirit of community eating and sharing – the vegetable world conjures up images in my mind and heart that seem to connect with my larger world.

Company: online

The community kitchen in her play becomes an image of a network of social relations that include cooking, feeding *and* the 'in-process' performance. Chowdhry's play may remind one, however remotely, of the Culinary Theatre's *Between the Bread – A Sandwich Performance* (2018), which is described on the flyer as 'a slice of work-in-progress lunch performance'. At the end of the sandwich performance, a mix of 'cutting recipes and carving stories', sandwiches were offered to the audience as 'a ritual meal' that helps them explore the diversity of a neighbourhood in taste and talk.

Early devised productions

Karen Jürs-Munby writes in her introduction to her translation of Lehmann's *Postdramatic Theatre* that Lehmann's methodical probe into the association between drama and new theatre and performance resulted in surveying a wide range of international productions 'from heterogeneous theatre and performance "genres" that are often treated separately under different names': devised experimental performance work and physical theatre are two of them (2006: 2). Deirdre Heddon and Jane Milling maintain in *Devising Performance: A Critical History* (2006: 6) that devised theatre remained marginal to the script-based or textual theatre even after it made its appearance in the 1990s. Citing the publication of the Kathryn Mederos Syssoyeva and Scott Proudfit-edited *A History of Collective Creation* in 2013, they note in their preface to the revised edition of their book that 'devising' took longer to become a regularly used form and terminology than its counterparts 'collective' and 'collaborative' in the US (Heddon and Milling 2016: vii). Interestingly, what is called 'devised' in British and Australian theatre criticism is still known as 'collaborative' in US theatre practice. In spite of many marked similarities between the two forms, 'devising' does not *necessarily* involve more than one participant, as Heddon and Milling say, while 'collaborative' obviously does.

A devised theatre piece, when taken as a collaborative creation, is expected to be non-linear and hybrid in form, with contributions from people (usually of diverse backgrounds and disciplines) running parallel to as well as into one another. Devising is an art of strategizing and contriving, and improvisation is central to it in terms of designing, choreographing, writing, rehearsing and intuitive exercises (Heddon and Milling 2006: 10). Devising is discovering a play by working on images and ideas, not fixing it beforehand, and generating a performance simultaneously. There may be a pre-existing play text which will determine the structure of the devised production but which will also be thoroughly processed nearly beyond recognition (Collins, in Pais 2014: 116). In *Devising in Process*, Alex Mermikides and Jackie Smart define devising as 'a certain playful openness: to a range of stimuli; to creative risk and experimentation; to the views and input of a variety of participants' (in Smart 2014: 101). Devising may also combine into 'a single performance text' disparate source material such as videos, internet, dialogue, choreography, physicality and 'the unexpected of the everyday life' (Pais 2014: 115). It often uses found texts, fiction, historical artefacts, interviews, testimonies and evidences – the reason that devised theatre is often described by various terms such as 'experiments in labs', 'workshops' and 'sessions'.

Devising may have histories that are special, if not specific, to a culture or can be inter-artistic in this globalized world. Devising is an inseparable aspect of classical Indian theatre which enjoyed a distinctive identity from Western theatre by not being representational. But in post-independence and contemporary Indian theatre it has taken on new dimensions in response to influences coming from other cultures and art forms. However, theatre-makers who devise may put different elements of performance: native or borrowed, in conversation with each other to see what the production finally arrives at. The creative excitement comes as scattered materials meet in an unforeseen, unplanned manner and fall into place with no sense of conventional artistic coherence. Devising does not preclude planning altogether – which in this case is more strategizing on the spot than preconceiving. Devised theatre does not banish text. In fact, the 'writing process has been in many ways another way of formalizing the devising process', John Collins maintains (in Pais 2014: 121). The writer may see many events happening during improvisation and weave them into a story. Supriya Shukla does it for Kirti Jain's *Baghdad Burning* and B. Gowri for Jain's *Aur Kitne Tukde* that I discuss below. The director and actors also take a cue from one another and develop new lines of action – something that Jain and her troupe members did for both the plays mentioned above.

Devised theatre is not necessarily devoid of a narrative. The constant 'devising of a single situation' (Jain 2016) through a series of improvisations may bring about a more live narrative than the playing of a scene from a preconceived text. Sometimes 'repetition of a motif based on central concerns of a play', says Jain in an interview, 'creates powerful images that provide a subtext to the main action' and create a layered story (ibid.).

Aur Kitne Tukde (2001)

In discussing the recurrent friction between text and scene, Lehmann underscores the importance of the 'body-text' in postdramatic theatre. He notes that in postdramatic theatre the 'body's visceral presence' with its breath and rhythm has predominance over the logos. 'The *principle of exposition*' as applied to body and gesture seizes 'the language material' and offers an experience predicated on a visual rather than text-oriented dramaturgy (Lehmann 2006: 92, 145–6). Words – even when they develop the plot – may not primarily form the tone and texture of the scene but rather depend on the body and its energetic movement for any relevance. To come to Kirti Jain's *Aur Kitne Tukde*, presented at the National School of Drama, New Delhi, in 2001, the body is placed somewhere between 'a carrier of meaning' and 'an *auto-sufficient physicality*' (Lehmann 2006: 95; original emphasis). Women during the partition of the subcontinent are presented as 'somatic texts' in the play (Menon 2013: 119). The 'binary between language and embodiment' (121) in performance nearly dissolves when the historical discourse turns into improvised 'physical actions' and 'chance conditions' that create a scene by interacting with space creatively (Jain 2019b).

Inspired by Urvashi Butalia's *The Other Side of Silence* (1998), *Aur Kitne Tukde* basically asks how people – especially women and children – have been devastated by the partition. Jain devises her work from 'two oral histories of Damyanti Sahgal and Basant Kaur' (all names are pseudonyms in Butalia's book), 'one newspaper account of Zainab and Buta Singh, and one dramatized version of Jamila Hashmi's short story "The Exile"', thus blurring generic boundaries in performance (Menon 2013: 124). The oral narratives in Butalia's volume have a storyline that articulates memories of violence as representation. Jain's project, however, explores 'how gendered selfhoods (as victims, survivors, martyrs, perpetrators) are performatively produced through iterative discourses of family, community, and nation' (ibid.) and thus goes beyond mimetic representationalism. There is enough 'language material' in the play, but mainly in the form of interviews and monologues to supplement the body-text, and not the other way round. Jain avoids the dramatic mode of storytelling by reinforcing the discursiveness of the past and the present-ness of performance. As there is no unmediated access to the real, staging the gendered subject is also to make the process of performative production self-present. Jain does this by making the dead in historical reality rise in the performance text as 'somatic materiality' (Menon 2013: 123), challenging authorial supremacy that both official history and dramatic narratives consist in. The narrative for the stage, according to Jain, should build on 'its displacement through the process'. A draft text (more like a screenplay with 'economy of words') emerges from a new kind of rehearsal that the devising often is (Jain 2017).

Theatre, for Jain, is 'a political act' (Jain 2016). As a theatre-maker, she has always taken pains to define this act through reflexive performance. Most of the devising process in *Aur Kitne Tukde* is 'about trying to perceive and feel the loss suffered by the victims', says Jain (2016). And 'women's bodies as sites of honour and absence of choice' are the connecting points between the four stories selected from Butalia's book. Jain with her group had to look for 'methods and exercises' to inscribe that sense of loss in the performing body. During rehearsals she would hide small belongings of the participants, watch their anxious reaction to such insignificant 'losses' and then explain the magnitude of people's dispossessions during the partition. As a group, the participants worked hard on different situations of loss to understand how appalling it was for those people to be dislocated and lose *everything*. So the performance was not going to be 'just acting', Jain adds, but also presenting an individual's story as 'a self-conscious narration' both facilitated and obstructed by the psychosomatic experience of loss (Jain 2016). A world damaged by a turn of political events and fraught with a deep sense of pain and incompleteness informs the very structure of the play. The action takes place in the liminality of outside and inside, which never allows it to be a 'dramatic fictional *whole*' (Lehmann 2006:12).

To make the historical trauma an experiential reality to the actors and by extension to the audience, Jain experiments with another set of exercises. She asks her team to imagine that there has been an earthquake and they each have run out of their house leaving everything behind. Then she asks them to suppose that an aftershock might follow in a short while, which can be terribly devastating, and they have very little time left to rush back home to retrieve what is most dear to them. There were different responses. One would come back with a diary, while another would go in and make her bed neatly and then come back because she wanted her bed to stay as it is even at the very moment of destruction. They kept working on such little things of life, 'more by way of exploring themselves and the different reactions possible in moments of crisis', Jain told the author. 'These kinds of exercises help us as a team to break out of stereotypes', she continues, by guarding against – for example – sentimental responses like crying 'that is not just the easiest thing to do in a tragic situation but also the most superficial' (Jain 2016). Such hard exercises, which are pure improvisations, helped her cast perceive what it means to leave one's home, get raped, have one's breast cut off; or what it means when one is not recognized by a person for whom one can die; or how it feels to be refused entry into one's home where one returns after a life of torture and alienation; or what survival is when one's attempted suicide fails. The whole rehearsal process became a kind of laboratory experiment for the team. The play's status as a devised piece may have as much to do with how it is made as with how it looks when it goes to the stage. To Jain, however, the process is sometimes more important than the end product.

The exercises offstage continue onto the stage, turning initially into a Punjabi folk dance involving women and men, accompanied by the playing of *dhols* (local drums), to celebrate *Basant*, the season of colour and bounty. The dance then changes back into theatre exercises as music plays on. The first exercise for the group on stage is to walk in lines and circles forming patterns of movement that remind one of the long snarls of refugees crossing the Radcliffe Line from either side during the partition. It is also meant to familiarize the actors with the performing space and with one another. The second is a set of uniform fitness exercises, together with whistling and shouting on the stage, suggesting the vital role of the body in performance and its energetic self-exhibition. Menon calls the second set of exercises mirroring exercises in which one person replicates another's movements (2013: 126). To me, both sets of exercises actually evoke memories of endless processions of people, one behind another. I would also add that the joyous dance in circles, hand in hand, with which the second set of exercises ends, is by contrast reminiscent of a time of communal happiness before faith was politicized to sunder the country into two landmasses and the bodies and hearts of people into countless pieces (*tukdre*). The body is not absolutized here in either case, as it sometimes is in postdramatic theatre, but is an important performance element that demands the discipline of hard physical labour that the refugees by contrast lacked when they suddenly found themselves in the crevices of Indian history in 1947.

Devising has given the play a rare flexibility in form and performance language. Monologue accompanied by movement and movement interacting with objects constitute the story of Saadia, whom a Hindu man abducted during the partition and forcibly married. The folk dance and exercises gradually turn into a scene of men and women moving in a circle with a *charpoy* (a jute-string bed) on their heads, a powerful image of rest in 'normal' times, and then leaving the stage to one woman who continues to move round, balancing the *charpoy* now on her head alone. The bare country cot as a 'poor' object is innovatively used for generating a variety of movements on stage, thus giving a sense of presence to a range of Saadia's reminiscences about events in another time and place – her ride with her brother on the turning wheel, running from one room to another over the furniture and through the doors, playing hide-and-seek by going under the bed or going up to the terrace. Each such activity finds a solo 'redo' in the movements without being mimetic. Saadia's story also plays out in the form of a monologue. She narrates both her pleasant past and unpleasant present while continuing to perform those vigorous physical feats. The hyperkinetic Saadia episode, as Menon observes, raises crucial questions about female agency in those days. What other way/s might these women have acted to liberate themselves? Postdramatic theatre, as Lehmann initially defined it, would be indifferent to this question because it does not believe in achieving a goal in terms of stage action (2006: 36). But *Aur Kitne Tukde* deals with (female) agency not only beyond the commonly perceived dramatic–postdramatic binary but also beyond the 'prevailing liberal conceptions of agency'. 'Caught within a domination/subordination paradigm', as Menon observes, 'these women *do* act', if only by struggling to stay alive (2013: 132).

Not only does monologue alternate with dialogue in the interview format, as in the encounter between the two sisters who meet after forty long years, but ordinary objects and government documents take on the personality of characters. In the Zaahida story, which crisscrosses the Saadia episode, Zaahida (Zainab in real life) is seen riding pillion on her lover's bicycle. The brand new cycle, sparkling in the light as it turns, and the woman often running beside it clutching its handlebars, serve as an effective stage object in narrating an intimate love scene almost with no words. Parked at a corner, the cycle becomes a witness to their dreams as they sit by its side and plan their life together. As the lover rides back alone when Zaahida's family decide to leave the country, their dreams fall apart – the cycle shining no more and the fading shine bringing in an atmospheric gloom. The projection of documents, on the other hand, jointly drafted by the governments of India and Pakistan on the exchange of population post-partition, is a way of reporting the real to the audience beyond the fictional reality of dramatic theatre. But the document looks striking in its arbitrariness about the citizenship law directly involving the fate of millions on either side of the infamous Radcliffe Line, the effect of which is still suffered by the peoples in the subcontinent. We are returned to the Zaahida–Kirtar story at the very end of the play, after the 'remaining' parts of the first two take place. When the abducted Zaahida had a happy home with Kirtar in India, she was sent back under the recovery and restoration policy to her family in Pakistan.

The format of game is also used to replay history: it is both presentation and representation. A group of women and men gather around a makeshift slide, climb atop it and then slither down as children do. The ground below suddenly turns into an image of a well and they start enacting the story of

Basant Kaur (Harnam here), a survivor of a mass suicide campaign by Sikh women in March 1947. Reportedly, more than ninety of them jumped into a well to avoid being raped by a group of Muslims. Harnam also jumped but did not die as the well had already filled up with bodies. The simulation of the tragic event, including Harnam's failure to kill herself, not only represents the historical real but also presents it in the form of a hard, self-referential physical act. The women jump in turn; but their cries lose the excitement and fun of the previous act of mimicking and acquire a serious ritualistic overtone. The devised act on stage goes beyond symbolism by virtue of its performance realism: it uses body and choreography to expose the social process of stabilizing the code of honour for women – *stri ka samman, rashtra ka samman* (the honour of women is the honour of the nation). The survivor lives a kind of death in life, constantly reminded by her own community of her failure as a woman when Mother India (nation is the supreme female body-text) demanded her sacrifice. A (female) rape survivor would be a disgrace to the nation because rape ironically pollutes her body and, therefore, desecrates the nation she lives in. Men were ready to honour-kill their women and daughters to save them from being raped by those who do not belong to this nation on the basis of their religion.

The crisscrossing of one story with another in *Aur Kitne Tukde* problematizes the straight official narrative of the nation with its erasures and elisions, while the visual-visceral presentation of the little narratives both makes the invisible visible and undermines the dominance of word that characterizes dramatic structure. Telling or showing in Jain's theatre is not a straight 'assertion of the real as such' (Lehmann 2006: 101) but a constant switching between the performed real and the assertive real that produces a double-bind of outside and inside, real time and fictional time, acting and performing. *Aur Kitne Tukde* shows how theatre can remind us 'of the space for *new* ways of producing meaning that diverge from the officially licensed rules', to borrow phrases from Lehmann, implicitly inviting 'not only performative acts that confer new meanings but also such performative acts that bring about meaning in a new way'. 'It is not the occurrence of anything "real" as such', Lehmann would repeat, 'but its *self-reflexive* use that ... allows us to contemplate the value ... of the extra-aesthetic *in* the aesthetic' (102–3). Jain's work does so in its very own way.

From the next chapter onwards the book examines Indian theatre's increasingly steady turn towards postdramatic forms.

3

India's Postdramatic I: 'Telling Stories Across Forms', Theatre and the New Political, Theatre of Scenography

This chapter deals with theatre between the arts (Gowri Ramnarayan's *Dark Horse*, 2006), theatre and the new political (Abhilash Pillai's *Island of Blood*, 2003), and theatre of scenography (Deepan Sivaraman's *Peer Gynt*, 2010) – the first two make non-dramatic performances out of poetical and journalistic texts, respectively, while the last de-dramatizes a dramatic text. The productions under study either bear traces or fragments of narrative which are staged in a largely non-referential manner or present issues more performatively than thematically. Readings from poems, interspersed with music and choreography; presentation of political realities in the form of interviews and video installations; and adaptation of a canonical play predominantly through visual dramaturgy constitute the variety of performance covered in this chapter. What puts them into the same folder is their common capacity to go beyond logocentricity, or the literariness of drama, and explore a variety of mediums previously kept outside of theatre's purview.

Between the arts: 'telling stories across forms'

Elinor Fuchs writes that postdramatic theatre 'turn[s] the performance out to the spectators without retreat into a closed dramatic world. Yet a return by whatever circuitous route to the embrace of the narrative ... invades much contemporary postdramatic work' (Fuchs 2011: 66). Fuchs cites several works in the American theatre, 'performance pieces' which are central to Lehmann's investigation, to substantiate her point. The Elevator Repair Service's *Gatz* (2010), a verbatim reading of *The Great Gatsby*, is one. In the work under discussion, the verbatim reading of Arun Kolatkar's (narrative) poems in a fictional setting, accompanied by choreographic movements, is what constitutes theatre. Fuchs concludes that the fictive cosmos is 'a hard thing to kill' (2011: 71), although she knows at the same time that it can surely be rethought and restructured to reinforce the performance dimension of storytelling in the new theatre. What is primarily important here is the theatre situation, theatre as theatre, 'within whose energy lines the elements of fictions... inscribe themselves' (Fuchs 2019: 27). This new fictive, as Lehmann observes, is 'not a site of transcription/copying' (2006: 32).

Theatre's relationship to storytelling has in fact changed in recent times, giving rise to newer modes of *telling* on the stage. Storytelling was discarded by high artists and theatre-makers for the most part of the postwar era, resulting in the creation of a new form of elite theatre rich in visual aesthetics. One steady development in the theatre since the 1990s, however, has been the revival of the art of (direct) storytelling that attaches less importance to meaning that nevertheless seeks to erupt within the performance moment. Storytelling in postdramatic theatre is both the reality of its telling and the fictional reality that sustains the telling (Borowski and Sugiera 2010: 2–7). Theatre thus goes beyond the dramatic without cancelling out the story element. When Lehmann says that dramatic and postdramatic theatre may *coexist* at times, he does not mean 'a return of drama to the center of theater life' (2016: online). His disillusionment with the plethora of visuals, coterminous with his identification of media society as the primary factor for postdrama's appearance, is accompanied by his hope for a theatrical form that would be postdramatic without being dominated by digitally generated images.

Storytelling and text have been traditionally interrelated. It should be borne in mind that postdramatic theatre pronounces the end of 'the control of the text' (Fuchs 2019: 26), but not the end of text altogether. It dismisses the kind of text with a claim to 'originary' meaning that undermines all the suggestiveness and sensuous properties of theatre. Lehmann notes as early as 1999 that by alluding to drama's literariness, the title 'Post*dramatic* Theatre' signals the continuing relationship and exchange between stage and text. Only later text came to be considered 'as one element, one layer, or as a "material" of the scenic creation, not as its master' (2006: 17). Lehmann's citation of the multiform theatre pieces of Heiner Goebbel, among others, as examples of 'between the arts' performance is appropriate in our context because Gowri Ramnarayan, like Goebbel (however far-fetched the comparison), is a composer, vocalist, 'collagist of texts' and director. Both ensure an interaction of text with 'visual material' and a range of performing arts including song, instrumental music and dance (Lehmann 2006: 111). While the *return*-to-text wave in the 1990s yielded many new texts for the contemporary stage (for example Sarah Kane's), durational readings of classics (for example *Gatz*) altered, or added a different dimension to, narrative text's relationship to theatre. However, the storytelling in *Dark Horse* does not relate to either of the two kinds of text usage mentioned last.

Dark Horse (2006)

Dark Horse, presented at the 8th Bharat Rang Mahotsav in New Delhi shows how stories can be told on stage by employing a diversity of performance forms and styles and as a conscious 'process of representation' that does not claim any 'authoritative validity' of the world re/presented but may seek to essay a 'poetic truth' above facts in an evocative language or through the body in motion over a space that itself turns dynamic (Lehmann 2006: 33). Such performances cut across formats and disciplines – dialogue and poetry, music and songs, choreography and dance – allowing 'a huge amount of flexibility' in theatre, to put it in the words of Brian Quirt, and 'adaptability in how [artists] work' (in Ferrato 2014: 54). Indian performance tradition has always had this flexibility. Episodes from the epics and the Puranas are still recited by a class of professional reciters (called *pathakas*) who supplement the activity of the actor-performer (Awasthi 2001: 2). Those from the Mahabharata, for example, are performed in multiple performance formats simultaneously – acting, recitation, dialogue, question–answer session and philosophical/critical discourse. In *Dark Horse*, these predramatic styles and formats receive a postdramatic orientation in a number of ways contingent on the overall design of the performance.

The form draws attention, primarily. The show is in the format of an interview, but different from the way an interview would be used for creating the 'dramaturgy of the real'. 'I don't know God. But Tukaram knows God, and I know Tukaram', says the poet-character Arun Kolatkar (1932–2004) in a semi-fictional interview with a woman journalist. As the journalist-character recalls her only meeting with this famous poet in his favourite Kala Ghoda (Dark Horse) area, Mumbai, 'Kolatkar's poems spring to vibrant, mordant, quirky, even tender life, opening windows into other worlds and characters, real and surreal' (Ramnarayan 2017a). Written and directed by JustUs Repertory founder and director Gowri Ramnarayan, *Dark Horse* is a 'multi-layered performance' centring on the real as well as imagined interview and creating 'an innovative musical soundscape' that ranges from Carnatic classical to Britpop. Theatre critic Shanta Gokhale observes that *Dark Horse* is 'one of the freshest scripts one has come across in a long time. It is fluid, imaginative, witty, and comes complete with a rich, wide-ranging musical score which is like a parallel script' (in Ramnarayan 2017).

The director's account of how the 'play' got made is an interesting comment on its form (Ramnarayan 2012: 6). After much effort, years ago, she succeeded in meeting the real poet over tea at a restaurant in Kala Ghoda. The conversation was never published for various reasons, which is 'not unusual in journalism'. When Kolatkar published his *Sarpa Satra* and *Kala Ghoda Poems* in 2004, her 'interest in the man' and his work revived. 'Those poems sang to me', she says. Trained in Carnatic music, she felt 'they were in the tradition of the revolutionary bhakti [poems] of India' and could be sung and performed (Ramnarayan 2012: 7–8). All the questions she could not ask the poet when they had met came back to her, and she imagined his answers besides those she had actually had. Thus the piece constructs its own Kolatkar; the performers create a Kolatkar as a theatrical reality in itself. There is no representation as such of what the poet was or any suggestion about how his poems should be read. 'My protagonist is . . . my own construct, based on my interactions with his poems. [His] poems resonate with my own doubts and traumas, asking troubling questions about the role of art and creativity in a fractured, consumerist, blasts-ridden world', says Ramnarayan (2017b: online). As the poet is recreated and presented in the form of a real-fictive conversation with the journalist, so do the poems, imprisoned otherwise between the covers, come to life only by being performed across forms.

'*Dark Horse* is not a play', says Ramnarayan. It is 'a performance text with a musical score weaving in and out' (2012: 6). It indulges in an impressive plurality of forms and performance languages, unhinging 'methodological certainties [of] previous assumptions of causal development' in the theatre long dominated by word and plot (Lehmann 2006: 20). The play is pure fiction, but self-reflexively so. Kolatkar's poems are recited by the actor playing the poet in the course of his conversation with the journalist or read by other performers who choreograph them in a way that their body at once becomes the site of 'meaning' and produces a physicality that is 'auto-sufficient'. Poems are read to the music played by Savita Narasimhan, a renowned Carnatic vocalist. *Dark Horse* primarily builds on 'the gestures and movements of performers . . . the qualities of the visual beyond representation [and] musical/rhythmic process with its own time'. The written/verbal text is cast into a new theatrical mould that changes the traditional idea of performance text (Lehmann 2006: 35, 85). Music, dance, choreography and sound contribute to word as nearly autonomous performance practices.

Every poem is steeped in music. 'Some had *swaras* [the seven notes in Indian classical music] scattered through the stanzas, others had *alaap* [the opening stretch of an Indian classical musical performance] and *taanam* [a special technique of melodic vocalization in Carnatic music]', Ramnarayan writes. 'Some were framed by songs from other saint poets' in Tamil, Sanskrit, Hindi and Marathi (Ramnarayan 2012: 9). Almost like Conrad Alexandrowicz's project, 'Dancing the Page', Ramnarayan's seeks, in Alexandrowicz's words, to 'retrace the path' poetry took 'from its pre-literate past, when it was sung and spoken', while keeping in mind which portions of a poem would 'best lend themselves to theatrical performance' that includes movement/gesture and music (Alexandrowicz 2015: 120–1). The poem dealing with the destruction of the primeval forest with all its wildlife and native human population is performed from Kolatkar's *Sarpa Satra* as a musical. *Dark Horse* takes only a few lines from the poem and follows them with 'an *alaap* in *raga* Latangi' which, to Ramnarayan, creates 'the same image of irretrievable loss'. She uses *raga* Varali to convey the image of the sacrificial fire which is lit to 'exterminate the entire race of snakes'. The serpent woman Jaratkaru, on the other hand, enters in the middle of an old serpent dance song, narrating the tale of the burning of the Khandava forest by the 'heroic' Arjuna (Ramnarayan 2012: 10). Poetry, song, myth, choreography, dance, reading, dialogue and visuals combine in an aesthetically plural space to bring out a vision that no dramatic theatre can do and create a 'recondite hybrid project in the current marketplace of representation' where poetry is hardly read (Alexandrowicz 2015: 126).

The varied types of text that the performance brings together demonstrate a new kind of writing for the theatre in India. The show begins with a *bhajan* (a Hindu devotional song) in praise of the four incarnations of a Hindu god, Rama-Krishna-Hari-Govinda. The song melts into lines read from a piece in Kolatkar's *Kala Ghoda Poems*. When Ramnarayan first read this poem, the poet was at his terminal stage of cancer. At this point, the verses recited offstage from *Katha Upanisad* 2.2.15 are heard, followed by a young man reading from a résumé of Kolatkar: 'Kolatkar shaped a vibrant poetic idiom that blends the searching tone of bhakti poetry with the imagistic precision of modernist poetry'. An excerpt from what sounds like literary biography is used as a component for performance, which mingles with a line from the poet's *Bhijki Vahi*, read by a young woman, and a softly read passage mourning his death. The whole biographical note reads at once like an obituary and a piece of literary criticism that revisits the controversy in the Indian academia over the changing nomenclature for Indian literary texts written in English ('Indo-Anglian' to 'Indian Writing in English' to 'Indian English literature'). Performance and pedagogy come together in this production – the former comprising recitation, choreography and montage-formation; the latter a combination of class lecture and question–answer session. The journalist introduces Kolatkar's *Jejuri* poems as required readings for a class where a teacher asks questions and students answer them one by one, the answers being stock answers usually written as responses to questions set from Kolatkar's work for under/graduate examinations.

The interview is in the form of dialogue, but the conversation serves to create performance works out of Kolatkar's poems. While the music style, as hinted at above, ranges from Carnatic to Hindustani to Christmas carol to the Beatles, the vocalist onstage changes her beat as performers enter in a parade gait, move in a circle, stand in a vertical one-behind-another row, and read some verses from Kolatkar's 'Pi-Dog', distributing the lines neatly among them. Music marks the change of stanzas and the difference between the performers' varied motions. The ideology of the right-wing Hindutva brigade across the country, and particularly in Bombay (now Mumbai), is cleverly questioned by performing the dog's tale that traces the pedigree of a canine species back to places outside of India. The way the poem is performed interrogates the received notions of origin and authenticity currently dominating the political discourses in India on religious and ethnic minorities. The pi-dog's soliloquy, when performed onstage, also makes of Kolatkar's 'position of non-belonging a condition of creativity' (Zecchini 2011: 248) and of plural identity. The poet plays with binaries to evade self-categorization: Marathi/English, original/translation, *bhakti*/secular, and the like. The performance of the poem to the accompaniment of music (vocal as well as instrumental), dance and drill demonstrates an amalgamation of forms and collapses generic boundaries in theatre and performance.

Dark Horse creates a new world of perception, thus reinforcing its status as performance. The performing of the poem 'Crabs' on the stage in forms of reading and enacting displaces habitual modes of reception. The poem as a performed text builds on the opacity of perception, juxtaposed with our expectation of something in excess of what we see in fragments: 'Do you see a crab there? / Not the whole crab perhaps, not yet, / but you did see something move?' The poetic-philosophical revelation is made on stage by leaving the theatrical image of the object (crab) incomplete. The object 'crab' is not there; but it is also *not* 'not there'. It is in a perpetual in-between state of construction. The theatre-maker knows what is to be revealed and what is to be concealed in performance to produce special effects or 'where we look from, how we look, and why we look away' (Johnson 2012: 1). Dominic Johnson asks, 'If we are accustomed to looking at bodies, what happens when they look back at us, in affectively charged theatrical encounters?' (ibid.). The crabs (played by actors) make the spectator 'look behind or under' as well as look back at them. Such critical encounters continue throughout the performance, interrogating the mimetic mode of action in theatre.

Dark Horse reviews the existing relationship between the stakeholders of a performance: author, director, actor, singer, dancer and the audience. It is done in a self-reflexive manner in the presentation of Kolatkar's *Sarpa Satra*. The poem begins with a summary of its narrative for the audience figure onstage who is supposedly not familiar with the ritual of serpent sacrifice. The aim is not only to familiarize the non-initiate with the outline of the 'story' and its cultural origins but turn audience attention towards the performance aesthetics of the production rather than the development of action. The introduction to the poem is followed by the director-performer's reading of select verses from it in a way *shloka*s are incanted. The two burning *diya*s flanking her lend a ritualistic overtone to the entire stage event that otherwise mocks the inglorious practice of snake sacrifice, sanctified by religion for those in power. As her reading is punctuated by the vocalist's *bols*, mnemonic syllables that define the rhythmic pattern of a musical style, the other performers enter the stage one by one to gesticulate the story. Soon the poet figure returns to join the group by reading some verses himself, thus reducing the distance between the functionaries of the theatre into a space where performance alone matters without any hierarchy of form or role, although all of them are cast as characters. But the way Kolatkar's poems are presented on stage – reading, dance and music forming an interactive performance mode – creates an experiential reality that is defining

Telling and showing becomes all when the page comes to the stage, and it is primarily in form that the political dimension of *Sarpa Sutra* comes through. The poem performed on stage brings up images of coercive power and colonization, anthropocentric development and destruction of nature, the doublespeak of godlike big-brotherly nations and their brazen capitalist interests – all in a way different from 'dramatic' telling since the issues are not narrativized or presented in the form of dialogue (see Ramnarayan 2004: online). Nor is the story told as a 'closed-off fabl[e]' staged as a representation of external reality; stories in *Dark Horse* are told within stories making theatre partly what Ginka Steinwachs calls 'an oralic institution' with a poetic quality about it (in Lehmann 2006: 18). Furthermore, word either has its musical counterpart or is replaced by choreography. *Dark Horse* acquires through its multiple performance forms a dimension that takes it beyond the 'strong action' of dramatic theatre. It makes no ideological intervention by trying to force any meaning on the audience. The activism in *Dark Horse* resides in its formal properties, in producing a presence that has a strong sensory impact on the audience.

In Ramnarayan's theatre poetic language occupies a significant space with word deliberately dissociated from scenic action even as both may apparently exist side by side. Staging poetry may ultimately be 'dangerous', as Lehmann warns after Maeterlinck and Craig – a note of caution sounded about the difficulty of amalgamating text and stage. In *Dark Horse*, however, the transaction between poetry and stage happens on a new performative level that is a step towards the postdramatic. We witness a '"poetry" of the stage' (Lehmann 2006: 59) that in some way reconstitutes 'in the modern mind a lost faculty, the sense of the mysterious' (Clark 1920: 228) and locates the poetic in the atmospheric quality of space. *Dark Horse* shares the lyrical aspect of the Symbolist theatre by outgrowing the domination of dramatic plot ('the role script') and eliminates imitative acting by choreographing the poems without making them mimetic action as such. Moreover, in *Dark Horse* the 'textscape' (Lehmann) runs parallel to the 'audio landscape'

(Wilson), created by reading and music respectively, building up 'a space of association' in the mind of the audience. Thus the performance 'opens up "intertextual" reference to all sides', to quote Lehmann again (2006: 148), and leaves behind the old issue of text–stage discordance to create a theatre that performs text (not only poems but conversations and commentaries) and non-text into a constantly interactive relationship.

Ramnarayan is cautious about the type and extent of movement that can go well with the spoken poems. All movements are determined by her improvisatory engagement with the kind of text being read. *Dark Horse* in fact operates by making a collage of word (speech and recitation), music and choreography, but without any strained effort to integrate them for meaning-making. A quest for rhythmic bonding and a conscious avoidance of forced integration at once create the poetic moment in the theatre. The telling and the showing are not always simultaneous. Ramnarayan maintains a delicate balance between the 'mode of telling' – as in narrative literature – and the 'mode of showing' – as in the movement of a pageant (Alexandrowicz 2015: 125). Through the visual and the aural, she keeps her audience between the domains of imagination and immediate perception. By giving Kolatkar's poems a multi-dimensional performative character, *Dark Horse* acquires an intermedial presence that is absent in the predominantly representational theatre. It is not without representation; but the embodied performance in it avoids the interpretive tendency of the dramatic theatre by way of traditional plot development. Different types and layers of perceptual reality compete for recognition in the audience sensorium and interact with text to create a meaning beyond the function of dialogue and the essaying of conflict.

Theatre and the new political

Margot Morgan observes in *Politics and Theatre in Twentieth-Century Europe* that the relationship between art and politics has never been viewed as unconnected until recently. In fact, 'an ecological conception of politics', as she says, had prevailed for thousands of years, providing a worldview that sees politics as 'part of a dynamic whole' that we call social life. This social life in a broader sense comprises art, history, religion, morality and politics – all of which are understood as interconnected and 'constitutive of one another' (Morgan 2013: 1). Drawing on Michael Walzer, Morgan holds the liberal 'art of separation' to be responsible for compartmentalization of the different spheres of human experience, critiquing liberalism as 'a world of walls, and each creat[ing] a new liberty' (2). To separate art – including theatre – from social life is to resort to formalism, to draw the spectator's attention (as formalism is generally understood) to the internal process of form-making where content is nothing more than a pretext or which, as alleged by scholars like Janelle Reinelt, disengages the viewer/audience from sociopolitical and historical issues. Birgit Haas has dismissed postdramatic formalism as 'postpolitical', while Reinelt finds it too close to 'theatrical narcissism' (in Boyle et al. 2019: 6).

All such allegations may not sound wrong since Lehmann seems fairly sceptical about theatre's potential to produce anything or effect any social change. That said, the anti-postdramatic stance has often failed to recognize Lehmann's approach to form as socially and historically shaped – an extremely crucial issue discussed in the introduction. What I would underscore briefly here is the need for a fresh understanding of politics, which I call the 'new political', in its relationship to theatre and performance at two different but interlinked levels. First, the question of 'issues', which Reinelt and some other scholars find absent in postdramatic theatre. That Lehmann is opposed to the thematization of issues in theatre does not necessarily mean that such theatre is postpolitical. When theatre is primarily organized around content, theatre as theatre fades into the background. It becomes an illustration on stage of a dramatic text, predominantly a literary form, or a preconceived story with a telos that is translated into action by characters in an illusionist setting. Lehmann later felt the need for a more immediate relationship between society and stage but still located theatre between activism that may not culminate in achieving a political goal and aesthetic practice that has lost its defined frontiers and become 'performative praxis' (2016: 6, 12). Theatre, therefore, stands outside drama, but not without a critical, reflexive gaze on it. As postdramatic *practice* has become *practices* in recent years by continually reinventing itself globally, artists in multiple locations are employing an array of international forms to engage with current issues of identity, class, ethnicity/caste and faith. Lehmann's objection to conventional political theatre is primarily due to his discomfort with its representational realism and closure. Mateusz Borowski and Malgorzata Sugiera's contention that contemporary theatre can be more relevant politically through 'specific means of representation' perhaps makes better sense (2013: 3) since the mode of representation, as Lehmann himself notes, reassuring us previously of '*an immediate morality*', no longer works in an information society or under late capitalism (2006: 177). At the other level, the relationship of politics to theatre in our times underlines the fact that contemporary formalism 'engages with the reproduction of social life beyond the specific sphere of politics' but is 'inseparable from the social conditions' within which it emerges (Boyle et al. 2019: 15–17). These conditions may be simultaneously economic (modes of production in a post-Fordist society), technological (hegemony of the media and voyeurism), spatial (types of space available to twentieth-century urban theatre-makers), cultural ('the ubiquity of video' and electronics) and ecological (posthuman understanding of the body as an extension of the world's thingness). The show under scrutiny combines the two levels of the politics–theatre relationship as noted above to foreground a new kind of performance in India that uses fragmentary text, television/video images and the performer's live body simultaneously to expose, and also provisionally to comment on, a political condition from multiple perspectives.

Island of Blood (2003)

Pillai's *Island of Blood*, based on CNN's former South Asia bureau chief Anita Pratap's book *Island of Blood: Frontline Reports from Sri Lanka, Afghanistan, and Other South Asian Flashpoints*, is a telling attempt at fashioning historical material for postdramatic theatre. Cast in the form of a seamless stream of television newsfeed, it brings onto two large video screens on the 'sandwiched stage' in a studio space at NSD (Pillai 2012: 268) harrowing images of killings and destruction, loss and trauma caused by ethnic and religious conflicts, civil and proxy wars. These images, also projected on smaller video installations on the sidewalls, are of a fragmented South Asian region and fractured lives of ordinary people, especially of the ethnic-religious minorities. The ceaseless flow of news in forms of live commentary, visuals and recorded interviews is accompanied by live action on a rectangular platform surrounded by the audience on three sides. Pillai's work does not interpret politics on the stage or project the dream of an ideal world through a political programme but rather 'elicits reflection on the dominant notion of "political involvement"' (Borowski and Sugiera 2013: 69). 'No dreams as such', Pillai says in an interview with S. Gopakumar (Pillai 2014: online).'It is more about exploring theatre in terms of life to bring it closer to life. And ... theatre becomes an extension of life itself', he maintains. A new sense of urgency is created by the exposition of reality through strategized performance.

Island of Blood is very different from the politically engaged works of Pillai's predecessors. Neither the global capitalist system nor the terror network arising out of a long history of repression and occupation ensures an economically prospering or a politically liberal society. This is as true of India and its neighbours as of many other parts of the world today. Apart from this, the media has not only rendered ideological siding difficult and moralism problematic but has become the dominant mode of (mis)communication. As a result, the status of theatre has also changed worldwide. Lehmann thinks that postdramatic theatre is 'a caesura of the mediatized society' (2006: 22), as already noted, in which scenic translation of external reality is rendered problematic by the new language of the media that poses a challenge to 'intuitive perception and cognition' (175). The world dominated by the media, and thus brought home to us, hardly provides any access to reality per se, as Pillai's work shows, and questions in the process the veracity of available reality. While Guy Debord's 'the society of the spectacle' interrogates the possibility of knowing truth in an age of representation, Baudrillard's 'simulacrum' strikes a more disconcerting yet relevant note in our context since it replaces reality with simulations. Baudrillard writes that '[t]he simulacrum is never that which conceals the truth – it is the truth which conceals that there is none' and thus makes resolution of issues difficult (Baudrillard 1988: online). Consequently, theatre has had to alter its art of showing. And this is what *Island of Blood* does.

The cognitive mechanisms at work in *Island of Blood* highlight the perceptual and the sensuous, re/presenting political phenomena 'synchronically, and not as a diachronic succession that could possibly show causal connections between them' (Borowski and Sugiera 2013: 711). The live action on stage also comes in a disjointed, fragmentary manner, suggestive of a barrage of fleeting images that we watch by surfing channels on the television, and thus makes interpretation difficult. Pillai's *Island* questions, at the same time, part of the political reportage motivated by personal profit and influenced by the suspect nature of memory in representation, inserting on the other hand 'new speaking subjects' into the performance (73). The two women actors (one Malayali and the other Manipuri) playing multiple roles hardly speak, literally, however. The rationale behind having them onstage from two far-flung states of India (Kerala and Manipur), as Pillai explains in his doctoral thesis, is that both the states (especially the latter) were confronting political upheavals when he made this production and there was little mention of them in newspapers or on the television since most of the journalists were more interested in other kinds of sensational, 'profitable' news. This brings a new politics into contemporary theatre that does not develop any political fiction through plot and character and leaves the action to the audience to decide where judgement seems feasible. Pillai's work both 'mimics and reflects the omnipresent media and their suggestion of immediacy', screening the pervasive sense of horror that grips the subcontinent and simultaneously parodying technology's hubris to define the world (Lehmann: 118–19).

Conceived for the Holy City Festival 2003 in Berlin, the production builds on the frontline reports that Pratap sent to the newsroom from Sri Lanka, 'a ravaged nation' reeling under the Janatha Vimukthi Peramuna (JVP) insurrections of 1971 and 1987–9, followed by the civil war (1983–2008); Afghanistan, 'the doomed land' under the Taliban regime; and from Ayodhya in India, lost in a 'cycle of revenge' beginning with the dismantling by Hindu zealots of the six-hundred-year-old Babri Mosque in 1992. Pratap later puts these reports together in her book interspersing them with self-congratulatory stories of her courage as a reporter. But Pillai's work deliberately disregards the chronological order of the episodes in print because it seeks to create the impact of media journalism on the spectators, presenting 'a multi-layered *picture* [my emphasis] of political and social turmoil' (Pillai 2012: 300–5). The scope for the actor in this show is purposely made subservient to the role of the media-as-performer which dominates perception (305). Pillai writes in his thesis that he used the media-generated scenes in this production as 'a parallel trajectory' that would 'exhibit visually [the] dismembered body' of a region by throwing up 'a plethora of ... [new] images', 'one against the other', which are 'all fragmented [and] compet[e] for attention' (305). Ethnicity, faith and gender crisscross the narratives of violence. The external world is present through its mediatized images, raising the question whether the new media is representational or constitutive of reality.

When it comes to text, it is meant more for reading than for acting. The two women on stage read aloud excerpts from two religious texts (one Hindu; the other Christian) written in their respective mother languages. The scriptures include, among other things, passages on the discriminatory code of conduct for women. The performers suddenly switch to readings from the Constitution of India, relating mostly to the principles of equality, liberty and secularism, thus building up a contrast between the two types of texts they read from. Their loud, simultaneous readings create a form of cacophony, compelling the audience to strain their ears to understand the content before its loss beyond recovery. The contentious interpretations of the lines/clauses from the scriptures and the Constitution suggest the indeterminacy of textual referents. But the most disturbing question from the outer world, 'What are you: Hindu or Muslim?', accompanied by fleeting pictures of Hindu gods and goddesses, points to a brazen parade of Hindu nationalism over the secular principles of India as a republic. The question was actually put to Anita Pratap by the late Shiv Sena chief Bal Thackeray as the journalist approached the Hindutva ideologue for an interview after the *kar sevak*s (religious volunteers) had pulled down the massive mosque raised by Babur allegedly in place of a Hindu temple commemorating the birth of the legendary Lord Ram. Pitted against the Hindutva version of Bharat is Gandhi's vision of Hindustan, embodied in the salt strip centre stage reminding one of the historic Dandi march for a free and plural India.

Recorded text and images converge to create an atmosphere of terror. The 'Mothers and Sons' section of Pratap's book is shown as video work, delineating the joy of motherhood in the face of challenges confronting a journalist working in conflict zones. If it is taken as representation, it enjoys the freedom and flexibility of the cinematic form, calling attention to the medium ('the medium is the message', as McLuhan would say) more than the content which is found in shreds. However, the focus abruptly shifts from the video display of products in shopping malls, marketed for mothers and babies, to two perambulators on the stage – one carrying tools that a media journalist needs for reporting and the other ferrying equipment required for terror attacks, both drawing equal attention (Pillai 2017a). As the journalist figure takes up the camera to shoot, blasts begin: images of the actual ones across South Asia flash on the screens, including the Bombay serial blasts of 1993 which happened months after the Babri Masjid demolition in Ayodhya. 'Hindu ke liye Hindustan, Musalmaan ko kabristan' ('Hindustan for Hindus, the graveyard for Muslims'), a Hindutva slogan, referred to in Pratap's book and related to these video images of devastation and its backlashes, contextualizes the politicization of faith in India for pure electoral gains. Another fragment of text on the soundtrack, 'Why should I go there [to Pakistan]? ... This is where I was born', serves as the pivot around which the Ayodhya segment of the show revolves (Pratap 2002: 187, 193). None of the episodes have a dramatic beginning or end. It is also important to note that neither of the actors on stage assumes the role of a character; each performs a series of discrete movements suggestive of a world gone wrong and confused but with no remedies in sight as power operates insidiously and escapes public survey or management.

Images and film footage, sound and fragmented action, and readings from the Pratap book are interwoven to present news from the conflict zones. The cover pages of reputable national dailies, carrying news and pictures of the violence all around, are projected on screen. Thackeray's defence of the acts of violence perpetrated by his men ('my boys are retaliating'), which demonize the Muslim community in India and assert the 'natural' innocence of the Hindu populace, finds an ironic counterpart in an offstage voice justifying the Islamist imposition of the Shariat rule in Afghanistan. The news and images from the 'Doomed Land' and the 'Island of Blood' crisscross into collages, sending the spectator back and forth in time and space. A performer demonstrates preparations for a suicide mission: she covers herself with strips of explosives and slings an AK 47 from her shoulder, while on the screen appear images of shooting and explosion. The voice offstage makes oblique references in newsreading style to the presence of the Indian Peace Keeping Force (IPKF) on Sri Lankan soil in 1987, the long-standing Tamil demand for the devolution of power, the JVP's unleashing of terror on the state machinery in retaliation against the IPKF accord, the emergence of the

Liberation Tigers of Tamil Eelam (LTTE) and the seizure of Jaffna, and to the failure of the second JVP insurrection (for details, see Sengupta 2014: 43–50). Pillai's presentation of the hyped LTTE chief Prabhakaran alludes to the mass popularity of 'heroes' in the Tamil film industry (Pillai 2017a). Pratap's interviews with the militant leader and the swirl of action since 1983 are randomly read out and digitally presented in Pillai's work. The performance becomes a complex of reporting, reading and dialogue on one hand, and of digital documentation and screening on the other, showing the shift towards technology as the dominant medium of art and culture including theatre.

Footage is shown of the rugged terrains of Afghanistan, invaded by the Soviet forces in 1979 and later freed by the US-created Mujahideen militia. With the Russians pulling out of the devastated land in 1989, the Mujahideen rolled their tanks into Kabul with much euphoria and, after a three-year-long civil war, the Najibullah regime fell. The Taliban invaded Afghanistan in 1996, 'filling the ominous vacuum left by the evacuating troops' of the Burhanuddin Rabbani government that came to power with the dissolution of the previous regime (Pratap 2002: 149). As video projections go on, the women on stage perform various feats that loosely connect Afghanistan, India and Sri Lanka along an axis of violence and destruction: toting guns, sharpening knives, wearing bombs – spectacular examples of the humans used as means to ends by the big powers that remain invisible to the public eye. The same women lighting lamps and reading stories, on other occasions, may be indicative of good times poised between wars. The images on screen and the offstage readings from the Pratap book, however, evoke a life under threat across the South Asian region.

The production is also a commentary on media reportage and its ethical dimensions and, by implication, on Pratap's book as a popular political treatise of an internationally acclaimed South Asian reporter. Pillai's attitude towards contemporary media culture is critical. He shows how the news is processed and perceived at large, or what 'reality' means, in the information society and how it affects people. The news and the video images were 'conceived on the lines of the popular visuals of the [electronic] media', Pillai notes in his thesis. There are visuals on screen and movements on stage that obliquely highlight the media's 'sentimentalism ... [about] violence', the director writes, and its popular representation of rebel leaders. While the production leaves little space to figure out Pillai's own position on the LTTE cause, the full picture of Prabhakaran on the screen exuding an aura about him is suggestive of the new media's role in making a mass hero of a man almost anonymous hitherto. 'Probably, [the media journalists] are after spicy news ... in the global market, and would like to play along with the[ir] power managers', says Pillai, often ignoring regional concerns such as the violation of civil rights in Manipur and the ethnic-linguistic strife confronting Kerala

(Pillai 2012: 304–6). It is here that a very short sequence, titled 'Reporter & Editor', acquires the utmost significance in the show: the image of a big hand comes down on the screen, probably to edit out portions that do not suit the business interests of the press. On the other hand, Pratap's dispatches on the training of Tamil Tigers in guerrilla warfare, the media journalist's journeys through the dense forests in Jaffna, and her reporting from Afghanistan, clad in a burqa, no less make a 'hero' of her. Without narrativizing politics, Pillai has shown how the very medium that rules the world today can be used as a performance form to critique it as well as the political culture of our times.

Ana Tasić argues after Greg Giesekam that in intermedial theatre, the simultaneity of the live and the mediatized forces us to re/examine conventional notions of liveness and presence. The use of video in Pillai's production operates, to borrow Giesekam's words, 'as part of a general interrogation of representational practices that pervades ... [postdramatic] work' and, particularly, as an instance of mediation and remediation (in Tasić 2011: 125). When the live on stage is mediated by mimesis, the mediatized spectacle in theatre is a case of remediation, suggesting that 'every medium is a medium' of another medium (ibid.). Contemporary experimental (live) performance also uses or references media, as Jürs-Munby says, 'not in order insidiously to "replicate" ... but in order to probe their status and impact on us in a self-conscious manner – including their history of remediating theatre' (in Lehmann 2006: 13). The issues of presence and authenticity in this perspective lie not in the bid for faithful representation but in the theatre's aesthetic strategies of performing the political in the form and manner in which it reaches us in present times.

Theatre of scenography

Many think that the multiform scenography in Indian theatre needs to be assessed by parameters different from Western standards. The word *'aharya'* in *Natyashastra* (arguably written between 200 BCE and 200 CE) means 'make-up' or embellishment, which is not exactly scenography by contemporary standards. Being presentational rather than representational in form, predramatic genres of Indian theatre, which are still practised, have 'scenes' described by stylized dance, choreography, and hand/finger gestures. The Renaissance-style Italian perspectival painting became 'Indianized' in Parsi theatre between the 1850s and the 1930s to recreate/represent a sense of place and atmosphere on stage – including forests, gardens, buildings and streets. The painting of a scene on wings and curtains became a popular aspect of theatre art. In Sanskrit plays in Hindi translation (1956 to the 1970s), again, the stage had elaborate sets for creating an environment. The use of painted masks and designed costumes in premodern folk theatre is another instance of visual art that might have contributed over time to scenography in modern Indian theatre. Scenography as stagecraft entered urban theatre in the 1940s as a distinctive discipline with Tapas Sen's pioneering lighting and Khaled Choudhury's innovative sets. On the other hand, Ebrahim Alkazi's staging of plays (especially in the 1970s) in old forts and the ruins of medieval structures introduced site-specific theatre in India and heralded an important variant of modern scenography. Scenography in Indian theatre took a still newer turn as women directors entered into theatre-making in the 1990s and went beyond the prevalent realist/representational practice by using visual arts – such as painting, installations, *kolams* (floral motifs made with rice flour) – and performing in unconventional spaces. Scenography became a dominant language of theatre in India at the beginning of the twenty-first century as a host of young theatre-makers, such as Deepan Sivaraman and Zuleikha Chaudhari, made several experimental productions (including performance installations) using their training in Indian theatre aesthetics as well as their exposure to theatre-making in the West. Set design, architectural patterns, use of natural elements such as water and fire, laying of text on different kinds of material such as cloth, glass and acrylic screens, transformative lighting of performance sites, and the use of sprawling lawns for real-time action constitute the new visual language in Indian theatre and performance.

Appreciation of scenographic theatre in India is not possible without trying to understand what scenography means today globally and how it is connected to postdramatic theatre. Postdramatic theatre attempts to dislodge the 'logocentric hierarchy' by assigning greater importance, as Lehmann observes, to 'elements other than dramatic logos and language', especially the visual and the auditory. When a *'visual dramaturgy'* comes in place of a text-driven dramaturgy, the former is less 'an exclusively visually organized dramaturgy' than a performance paradigm that can develop its autonomous logic (2006: 93). Visual dramaturgy, which forms the core of the postdramatic theatre of scenography, is largely defined by 'optical data' (93) and, therefore, has its own system of meaning-formation. This theatre comes very close to visual art, and it is no coincidence that many postdramatic theatre-makers are from visual art or have collaborated closely with visual artists. Modernist visual art forms have generally rejected representation or any kind of signification and focused on their self-reality instead. But one should also recognize that theatre, even when scenographic and therefore predominantly visual, is also a world of human action that makes this attitude towards aesthetic reality more difficult (94). One possible way to overcome this difficulty is to present the 'all too "dramatic" events' (torture, war, death), as Kantor does, by creating 'a pictural poetry of the stage' (72), a de-realization of the human figures, and thus avoid the illusion of representational authenticity.

However, this is not a prescriptive approach to scenographic theatre. Scenography today has expanded and pluralized its forms. As regards India's scenographic theatre, I would like to discuss only the theatre of Deepan Sivaraman in this section, although I probe the works of others in the field (in other chapters) but under separate rubrics. Director Sivaraman prefers to call himself a scenographer and considers his work as a variant of the 'theatre of scenography'. He has admittedly been influenced by the works of several theatre-makers of the West during his education abroad and his tour of European countries with his own – Kantor being one of them. Sivaraman also pays tribute to Alfred Jarry while explaining his dramaturgy:

> Theatre of scenography is actually more than 100 years old; it dates as far back as Alfred Jarry who shook the art world with his play *Ubu Roi*. But in India, as it is with also other countries like the United Kingdom, many viewers still consider theatre to be all about the written text. If audiences read an object in my play as a visual device, then they are failing to understand the language I am trying to explore and the dramaturgy I am creating through design. The very 'device' they are amused with is an integral part of the dramaturgy I create. Sensibilities need to be developed [for this language of theatre].
>
> Sivaraman 2013: online

The tradition of storytelling in theatre is old in India. Sivaraman would never be blind to his context and audience expectation. He therefore distinguishes between influence/inspiration and imitation. He notes this in an interview with the author:

> I do like narratives; Indians love stories – but I do not tell my stories in a 'dramatic' way. Many Western theatre-makers – such as Foreman, Kantor, Wilson – have told stories, but in a de-dramatized, fragmented manner. Further, the situation in India is more complex: the audience here, especially in villages, are not familiar with the language of the new theatre. So my art is neither fully non-representational nor fully representational. I don't want to repeat the linear structure, and the objects used work very well by themselves within their context. The text is there; but it is not the centre or the primary material. It gives you only a fluid storyline that you develop through scenography.
>
> Sivaraman 2016

Sivaraman maintains that only when the transition takes place from a dramatic text to a performance text, is it possible to move away 'from a textual performance to a visual performance' (Sivaraman 2014: online). His attempt is to 'transcend ... the strict boundaries between visual art and theatre – and

Figure 3 *The Legends of Khasak* (2015), directed by Deepan Sivaraman, presented by KMK Smaraka Kalasamithi, Trikkaripur. Photo credit: Ameer Ali Olavara.

provide an experience beyond conventional drama' (Sivaraman 2013: online). He often devises his theatre during the rehearsal without any written script. He would draw his 'ideas out on paper, make three-dimensional models of my drawings, and make a blueprint of actions, which at some point take physical shape through the interaction and collaboration with the actors'. When the action begins, he often adds text to it and keeps 'reforming it in tandem with my visual ideas' (ibid.). His goal is to find a scenographic language which 'explores space while collaborating with various art disciplines'. Sivaraman sees the 'future of Indian theatre' in our ability for such 'intermingling' (ibid.). A visual object, for him, may momentarily signify something, 'but you don't prolong the process of signification' (Sivaraman 2016). He creates unconventional designs out of used and found objects with their emotional and cultural associations, and aims at 'a visual texture which is closer to the times we live in'.

Peer Gynt (2010)

Deepan Sivaraman's *Peer Gynt* was commissioned jointly by the Norwegian Embassy and Delhi-based Dramatic Art and Design Academy (DADA) for the Ibsen theatre festival of 2010 and produced by Oxygen Theatre Company. 'My play starts where Ibsen's [1867/1876] ends, with Gynt's death. Gynt asks God to give him another chance to be a better man. The Devil, however, is convinced that an evil man will never change', Sivaraman says in an interview with Dipanita Nath (Sivaraman 2012: online). For the scenographer-director, the project was an experiment in spatial design, in the physicality of performance, materiality of objects (including the puppets that replace human actors intermittently), ritualistic structure, music, costume – elements, in short, which more speak their own language than simply illustrate the text or do 'scene painting' according to 'the needs of the text' (McKinney and Palmer 2017: 1). Sivaraman's scenography in *Peer Gynt* might not have gone so far as to be a fully autonomous art practice, but has certainly established itself as a 'performance design' in its own right. It is an attempt at 'a multisensorial and dynamic' scenography which is both contributory to and constitutive of theatrical action, both self-reflexive 'and capable of a dialogue or even a confrontation with other elements of theatre' (ibid.: 5). In *Peer Gynt*, either Sivaraman's visual imagination dictates the text or his visual statements develop independently of any text, leaving much for the spectator to make sense of.

The scenographer's preoccupation with space and material, and the show's relationship with the audience, is self-evident in his email to the Bharat Rang Mahotsav (BRM) team at the National School of Drama in 2011:

> Please note that *Peer Gynt* will not be performing on the proscenium setting using the usual spatial design of Kamani[;] instead we are planning to build a four-sided gallery on the stage and [the] audience will be sitting around the squ[a]re performance space ... Also note, as part of the scenography a 25′ × 25′ metal structure with a height of 9 ft. will be constructed in the middle[,] which means the subtitle screen should be above the structure in order to avoid any masking.
>
> Sivaraman 2018a

Sivaraman wanted his audience to have a wider view of objects that speak for themselves all over the space. The behaviour of the material in space, in fact, becomes in such case 'a performative act' in itself (McKinney and Palmer 2017: 8) and also an encounter for the audience who see their own 'desires and fears' (Maaike Bleeker, in ibid.: 7) in the material presented. *Peer Gynt* makes little attempt to put material in a mimetic correspondence with the text and thus fix a meaning, but instead gives it a context in such a way as to generate 'multiple contingencies of subjective response' (Freshwater, in ibid.). And the material the scenographer uses – whether it is an object or costume or light – is decided and developed through workshops with others in the team. I would use an example Sivaraman cites himself to substantiate this point.

> I thought of using the character of a devilish dog which chases Peer Gynt throughout the play. I took this idea to my object designer Anto George, and he started to improvise a puppet dog and came up with a prototype which he handed to the actors. They improvised with it for several days and handed it back to Anto asking to alter it according to the sequence they had developed. Concurrently I wrote the dialogues for ... the Devil, closely watching the communication that had developed between the actors and the design team.
>
> Sivaraman 2013: online

It was difficult to present *Peer Gynt* scenographically because it was conceived in the form of a tussle between God and the Devil over the fate of a human being. But the conflict informing the project is presented through an expansive scenography that brings political commentary into theatre in a postdramatic way. To go by his words, Sivaraman adapted the Ibsen play by letting his 'imagination run wild', by opening up 'the tremendous possibilities of visual exploration' (ibid.). Non-human creatures (played by actors) and surrealist objects dominate the opening of the show, generating 'a ritual mode of perception' (Lehmann 2006: 58). Ghosts and animated objects fill the stage, invoking the old element of fate, but through a new dramaturgy. The dramatic structure is dismantled by dismissing linear time and rationality as factors central to discourse formation. The objects have their symbolic value but do not make *Peer Gynt* Symbolist theatre because the correspondence between them and the non-aesthetic real is not denotative or congruous. This breaks down the conventional terms of communication in theatre, asking the spectator to participate in meaning-making. The skeleton of the devil dog chases the doll that opens the show with its robotic movement, manoeuvred by two people. At the centre of the performing area, which looks like a morgue, is a bed on which is laid the body of Gynt, covered in a plastic sheet, his heart lying on the floor close to his bed, with a pool of light focused on it. An anxious, insomniac God enters in the surgeon's apron with an operating-theatre trolley with jars on its top shelf filled with human hearts. God has collected them to find out in the lab how these hearts turned to the Devil during their lifetime. When asked about the use of such an object (Gynt's synthetic heart), Sivaraman said: 'When the objects refer more to themselves, that's a moment of presentation which is however not totally disconnected from representation' (Siavaraman 2016).

The story of Peer Gynt is told by his old mother, who comes out of her grave only for the sake of the telling. The dead intervening in the life of the living is not only a part of the Malayali tradition but also reminds one of Heiner Müller's famous saying that theatre is a 'dialogue with the dead' (in Lehmann 2006: 70), a ceremonial act that has passed from high modernist drama to contemporary theatre, or of the Japanese Noh that celebrates 'the return of the dead with a minimum of the mimesis' (Lehmann 2006: 70). Gynt's notorious early life with his mother is narrated through a long dialogue between them, parallel to which run scenographic explorations. The mother, played by C. R. Rajan (a male actor of repute), enters carrying her own skeleton on her shoulder, along with a broom, a bucket and a plastic sack. The palimpsestic image of a person at once living and dead, living in the sense that she is recalled to life for a ceremonial performance and dead as evident in her bearing of her own skeleton, is a radical departure from conventional image-making and scenic representation in Indian dramatic theatre.

The teller is not always present on stage, but the telling happens mostly via visual dramaturgy. The wedding scene de-dramatizes the Ibsen play in a way that evokes a phenomenological experience of atmosphere and events and presents materiality as immediately influencing our regular, normative perception. A number of low benches are so arranged as to form the pattern of a cross laid on the floor. Close to the intersection of the pole, staff stands a priest in a white robe reading passages from the Bible to the gorgeously dressed wedding couple who stand at two ends of the crossbar. Two nuns also stand on the floor with the Bible in hand, one behind the bride and the other behind the groom. At either end of the pole/staff is a person who is cooking food (real-time action) on a gas stove, presumably for wedding guests. Two lamps with bluish flames also burn on either side of the priest. The hollowness of the ritualistic extravaganza is suddenly exposed by the priest's exhortations to the bride, 'even if your husband gets angry at you, he is your guardian', and by Gynt's elopement with the bride (Ingrid). The fragmentary visuals, theatrically manipulated, rupture the logic of mimesis and the profanation of the sacred embodied in the institutionalized ritual is a figurative break-away from the holy institution of dramatic theatre.

Sivaraman's scenography acquires an autonomous agency, even as it contributes to the storyline, in the scene following Gynt's desertion of Ingrid in a hotel room. The presentation of a scene without words and solely by way of visuals and music is new to the postindependence theatre in India. Gynt's sexual fantasy runs wild as three dolls (actors so dressed) dance to fast drumbeats and the blue-and-white beams rotate around them. An aroused Gynt is seen running across the floor and traversing the dancing dolls who sing 'Oh, you naughty bee, / Searching for nectar-laden flowers / Crush my inner petals / with your rough footsteps'. As the dolls exit and a tired Gynt lies down on the floor, the drumbeats slow down and the accompanying flute music transports us to a fairylike world. Enter an alien female figure in a leafy green top, with thick/juicy petals beneath her ears and the lower half of her body in a loosely flowing gown. She is holding an artificial lotus, trying to wake Gynt up by tearing off its petals and throwing them at him. The human and the non-human coexist in the same figure and in such a way that the logos would fail to re/present the 'reality'.

Sivaraman's scenography in *Peer Gynt* breaks new ground when the troll woman's father enters, seated on the metal skeleton of a horse fitted onto a trolley, followed by his armed men. The chief's horse is drawn by a bird (an actor dressed in a frilled gown resembling wings) with a long red beak and a grey head. The chief's army (the aliens) begin the tortuous process of turning Gynt into a troll by embossing the gang's emblem on him with electric drilling machines. A bloody, groaning Gynt is left on the floor at the end. The devil dog enters, hissing and gasping and chasing Gynt again. Such surrealistic presentation of quasi-human figures in a post-anthropocentric setting, composed like sculpture in an architectural space, contributes to the diversity of India's postdramatic. Acting, puppetry, choreography, music and gadgetry combine to build a theatre where human bodies intersect with a range of material and space to configure a reality that defies preconceived meanings and proposes 'an understanding of design as process in which things and ideas come to matter together' (McKinney and Palmer 2017: 125).

Scenography of this kind points to 'new configurations of design and performance' (2), to new stage compositions where pre-existing narratives, even when available in fragments, do not make them their illustrations. Such compositions develop and unfold according to their own visual (and auditory) logic (125).

Sivaraman's experimental scenography reaches its apex in the hospital scene where space, body, material, geometry and text work autonomously and yet do not refuse connection in difference. The performed acts within the scenographic frame are self-reflexive. Gynt's mother lies on a mobile bed with her skeleton next to her. She has to die again in her story, the story for whose sake she came out of her grave. A lamp is burning on her chest, held by her hand. Three more empty beds on wheels are rolled in by three men clad in milky white *dhotis* and coughing incessantly. These people are actors as well as performers who set the stage and ready themselves for action, thus breaking down theatre's illusionist atmosphere. Lamps are burning at the edge of each bed, arranged in geometric proportion to one another. The three men (terminally ill patients) keep the lamps down on the floor, spit into the boxes provided to them, pull up the catheter bags attached to their genitals and lie down on their backs. Sivaraman's scenography creates a whole atmosphere of disease, illness and morbidity – destabilizing the traditional notion of audience comfort in the theatre that is supposed to offer beauty even in pain and suffering. The tension between life and death, good and evil is painted in a language that functions 'as the sum total of the visual, spatial, and aural components of a performance' (Aronson 2017: xiii) Instead of taking the dialectical, dialogical route, Sivaraman's *Peer Gynt* collapses categories on stage – animate and inanimate, human and non-human, 'man' and machine, mind and body, painting and architecture, and, most importantly, presentation and representation – and in so doing lets scenography mount the performance.

Ludwig Jáger's 'epistemology of disruptions' should prove relevant to understanding the underside of the business world Gynt joins. The scene is portrayed as an opaque atmosphere positioning the audience as part of it and narrating the events as 'transcription' or 'transition from disruption to transparency' (Jáger 2010: 82). Although Jáger developed his theory to analyse the mode of communication in media, 'transparency' and 'disruption' as 'two polarized functional conditions' – the former as 'unproblematic recognition of meaning' and the latter as its 'recurrent reconceptualization' – should help us understand the condition of visibility in the scene and, therefore, the dynamics of meaning-formation in it (83). The rectangular structure built on the stage, covered on all sides with a foggy plastic sheet, has a number of businessmen assembled inside. The criminal world of vulgar money is given a visual quality that supersedes in effect any 'dramatic' sign system. The interior is lit red. The men get drunk and end up fighting over the conditions of the proposed deal. Gynt is assaulted, his briefcase seized, and the currencies inside go flying about. The transition from the sign making itself invisible in performance, and thus making the mediated transparent, to the sign making itself visible, and thus disrupting the interior's transparency, defines the scene. Sivaraman's theatre of scenography may be said to reside within a large 'framework of art, architecture and social practice', redefining the approach to presence which, in order to present itself, has to go through a chain of mediation and remediation (Aronson 2017: xiv).

Sivaraman's scenography moves 'from background to foreground' and presents itself as 'the generative element of performance'. The dog revisiting Gynt, barking loudly and chasing him to death, becomes a 'visual-aural-spatial construct' that turns allegory into experiential reality (xiv). In the scene of his funeral, his body is laid on a makeshift hearse, with his skeleton lying next to him – a hyphenated visual image where the exterior (lifeless body still appearing intact) and its decomposed interior (the bare skeleton) exist side by side to provide an experience of the 'deficient body' (Shearing 2017: 148). The burial ritual, conducted elaborately, not only suggests the liminality between life and death but brings scenography and architecture in an intricate relationship. God appears for the last time, cordoning off the site of burial, as of a murder, with a long 'caution' tape that separates the enclosed space from its outside as if for ever and evokes Jacques Herzog's 'horror' of a durable built place (architecture) as well as Thea Brejzek's ephemeral 'aesthetic imprisonment' (scenography). Working both architecturally and scenographically, Sivaraman welds the 'time-based art of scenography', basically aimed at producing 'atmosphere and effect' for the duration of a performance, with the 'built reality' of an enduring architectural space. His scenography eventually rethinks material, design and space towards an 'interactive architecture' and irreverent fracturing of beauty on stage (Brejzek 2017: 63–4). God says, 'Life is not that easy to live', and then exits pushing along the laboratory trolley with the jars atop still containing the hearts. The scenographic re/writing of the moral yields an experience very different from how it would be in the symbolic representation of modern unified scenography.

4

India's Postdramatic II: Monologies and Theatre Solos

Theatre solos/monologies

Solos and monologies (not monologues of the dramatic type) are considered a significant part of the postdramatic panorama. A monology, as Lehmann broadly defines it, may be the self-presentation of an actor, a playing or speaking of all the roles in a dramatic text, the rendering of a play text or a non-theatrical literary text into a monologue, and so on. The monologue or solo performance in this new sense succeeds with its directness and immediacy, where the dialogue-based play doubly fails for being a fictive substitution for the already failed communication in the world offstage. This should not imply, though, that monologies/monologue theatres do not tell stories or build a fictive world on stage. The act of *telling*, however, takes the audience into the very process of story-making, and it is here that it deviates from the dramatic theatre which is predominantly illusionist as a finished product. Monologies can help theatre exist as 'an "external communication system" ... almost without the construction of a "fictional internal communication system"' (Lehmann 2006: 125–8). Their distinctiveness is in this communication system, or presentation, rather than in the fictionality or non-fictionality of their material.

Lehmann cites a number of productions to substantiate his point, which are translations of classical or Shakespearean plays, or of other narrative/dramatic texts, into monologues: Klaus-Michael Gruber's monologue version of *Faust*, Hermann Broch's *Story of the Maidservant Zerline* and Robert Wilson's *Hamlet – A Monologue*. Of the other performances constructed as monologues and which are performer-centric, Lehmann also mentions Edith Clever's *Penthesilea* or her *Marquise of O*, directed by Hans Jügen Syberberg, and Marisa Fabbri's role in *Bacchae*. The Wooster Group's preference for Eugene O'Neill's plays, such as *The Emperor Jones* and *The Hairy Ape*, is referenced for their inherent monodramatic qualities. Formalism informs these performances, especially Wilson's, in the sense that things are defamiliarized formally; yet articulations of personal emotions with a lot of psychology and poetry are not rare either. What is more important is that when a *'real theatrical situation'* ensues from the violation of the order of *'the imaginary dramatic universe'*, a perception is reached that is more authentic in terms of the performer–audience relationship (Lehmann 2006: 127).

Theatre solos of twenty-first-century India have partly descended from various types of non- or semi-dramatic forms that had existed in an ancient culture before the arrival of the dramatic via colonial routes. In his book, *Performance Tradition in India* (2001), Suresh Awasthi discusses some such forms of performance in a chapter titled 'Itinerant Performers and Wandering Bards'. Following the decline during the ninth and tenth centuries of Sanskrit drama, which was different from the theatre of Racine (who, for Lehmann, inaugurated the dramatic phase in Europe) in invoking *rasa* (sap) as the target of *natya* (theatre) and pursuing *ananda* (pure delight) beyond all pain and pleasure, theatrical activity in India 'manifested in many types of semi-dramatic forms' including painting recitation, oral narratives, Burrakatha, and so on. Of these, some are solos (*Akhyan* with one reciter-narrator), some feature two performers (painting recitation) and a few others are performed by a group (*Pala*). But what is common to several of them is 'the intricate stylistic interweaving of a number of performance elements' – question–answer, monologue, stylized gait, dance-like movement, musicality of structure, the combination in one person of the multiple roles of storyteller, reciter, singer and performer (Awasthi 2001: 26–7). Many of these performance elements largely inform some theatre solos in present-day India that are nevertheless different from the original semi-dramatic performances by being modern in form and style or postcolonial in spirit. Those ancient performance traditions are used for the contemporary stage primarily to do theatre beyond the dramatic type that had dominated the Indian theatre scene for over a hundred years since the middle of the nineteenth century.

The theatre solos that have come up in India recently may be called postdramatic in form since they violate the organizational order of the dramatic theatre by creating a theatrical situation with its focus on performance reality and, therefore, on the presentness of happening. Of a large body of such theatre solos and monologies in India, the following stand out: Sudarshan Chakravorty's solo performance based on female impersonation (2016); the theatrical solo by Kartikey Tripathi, based on Divya Prakash Dubey's *Class Nine B* (2016); Sujayprasad Chatterjee's reading of 'Vagina Monologues' (2016); Kalyanee Mulay's non-verbal *unSEEN* (2016); and the works of Maya Krishna Rao and Jyoti Dogra. Each of these productions has pushed the boundaries of theatre in India. 'The focus has turned to solos as a genre in itself', says Rao. Apart from being part of the general pull-away from the dramatic theatre tradition, theatre solo as a form suits (Indian) performers since it does not require bulky funds or elaborate stage arrangements and is portable enough to tour places. I discuss below two solo performances of Maya Krishna Rao, arguably the most renowned solo theatre artist in contemporary India, and one by Jyoti Dogra, who makes devised pieces that are not text-based and, therefore, not narrative in structure either. For both, the self/body is the starting point for performance.

Maya Krishna Rao

Rao's theatre solos are a mix of cross-media performance, monologues, stand-up comedy and dance theatre that includes cabaret and Kathakali. She often begins to make a performance from a blank slate: 'The theatre-making process for me is about letting myself into a series of experiences. The trigger could be a short story, an event or a single prop. Improvisation is at the core ... the performance, as it takes shape, is its own reality'. The improvisations are shot on camera, and when Rao watches them on her laptop, she begins to see what is emerging as part of her theatre (M. K. Rao 2019: 55). She trusts 'the gut more than the head', she says. Meaning is born only within the process of performance-making, though interpretation is also somehow embedded 'in the random selection of material that I play with'. And that, for Rao, is politics because ultimately 'we bring our baggage of gaze and experience to bear upon the work we produce for the stage'. But 'the primary appeal' of her work, Rao notes, is to 'the emotions and the senses' (2016). This is, however, not to delink thought, emotion and feeling because cognition and emotion are interdependent, as Jackie Smart argues after Joseph LeDoux, and the central theory of neuroscience today is that emotions are not only 'ancient in evolutionary terms' but form 'an essential part of our interpretation and evaluation of situations and events' (Smart 2014: 103).

It is not after all difficult to see why Rao's work is far from dramatic theatre. It is more connected to body, sound and image than text. She calls her work 'theatre', and not 'performance art', in that the starting point for the performance artist is not the body but the visual (Rao 2016). In Rao's case, the visual, in spite of its functional presence in her work, mostly supplements the theatrical situation that arises out of the body. In a conversation with the author, Rao refers to *Cut Piece* (1964) where Yoko Ono has her dress cut off piece by piece on the stage by members of the audience with a pair of scissors. The performance artist begins with her dress, and the cut pieces turn into images or visuals, although they finally 'interact with her body'. But Rao improvises her performance with her body as the primary and enduring medium. This for her is 'a Lehmann moment' (Rao's phrase) in the sense that what gets made through the different stages of this process is 'a real moment' for the performer (Rao 2016). She has often wondered with her cameraman and sound designer (whom she calls collaborators) why they do not 'invite audiences to ... [their] improvisations. "What's this idea of 'rehearsing'?"' (M. K. Rao 2019: 55). Rao does not sometimes feel comfortable editing out portions of her improvisation for the final show. But she also accepts the inescapable paradox that the 'refinement' that the improvisations undergo is necessary for the time-bound performances (Rao 2016). In the real theatrical situation she creates on the spot is the distinctiveness of her theatre that is postdramatic in its expanded contemporary sense.

Rao's basic training as a theatre/performing artist is in Kathakali. She does not think of herself as a Kathakali dancer when she performs as a theatre artist, although she knows that Kathakali comes to her 'naturally, especially in the form of (creative) energy ... which impacts the imagination and the confidence you start with' (Rao 2016). Her Kathakali aids her in breathing, and her exercises and practices over the years as a Kathakali dancer help her perform the way she does. However, Rao keeps talking through her shows, whereas a Kathakali artist does not open her mouth during the performance. This classical dance form often enters into her theatre only as improvised movement, but not with its normative 'purity'. The Kathakali in her solos comes in bits and shreds, sometimes hybridized with other contemporary forms of dance. As Karin Shankar notes, Rao simultaneously de- and re-territorializes a centuries-old South Asian/Indian dance form's 'gestural and expressive vocabulary' (2019: 125). In her improvised work, the performer is at once a Kathakali dancer and not so. This double negative carries 'convention to unconventional spaces', creating new modes of storytelling in theatre that exploits the kinaesthetic and rhythmic elements of the ancient dance-theatre form (132). Two other mentionable aspects of Rao's solos are music ('without music I am nowhere; it moves me into action') and the camera that plays a vital role in her intermedial performances (Rao 2016). Rao says to the author: 'During improvisations, my collaborator usually chooses something within the room to zoom into and projects it large on the screen, and then I respond to the image and carry the improvisation forward. So it becomes a dialogue between performer and image' in those moments (M. K. Rao 2019: 55). It took the artist nearly three years of meditation and suffering to come up with her first solo – after a long career as an actor in dramatic/street theatre and as a Kathakali dancer.

Theatrical form is always influenced, if not determined, by the cost of production, availability of space, modes of circulation, development of other forms of performance and, in some cases, also by the performer's personal conveniences. Rao's choice of form has had to do with most of them. She started evolving the form after she left the National School of Drama (NSD) as a teacher and had to stay home for a long time with a broken back. She developed it at home as a young mother of a little daughter, collaborated later with a handful of people from other art practices, and made it suit her budget, time, social needs and the artistic taste of her audience.

Are You Home, Lady Macbeth? (2010)

Postdramatic theatre's preference for monological forms comes from the theatre of the Symbolists, historically (Lehmann 2006: 57). Here one may remember, as Lehmann suggests, Stéphane Mallarmé's idea of *Hamlet* as a play with a tall hero who relegates all other characters to 'the rank of "extras"', or Robert Wilson's *Hamlet* as a specimen of the neo-lyrical theatre that 'understands the scene as a site of ... [poetic] "écriture"' (57–8). In Maya Rao's *Are You Home, Lady Macbeth?*, first performed at the NSD in January 2010, the verse lines are devised and spoken in a style that suggests no kind of neo-lyricism or 'empty contemplation', the term Lehmann uses to mean immobilized action. But the production certainly renounces the whole *dramatic* paradigm of suspense, story and mimesis (143).

Are you Home ...? is a de-dramatized form of theatre after all, an interface between the turn to performance (based on a mix of Kathakali movement and multimedia projection, in this case) and a play text largely 'rearranged into a monological structure' (Lehmann 2006: 126). Lady Macbeth in Shakespeare, however influential, does not push the other characters off to the margin, and Shakespeare's play centres on her husband. But Rao performs her conception of the lady as 'a creature of nature' (Rao 2016) by selecting sections of texts from *Macbeth* where she is at the very centre. Rao also leaves the scenes unconnected, leaving it for the spectator to make any connection, and presents her show as 'scene and situation' (Lehmann 2006: 76) where less speaking and more (stylized) performance define the moment of reality in a considerably non-representational manner. This performance includes the playing of multiple roles by one performer, often accompanied by live video relay. When it comes to speaking, Lady Macbeth's sentences from different scenes in Shakespeare come together, as Hamlet's in Wilson's *Hamlet*, 'and illuminate each other in a new light' (126). Rao has also clipped and modified some speeches to suit the necessity of her show. They are defamiliarized as she adopts different voice patterns for different speeches and also changes her pitch, at times even croaking and growling. Music – a mix of Indian Kathakali drumming and selections from Pink Floyd – and costume of various designs and colours equally shape the performance.

De-dramatization happens through devising. The show is organized into thirteen loosely connected scenes and situations devised from Shakespeare's play. The titles of the scenes are suggestive of their deviance from the traditional stage adaptations of the masterpiece: Steam Iron, Massage, Telephone, Fork and Knife, Teranoke – Curtain Look, Forest Walk, Palace Walk, Make-Up, Dinner, Meat ... Cards ... Model, Red Iron, Brooming, and Back on Back. The set is simple: a portable panelled screen (a variant of *terashila*, a curtain behind which characters of Kathakali dance theatre appear), a focus light fitted onto its top bar, and a semi-dark stage. Rao turns the light on and moves a 'steam' iron over the blinds hanging from the panel bar and serving as a screen. There is music, and the second witch's words appear on the blinds, one by one, on each stroke of the iron: 'By the pricking of my thumbs, / Something wicked this way comes'. After a pause Rao mixes her own words with those in the original: 'Cruel are the times when we do not know ourselves'. The implication is that Lady Macbeth knew herself little when she came under the influence of the witches. Her words from the original follow, but uttered in a distorted manner by Rao playing a witch and addressing the skeleton of Lady Macbeth (a doll), placed under the screen panel:

Come, you spiritless woman, let me unsex you here and fill you from the crown to the toe top – full of direst cruelty ...

Make thick your blood ...

And drown her in the blackest smoke of hell,

That her keen knife see not the wound it makes,

Nor heaven peep through the blanket of the dark, to cry 'bas, bas, haraamzaadi!'

Rao feels no obligation to quote words verbatim from Shakespeare because the performer is not a cardboard character and therefore not obliged to fit into a predesigned groove. Instead, she is building a character on the spot by playing around it, especially by way of an irreverent handling of speeches assigned to Lady Macbeth and others in Shakespeare. The profaned text from this perspective serves as *one* of the elements of de-dramatization of a canonical play.

The second scene is not only characterized by a reshuffling of words from Shakespeare but also by their reassignment to speakers, accompanied by the physicality of improvised action. It begins with Lady Macbeth turning off the light attached to the panel and moving to an empty chair at the centre of the stage. There is music again, somewhat eerie, mixed with howling and screeching sounds. She starts massaging the body of an imagined Macbeth, seated in the chair. Music snaps out, and Lady Macbeth says to her husband:

Ay, in the catalogue you are listed as 'man'.

As hounds and greyhounds, mongrels, spaniels, curs,

Shoughs, retrievers, rottweilers, water-rugs and demi-wolves,

Are clept, all by the name of . . . dogs.

It is not hard to notice that the words quoted from *Macbeth* Act 3, Scene 1 are not only (deliberately) distorted, but they belong to Macbeth originally, and not to his wife. Rao tells the author in an interview that the whole show was conceived as Lady Macbeth's 'journey to discover the witch in her . . . in the alien corridors of power' (Rao 2016). To Rao, it is not a question of gender, but one of exploring, and exteriorizing, through performance how an individual, when alienated from the law of probability, can turn evil and destroy themselves and others eventually. It might still be difficult for the artist to escape feminist criticism, especially on the ground that she transfers all that is 'witchy' in Shakespeare's play to Lady Macbeth alone, including the sentences uttered by other characters in pejorative contexts. The impression may, however, change if we consider the following lines on her blog and focus more on the making of the character in the here and now of theatre: 'a woman playfully creates the character of Lady Macbeth but somewhere along the way she finds herself drawn into her skin . . . So she must either "rub herself" out of existence eventually or "re-find herself" in another form' (Rao n.d.: online). As the performer is careful to keep from total immersion in the character, the 'Lady' and the 'witch' do not look eventually conflated as we consider the playfulness around the role performed.

The de-dramatization, therefore, works not only through the free use (or re-seizing) of text but through the reconfiguring of the actor–character relationship into the performer–actor relationship. If the actor is playing a role, the performer comes in between, as if to turn the acting self-reflexive. Music snaps out again, and Lady Macbeth speaks more of Macbeth's words as her own: 'Stars hide your fires, / Let not light see his deep and dark desires'. The mixing of characters in one figure undermines the illusion of 'autonomous character' (Fuchs 1996: 31) that builds on the distinctiveness of identity, psychology and moral attitude as well as on differentiated acting methodologies. It becomes difficult to maintain the 'through line' of the Stanislavsky system when Lady Macbeth speaks lines from the other characters, resulting in the blurring of identities and breakdown of the concept of (individuated) character as the bearer of marked-off action that is part of a broader scheme of mimetic representation. More interestingly, Rao as performer maintains her distance from the actor and keeps intervening in the actor's playing of Lady Macbeth. The acting, as a result, purposely lacks emotion and psychological depth. In other words, when Rao as actor plays the character, the performer in her demonstrates that the actor does not belong to the character she is portraying.

The body is a vital medium in this process of theatre-making that does not dismiss mental state altogether but approaches it in terms of devised movement. In the scene 'Telephone', a violent state of mind is brought out by producing the *bhayanaka* sentiment, one of the eight sentiments of the basic four in the *Natyashastra*, in the body itself. Lady Macbeth runs to the panel, picks up the phone and talks, only gesturally – twitching her lips rapidly, shaking her head, moving her eyes, making frightened facial expressions, throwing up her hand, raising her fingers and biting them – and all of this to different kinds of loud sounds. After she hangs up, she looks at both of her hands, rubs them on a piece of cloth, rests them on the frame bar, takes off her scarf, and comes before the screen whose texture now looks different with the changing light. What happens on stage is a '*transaction of sentiment*', to use Prasanna's words. There are three participants, according to the *Natyashastra*, in such a transaction: the actor, the character and the audience. In Indian dramaturgy, Prasanna notes, 'the emphasis [for the actor] is on the skill of acting rather than on the capacity to feel' (Prasanna 2013: 180). The actor does not become sentimental herself but only physically manifests the sentiment. This is far from the predominantly Western technique of acting that asks the actor to identify with the character emotionally for the sake of faithful representation. While the actor in our context constantly negotiates with the character in a detached and critical manner, she becomes more of a performer. What Lehmann says of an actor in postdramatic theatre, that they are now less a role-player than a performer offering their 'presence on stage for contemplation' (Lehmann 2006: 135), may not be wholly applicable here because Rao the actor is *not* 'not doing anything to show that [she is] a character' (Kirby 1972). But the self-reflexive acting, which does not fuse the actor and the character, makes an interesting Indian variant on the global postdramatic by emphasizing the actor's presence more as the performer's. This is also a postcolonial appropriation of the Indian predramatic for a technology-driven experimental theatre where the European/colonial dramatic is thoroughly deconstructed in form, structure and mode of representation.

Devising takes on a different form in the scene that follows, 'Fork and Knife'. It embodies a type of performance that redefines live action in theatre by showing its interface with technology (live video projections). Rao sits before the screen. Multiple (broken) images of her hands appear on it, as if fracturing all possibility of building an integral character, which an actor trained to lose herself in character would aim at. This is again a destabilization of the dominant concepts of character, action and acting. The character is not

Figure 4 Are *You Home, Lady Macbeth?* (2010), conceptualized and performed by Maya Krishna Rao, presented by Vismayah. Photo credit: S. Thyagarajan.

only refracted but becomes the performer's medium to experiment with her performance style. Rao makes diverse *mudras* (hand and finger gestures), and the live video relay creates a brilliant performance dynamic that is accentuated by lighting and Rao's costume made out of tattered multi-coloured cast-off garments bearing memories of those who once wore them. The digital media gives the performer an opportunity to engage most intimately with her body. Alongside the full live body onstage, its tiny fragments and details including veins, otherwise not visible to the eye, now come into distinct view on the screen, affecting acting / performing as well as spectating that involves not only the audience but the performer too. Lady Macbeth's obsession with her hands, after the murder of Duncan in *Macbeth*, is given a new twist in *Are You Home …?* By expanding on the 'hand' image and extending it to the Banquet Scene, Rao puts the following words into Lady Macbeth's mouth:

> There was a time these hands knew not how to hold a fork, a knife, a plate, eat out of a plate,
> *She takes a hand out and brings it in again.*
> Wave a flag (*bring in other hand, take it out*)
> Hold his hand, marry a man, lie on a bed. (*take out one hand*)
> Close the door, rub this hand, look out of a window, to give orders …

repeat lines quicker with left hand, change text a bit

...

Meet myself ... call myself to myself ... (*hands calling, cup face with both hands; video: still image on screen.*)

Live gestural action and the accompanying audio-visual relay make 'a new kind of perceptual sense' in which different mediums are 'conceived and perceived together' (Cooke 2010: 193, 203). In such scenes, to borrow words from Markos Hadjioannou and George Rodosthenous, 'theatre's stage becomes the backstage for cinema, and cinema's construction ... a live performance' (2011: 43). When the two diverse mediums are brought together, the result is intermedial performance generating what Mitchell Whitelaw calls 'cross-modal' perception that involves interaction of two or more different sensory pathways (in Cooke 2010: 203).

The show shifts to the next scene via the performing body again, which now goes behind the screen (*terashila*) with its still image lingering on it. The simultaneity of the live in motion and the projected live, the stillness in movement and the movement in stillness creates a moment of presence that reveals itself in a fleeting present. Lady Macbeth withdraws herself from the banquet, and Rao devises a monologue for her that virtually splits into a dialogue between the Lady and her husband. Rao brings in the 'knock, knock, knock' of the Porter Scene from Shakespeare as a prelude to her thorough reimagining of the preceding scene (*Macbeth* Act 2, Scene 2). She begins the present scene by playing Lady Macbeth, murmuring 'Knock, knock, knock / Who comes here? Has he asked for me? / Knock, knock, knock'. The performer-actor appears to be trying to remember her speeches, and then, on 'failing' to do so, improvises an imaginary exchange of words between Lady Macbeth and her husband (actually a monologue), drawing loosely on the words and phrases that are attributed to the Lady alone in Shakespeare.

You will say ...
'It was the owl that shriek'd' ...
I will say 'Alack!' I am afraid they have awak'd.
'Knock, knock, knock' ... then you will say ...
'I go and it is done'.
Then I will say, 'Had he not resembled my father as he slept, I had done it'.
Then ... then you ... no I ... you ... no I will say, 'there comes my fit again: I had else been perfect but now I am cabin'd, cribb'd, no teeth for the present'.

There are very few examples in contemporary Indian theatre of such fracturing of a canonical text, attended by 'the materiality of performance' (Jürs-Munby 2006: 4), corporeality of movement, multi-design scenography and live video play. Moreover, the way the text forms on stage, swerving between a string of words and roles to speak them, shows its self-referential quality and highlights the 'making' process of the performance.

Improvisation and choreography build the next scene, where a radically modified premodern Indian theatre form (namely Kathakali) creates an energetic performance . Two women come on stage, holding a cloth curtain at its ends, and Rao wears her 'curtain look'. As music (Pink Floyd) begins, Rao devises a seductive movement for Lady Macbeth, which is similar to the choreography for an evil character in a traditional Kathakali 'curtain look' (*tirnokku*) scene (for details, see Zarrilly 1984). As the Lady moves ahead vigorously to woo the spectators, the long curtain held before her by the two women on either side restrains her. The performer moves up and down the stage in a 'ring-a ring o' roses' gait, uttering comically, and partly distorting, the words of the weird sisters in Act 1, Scene 3 of *Macbeth*: 'Weird sisters we go hand in hand, posters of the sea and land'. In her irreverent, parodic posturing and utterance, the solo clearly leaves all anxiety for mimetic representation and replaces it with devised presentation. The parody is not only a reaction to the colonial dramatic form but presents the performer as the subject of the show. Alluding to Lehmann's description of Robert Wilson's *Hamlet*, although here is no intention to compare the two performances, *Are You Home . . .?* could be retitled 'Maya Rao: Performance in the Mirror of the Lady Macbeth figure' (Lehmann 2006: 126). Rao performs herself here; the show is a form of her self-presentation as a solo performer.

Alan Read's 'parallax view', which he developed to explain the dissonant relationship between theatre and politics, may be deployed to explain the defamiliarized presentation of a major Shakespeare character in a hybrid/ized performance language (Read 2008: 7). In Rao's tragicomic presentation of the Lady with her ambition, fear, anxiety, boredom and immaturity, the dramatic properties of the Shakespeare play stand in dissonance with the performative exuberance of cross-media theatre. Those properties are overturned to pave the way for a postdramatic presentation of the character, which evokes a wide range of audience emotions, often cancelling one another, and generates an openness and flexibility of form by way of intermedial hybridity (speech, dance, live movement, simulated visuals). The scene 'Forest Walk' is a case in point. Rao suddenly lies down on the floor and lifts her legs, crossed, and then moves them in a walking pattern. The moving legs, thus inverted, are 'corrected' positionally when projected on the screen, creating a dynamic image of walking (in the forest by night) and making live performance and its simulation simultaneous. In this scene, the words of the Lady in Shakespeare, 'I heard the owl scream and the cricket cry', come back as 'The owl watched over me, the crickets led the way, the raven sang for me. I was a child of the night, they call them witches'. Rao's Lady clutches 'the length of the forest' between her feet, spectacularizing her relationship with the wild and the dark. She walks in the forest, indirectly referring to the Sleepwalking Scene of *Macbeth* but not integrating the two anyway. The scene achieves a new feat in theatre and performance art, subverting the old dramatic paradigm and inaugurating a new performative reality.

Walking has been a recurring motif in Rao's work, underscoring movement as central to her performance. Gestures and movements in space, without any determinate referent, create a fluid, floating semiology out of the performing body. Movement becomes the reality in itself, which does not require a mimesis of things from outside. The media-supported reproduction of the live 'walk' radically changes the terms of relationship not only between the original and the copy but between happening and spectating – spectating becoming a difficult exercise as the spectator has to constantly negotiate between two levels of movement (on the stage beneath and on the screen above) and two modes of presentation creating two different sensory modalities. The 'Forest Walk' leads up to the 'Palace Walk', the seventh scene in Rao's performance. The palace appears in the form of lines gradually building up a map over a projection board laid on the floor. This is the only scene where Rao is not alone. Media designer Amitesh Grover walks in, in his regular trousers, and drops a knife in one box on the map on the board, which stands for one of the rooms in the palace. Duncan is dead. Macbeth loses his balance and Lady Macbeth finds the palace 'too cold for hell'. Rao and Grover turn about abruptly and walk away.

The show, through fractured text, unpremeditated movement and use of digital media, now taps the Kathakali reservoir to use the tradition of putting on make-up in front of the audience, highlighting the process of theatre-making in a changed context and time. The actor does not appear before the audience as one who is already a character. The audience instead is provided with access to the preparing of an actor for a character in the theatre. In this scene (Eight), Rao goes to the dressing table and paints her face and neck with a brush – the whole action projected in its details on the screen by the side of which she is seated. The transformation of the actor into a character happens ritualistically; yet the transformation is far from complete for being self-reflexive. The back-and-forth movement between actor and character is a processual exercise that not only pronounces the predominant role of Rao as the performer but exposes re/presentation as a constructed act with its inherent inadequacy and yet uses it self-critically to build the theatrical world. At the end of the make-up, Rao watches herself carefully in the mirror and sets out on the performer's passage to actorship. The image of her face freezes on the screen while she moves over to the other side of the stage and draws out through the slats of the portable panelled blinds the props for her subsequent scene – a laptop, paper rolls, a doll and so on. Acting becomes performing a game of sorts.

Objects occupy an important place in Rao's scheme of things, not only evoking personal memories but underlining their own agential potency to bolster the performative moment. Rao appears with the above objects to reconstruct the Banquet Scene in a non-mimetic, playful manner. The banquet is laid elaborately as music (Kathakali drums) continues through the scene. Rao opens her laptop, places it by her side, picks up the paper roll, spreads it out on the floor like a runner over a dining table, takes off the array of plastic spoons tied to the laptop monitor, puts them in two rows on the paper roll, and then puts the *kireedam* (crown) in the middle. She as Lady Macbeth talks to herself, imagining herself in different roles and moods, and enjoys the role-playing even while exteriorizing the character's worries. Rao's Kathakali moments bring out the frightened and confused side of the Lady steeped in the blood of others. As Rao waves her hand to stop the music, media designer Grover's video projections come up. There is water in the palace hall, digitally shown, and objects (chosen by Grover) are seen being thrown in and floating there: house parts made of paper, forks and knives, milk, elephant, camel, and the like. The disintegration of Lady Macbeth as a stubborn aspirant for worldly power is shown through an ironic inversion of domestic and royal possessions into scrap.

As the performance comes to an end with Lady Macbeth mopping over the paper roll, supposedly trying to cleanse the stain of blood all over, and with the petals video playing, suggestive of the effort to 'sweeten these little hands', Rao takes off her chest bandages and knee pads that she wore for the performance. The taking off of her performance accessories that include some items of her clothing is partly visible to the spectators as the light dims out. The show began with the performer preparing for her role in it, a role that never goes without interruptions and interventions; it ends with her coming out of the role fully. The panel sans the blinds now enframes the performer ending her show. 'A multimedia production that swings from the comic to the tragic, and all that lies in between, seamlessly', as Rao's blog reads, the 'show was first created as a performance art piece (for Khoj, Delhi, in 2008) and evolved into a cross-media show' in 2010 (Rao n.d.: online). It is important to note that what Rao calls 'tragic' is without the closure of the dramatic form. The 'protagonist' has no visible adversary to fight in this solo but an imploding ego beleaguered by confusion. No wonder there is little drama in the absence of traditional conflict or plot (see Lehmann 2013: 105).

Heads are Meant for Walking Into (2005)

Maya Krishna Rao does not begin her theatre with a story but with her body as a site from where comes her story, if it can be called a story, in shreds and bits. Rao also begins her theatre with materials blown as images on the video screen onstage. If there is a tale in it, it is more a by-product than a generative element. The camera in her theatre is a co-actor rather than a mere tool. 'Surajit Sarkar uses closed-circuit cameras to create visuals', Rao tells this author, that are 'live projections of bits of my own body – limbs, hands, including my veins which look so unfamiliar when they are so enlarged on the screen. It's exciting ... suggesting that the spring of my performance has always been here, my body!' (Rao 2016). Similarly, her use of objects and materials on stage, most of which are turned into animated presences by video projections, gives her performance a new visual turn in contrast to the linguistic turn that once emphasized the construction of 'reality' by language. The minimal text that *Heads are Meant* has is prompted by the visuals I discuss below rather than the narrative creating them. In Rao's multimedia theatre and performance, the projections with 'multiple surfaces' (Rao n.d.: online) work in tandem with a wide range of music (from Indian Kathakali to Western pop) and improvised action to produce an experience of the everyday. And the experience comes through perception combined with 'instantaneous recognition' (*Erkenntnis*).

Rao's blog describes *Heads are Meant* thus: 'A woman sits at her desk with bits of her puzzle – a puzzle that is indeed the world, where life can be hard and its contradictions sharp. She must figure out her puzzle, so she must leave her desk and step out into the world to make sense of the pieces' (Rao n.d.: online). The story, which is less a story than a game with toys and other objects like building blocks, gets constructed slowly as Rao improvises action using them. The show developed over a long time as Rao, being her own director, reviewed her improvisations on the laptop and revised them time and again. The woman at the desk can be imagined as 'a writer who, while working on her manuscript, goes out into the world and meets life face to face', says Rao. The objects the performer was playing with 'start speaking to her' as she 'blow[s] them off on the screen, and the narrative starts building in your head' (Rao 2016). The show is all about '[a] world of power, of degradation of women's labour and being, of economic hardship, of living under martial law, of people being pushed to the brink of desperation. And of those who survive it through work' (Rao n.d.: online). There are episodes from a politically restive Manipur and about the starving farmers of Andhra Pradesh, although the segment I discuss here is primarily about the failed dreams of a female construction worker and the writer's reaction to it. In spite of engaging with politics as played outside the stage, Rao's production is not the conventional political theatre dramatizing issues; its theatreness lies in its performance aesthetics, in its form and style that are not, however, disconnected from the society she encounters every day. As a performer, Rao demonstrates what the female writer of her narrative thinks and does, without becoming the role.

Character, action, object and re/presentation are found in an unconventional relationship to one another. The stage is dimly lit – the focus being on Rao arranging her objects that will be blown off on the screen. Notably, once they are projected on the screen above, the stage beneath becomes a second fiddle. The performer leans over the building blocks with which she is trying to build a house for the poor worker. The answer to why a house for the labourer comes from Rao herself in an essay she wrote for Amal Allana's *The Act of Becoming*: '[C]onstruction workers who will sit here for six months to build... once the building is ready, will leave and never again enter there' (Rao 2013: 271). They remain mostly homeless. The projection of the house under construction problematizes the dramatic conception of the subject and space. The builder is not a character but a performer who keeps adjusting the blocks and pushes into the frame of action a doll with a basket on its head. The screen being the performance space now, the worker's image is doubled: Rao building the scene of the construction and the labourer (doll) carrying out her work on the construction site. Representation is problematized since no part of it is mimetic – there is no human actor essaying a role (Rao is playing with objects and, therefore, not playing a role); nor is there any speaking-acting human subject to play the labourer in the show (the doll is a toy that acquires performative agency in a world of things enlivened by technological improvisation).

Heads are Meant is not 'object theatre' in the sense Paul Zaloom and Christian Carignan have practised it since the early 1980s. Yet Rao's work somewhat shares their style and method in playing with objects and giving them a life of their own. It establishes in the process a reciprocal relationship between the objects and the performer. Rao's assembly of objects as images blown on the screen with the camera, in fact, encourages a new materialist reading of the production. 'Contemporary questions about the agency of objects and the forces of materialization', as Rebecca Schneider observes, 'have increasingly blurred the borders modernity had built up between the animate and the inanimate' (2015: 7). New materialism believes in the presence of agency in all kinds of material – which include here the building blocks, the battery-operated car, the doll with a basket on her head, compact discs *and* the performer's body. When the non-living materials are viewed in terms of their relationship among themselves, the whole process of meaning-making is recast by exposing the spectator to a new tribe of images in theatre through shocks and flashes, by forming a transient constellation out of them and thus avoiding 'dramatic collision' altogether. Rao's assemblage of hybrid objects may be said to have rethought 'subjectivity by playing up the role' of non-human forces within the human, flagging off the autonomous powers of 'several non-human processes' and thus explored through 'dissonant relations', in William Connolly's words, the extent of material's ability to partner with the affective turn (in Schneider 2015: 7–8). This is certainly a new configuration in theatre of the relationship between body, matter and technology (Clough and Halley 2007). The objects Rao uses for her production are not considered pieces of art in a conventional way. *Heads are Meant* may bear some resemblance to the 'anti-art' avant-garde movement in early twentieth-century Europe, but Rao's solo stands out for its intermedial political inquiry.

More objects enter into the playing area. Suddenly a speeding (toy) car enters the stage where the house for the worker is close to completion. Rao tries frenziedly to save her work from the car's destructive course. The conflict and collision that takes place is not between characters or in the form of dialogue, as in dramatic theatre, but between objects as mobilized and manoeuvred by the performer. Rao hangs a talismanic lemon-and-chillies strip from the building to protect the house from evil gaze as well as places some medicinal capsules near the house pillars, allusive to people's search for a cure in superstitious beliefs and science at once. But then she shrieks as the car, now projected on screen, hits the building, which cannot withstand the impact and collapses. The doll with a basketful of building material on her head stands silent. Rao picks up some flour (denoting sand) and begins to sprinkle it all over the site until the site looks dusty and the doll is covered with it. The music changes to hard, noisy beats and Rao cries aloud in rage and pain, sprinkling more flour, faster now. The 'acting' is not emotional, but the flurry of activities and movements inscribes a performative reaction to the deplorable state of migrant labourers in India as evidenced offstage by the recent searing images of millions of them trudging hundreds of miles, hungry and penniless, during Covid-19 lockdowns in order to be home from construction sites located in far-flung states.

Improvisation is the core of Rao's theatre, including the text she creates for it. The impromptu scripting and delivery of words dislodges traditional structuring of a play text and its dramatization. Rao picks up the doll and thinks aloud the possibilities of doing the show in varied ways: 'I wish I could / I would, I should, I would, I could / ... I knock on your door / Would you let me in there ...' As she speaks these lines and moves the mound of flour onstage with her hands, possibly to rebuild the house, the whole action with its palpable materiality is projected on the screen. The reciting of the lines below is indicative of a musing over the constant shifting of roles between performer and actor, and between actor and character: 'Watch the sky / The birds all fly ... / Will I ever get there / Please let me in / Just let me lie, let me sit, / Standing up let me free / And close your eyes, you open my eyes'. Rao asks the doll her name and whether she can write her name, wondering if her plight will be published in any newspapers ever or whether it will be read by anyone. 'I bring her back home', Rao says in an interview with the author. She will not let her be homeless again (Rao 2016). What happens onstage (and on screen) may not translate into action outside. But Rao must seek full control of her act on the stage then. Things do not always work on the stage either, but her politics come through via her formal and aesthetic strategies.

Architecture, photography, text and performance comingle in the last scene. 'My sister is an architect. I found a contact sheet that she had prepared as a student', Rao tells the author. 'She had taken pictures of the Rashtrapati Bhavan [the President of India's residence] from various angles' for one of her projects. Rao places the doll finally on the contact sheet, and when she focuses her camera on it, the scene, now self-consciously utopian, becomes moving otherwise. The text reads: 'You are finally home. I don't need to build your home. Your home is this Rashtrapati Bhavan' (Rao 2016). The performer has also become exhausted by now and rests her head next to the doll. 'All you see here is my white head', says Rao to the author. This is neither propagandist nor programmatic, but a kind of political presentation by way of a new performance aesthetic that undermines logocentricity, or theatre's lexical supremacy, as well as the element of rationality so long used to forge conclusions mostly not supported by changes in the external world. Theatre's 'purity', so far defined by the text's translation into scenic action, is 'contaminated' by 'interactive technology' releasing 'a whole new range of semiotic possibilities for the theatre' (Mitra 2014: 83).

Even when Rao becomes political by referencing the external event, she resorts to an avant-garde, feminist-cinematic (Dalmia 2009: 314) aesthetic to create an environment within the theatre that sensitizes spectators by shocking them. There is no pretence of a targeted impact of the theatrical event on lived life; yet the sincerity of the radical *artist* is outstanding. Activism in theatre finds a new form by dismantling established structures of communication: it neither imposes an ideology on the spectators, asking them to live or die by it, nor creates an anger that does not last long after the show is over. Rao's politics as an artist is to expose the holes in the system and lay bare its ugly grammar with a view to changing the audience perspective on things and questioning the excesses that have acquired the status of a new normal. The clip of a protest staged by Manipuri women against army atrocities in their state, which Rao intersperses with her other body narratives, stands out in another part of *Heads are Meant* for its power to affect through the senses without being dogmatic or interpretive. She 'wraps around herself a cloth on which is screened the visual of naked Manipuri women' in protest against the Indian army's rape campaign (in Rao n.d.: online). Invested with absolute powers to quash the subnational movement (interpreted by the government as 'insurgency') in the state by force, no action by the troops on the ground, however wrong, could be questioned by the public or challenged in the court of law. Rao's political gestures are layered, usually, including in her popular protest show *Walk* (2012), an improvised performance around the rape of a young female medical student and her subsequent death in the same year. *Heads are Meant* demonstrates how the protest theatre can be formally turned 'into a solo performance that has no storyline, [into] a monologue which is indirectly confrontational or deeply reflective' (Nath 2017: online).

Rao's production of images in *Heads are Meant* is not directly linked to representation. Here a reference to Walter Benjamin's imaged-based epistemology may not be out of context, although his engagement with image is not basically related to what we currently mean by visual studies. Rao's images show what Benjamin associates with 'a way of thinking and writing': a 'simultaneity and constellation over continuity, similitude over representation or sign' (Weigel 2015: 344–5). Benjamin's reading of the modernity of image-making through exposure to shocks and fractions and flashes may refer more to the shift from oil lamps to electric lights or to his 'nascent engagement with photography and film' (ibid.: 358, 361); but Rao's multimedia performance works out those notions of simultaneity, constellation and similitude by expanding, if not redefining, the idea of what constitutes image-making in our times.

Jyoti Dogra

Jyoti Dogra's entry into the world of theatre solos is purely circumstantial. The 'non-availability of people who would be willing to come on board' with her for a long-time research on topics for making new shows was the main reason for her becoming a solo artist, she says. The lack of 'an affordable rehearsal space for a long period of time and of sponsorship or funds further added to the difficulties of working with a group' (Dogra 2019). Working alone in different capacities for a show turned out to be the only possible option for Dogra. She came into prominence with her *Notes on Chai* (2017), a performance on the 'ubiquitous beverage' (tea) evoking many associations and feelings and finally sending her into portraying several people who at one point in her life 'caught [her] imagination' (Punjani n.d.: online). It has also been described as 'a collection of snippets of everyday conversations interwoven with abstract sound explorations' (programme note). No less mentionable are Dogra's earlier works: '*The Doorway* (2009), where she used a doorframe to explore concepts of open and closed spaces, or *K°* (2011) where she brought to life Kafka's characters' (Lakhe 2015: online).

Black Hole (2019)

What inspired the solo theatre artist to conceive and perform *Black Hole* (2019) is her long-standing desire to work with something beyond the immediate, her interest in a theatrical connection between astrophysics and the human world. The questions with which she began devising the show include whether stories and their linear telling are essential to theatre, if scientific facts can ever be the subject for performance, or when a lecture on science can become an intimate conversation where emotion, cognition and movement weave an intricate tapestry. The date of 14 September 2015, alluded to in the show, goes down in the history of astrophysics as the day when scientists had the first proof of Einstein's theory of relativity following the collision of two black holes. Nevertheless, Dogra had in fact begun her preparation for *Black Hole*, as she says to the author, long before the discovery of that great event in space. Her project seeks to stretch a 'basic [point] of science' to a very 'human context', thus providing a perspective where meaning-making becomes a process of constant performative negotiation between two otherwise different worlds (Dogra 2019).

The ninety-minute show centres on the mystery and attraction the black hole holds for a terminally ill woman in a hospital and her daughter's explanation to her mother of the cosmic phenomenon. At one level, the performance has the lecture form, but the 'lectures' are often interrupted by the mother's naïve but humane questions and the daughter's fragmented memories of their conversation in the hospital room. The performance as an event-cum-narrative takes place after the woman's death. But it is not a memory piece because memory usually demands representation, and dramatic theatre, even when expressionist, represents it by referring back to another place/time where/when the characters lived and the events occurred. *Black Hole* creates a performance moment of its own kind where the story belongs to its time of telling and so do the intervening explanatory notes. Nothing is scenically narrativized. The choreography forms on the stage without referring to any 'there' even though the story begins after it is over. The present act of telling and showing, rather than the story itself, and the moving body which is barely, in Michael Jackson's words, 'reducible to cognitive and semantic operations' (in Kringelbach and Skinner 2012: 8), create the experiential reality for the audience in Dogra's performance.

Cosmic reality, which cannot be experienced in one's imaginative engagement with it, becomes differently perceptible when made to interact with human feeling and sensation. Dogra's presentation of such reality in *Black Hole* shows the power of theatre to create an intimate experience of the distant phenomenon in the very sensuous making (not remaking) of it. The simultaneity of narration and movement, together with the playing of roles by the performer who does not become any of them, accomplishes this feat. Available information about events occurring in the universe does not provide any conversance with them even as we can measure or study them scientifically (Dogra 2019). Presented through a humane prism and in a theatrical language that makes no attempts at mimetic representation, they offer a subjective, spiritual and sensorial estimation of the enigmatic cosmos. Things that we hardly notice about the universe or can ever sense in our familiar environment, such as the collision of black holes when 'one is doing the laundry here' (Dogra 2019), are made to interact with our everyday desires, fears, hopes and fantasies. Dogra's solo with its setting, atmosphere, text and choreography offers an experience of events very different from our exposure to happenings in a story staged in terms of plot and dialogue.

The will to live, paradoxically coupled with the wish to return to particles, is theatricalized in terms of a choreographic negotiation with the black hole. In her theatre, Dogra does not 'work with an idea. I simply start working with the process and as the process continues, the material starts to grow and organically move, which was also the case here', she says (in Rao 2019: online). She uses the body and voice as the sole instruments for her theatre. Dogra says that she begins with an impulse in the body and then translates 'that impulse into a sound, into a text, into breath, into a performative segment of any kind' (in Khurana 2019: online). The show opens with the performer feeling the contours of her body with her hands and marking boundaries for different limbs. The attempt to break up the body virtually by setting limits to its notional fragments fails. This makes the performer declare that boundaries of any system collapse so easily. This is simultaneously shown to be countered by the human instinct to preserve the 'self', cordoning it off from other people and things. The mother stands at the edge of the black hole, a white sheet onstage tweaked by the performer's feet into a circle with a hole at the centre, but fears jumping into it. The opposing pulls of the desire to return to the centre of the black hole in death and of self-preservation create a liminal space that uses science to make an existential point theatrically. Whatever meaning comes of it is incidental to the form, though.

The show introduces the idea of singularity in both scientific and human terms. In science, singularity is the result of the force exerted by the black hole on matter which in such conditions is condensed into a single point. Anything inside a black hole, including an entire planet, can be compressed to a single point with no time and space and, therefore, with no reality as we know it on earth. Singularity in a black hole is 'inaccessible to anything but itself', says Dogra (2019). She extends this idea to the singularity of the individual which is inaccessible to others and accessible only to the 'self'. Nonetheless she wonders if it is accessible even to the 'self' or can ever be realized by it. Singularity takes on yet another dimension when it is considered as a divide between the black hole and the world outside (scientifically, whatever lies on this side of the event horizon), between life and death (a black hole is also called 'the point of no return'), with no points of intersection between the two. Dogra maintains:

> Scientifically, the world inside a black hole and the world outside it never meet. Similarly, in the case of death, there is always a stark divide between those who are dead and those who are not. No one from the world of the dead can bring information to the world of the living, and vice versa. You need to be dead or alive, and depending on where you are, you belong there. I feel death is a great divide, the event horizon of a black hole is a great divide, [and] so those ideas are connected.
>
> Dogra 2019

It is always wrong to look for a mimetic correspondence between facts outside the stage and their performed images in the theatre. The show, in freeing the audience from the long-standing practice to discover form as an expressive medium for a preconceived content, creates a different sort of theatre that is postdramatic and yet one of its own kind. The scientific idea of 'entanglement' is now explored to flirt with the idea of oneness or inseparability in human relationship after death. The mother, while envisioning the post-death 'space travel' as a disembodied journey, wonders if any substance in the human body, when dead, can go up to outer space and maintain a connection with those left beneath. Apparently pitted against the idea of inaccessibility of one person (or the black hole) to the other (or what lies outside), the comparison being purely imaginative around the concept of 'singularity' in astrophysics, the mother's impassioned question takes its fanciful cue from the theory of quantum entanglement. Quantum entanglement occurs, as Claudia Tesche defines it, 'when two systems share a common quantum mechanical state [and] ... also share a common fate, even if they become physically quite separated' (n.d.: online). While the dying mother asks her daughter (both 'played' by Dogra) if the humans are also entangled, the daughter clarifies that this is a theory of particles, not applicable to people. But the mother has her very own way of seeing the connection: 'But, human beings are made of particles'. Dogra takes artistic liberty to imaginatively establish a 'quantum entanglement' between people separated by geographical distance in life or by death. In an interview with the author, she emphasized this point of extension in her performance alongside the correctness of scientific facts presented.

The show is an experimental attempt to establish a direct relationship with the audience not so much by frontal address as by asking them to rethink the notions of death, loss and absence on a cosmic scale. Dogra says, 'The mother dies as a person but does not die as matter'. She is inclined to transform the scientific view of matter into 'a philosophical, existential idea', as if to explore how the two different worlds can meet and the meaning of loss or absence changes (Dogra 2019). Evidently, no pre-fixed meaning is imposed on the audience. Meaning-making, if you will, has been an arduous journey through form that includes monology, movement and play with a single bedspread. The interface between the world of science and the world of human relations is not forged but kept imaginative, tentative and fluid in contours and implications. The show thus questions the boundaries between forms of knowledge and experience. It puts things out of familiar perspectives only to bring them into a new creative field of view, thus influencing the mode of spectatorship. Audience engagement keeps changing throughout the performance between two modes: to engage with facts and aspects cerebrally and react sensorily and imaginatively to the constructed situations. The spectator is not allowed to enjoy a coherent illusory world, although the show builds on imagination in its intriguing relationship with science. Dogra talks about her visit to CERN in 2017 to elaborate on this point further. The visit helped her realize how scientific facts are today put together in exhibition formats for the general public, which include animation, film, audio tapes and the like. Dogra's production is different from all of that; but her impression that popular demonstration of scientific phenomena may ask for an imaginatively rich performance form might have reaffirmed her faith in the feasibility of her project at its formative stage.

Asked how she makes her shows that have no prewritten text, Dogra says:

> Through precise physical techniques one is encouraged to think and imagine with the body. Techniques that help one access the vast store of

real and abstract material that lives in us – images, fragments of text, bits of sound, happenings, stories that are stored in the body. Exercises allow the muscle, bone, hands, feet, pelvis, chest, to become tools to think and imagine and then find ways to translate these impulses into physical and vocal actions. This in turn is fed by continual research and reading that one begins to inhabit. So the making becomes an organic meeting of the material within the maker and the material that one is researching and working with and the two feed on each other.

Dogra 2020: email

This sounds Grotowskian. That said, while a performance can grow out of the performer's 'body memory', the practice of devising a piece over a long span of time can also sink deep into the performer's being. As Dogra's relationship with her performance is not primarily through the text, so is it not exclusively through the body. It comes through all kinds of material that have become part of her through her constant interaction with them as a performer. Besides body and text, they include space, objects, light, sound, costume and the audience. When it comes to text, Dogra had to work hard to find a language for *Black Hole* that would be neither too specialized nor too colloquial. It is a combination of scientific language and casual conversation that dismantles the fourth wall.

Nevertheless, the body plays the most important role in Dogra's improvisation that is central to her work even as concept partly builds the narrative. 'There is no ideation before, but preparation [for the piece]. I have read several things about the universe, about the black hole, which are not in my show, but may enter into it later – and I would keep my piece open to them all' (Dogra 2019). The body, 'which has soaked in all that I read and thought [in preparation for the show]', articulates the material by choreographing it. To Dogra, theme or character is less important than 'how I am going to make my performance elements work on stage'. 'The performance material is tangible', she adds, and dealing with it means 'whether I am going to read my text looking at the audience or away from them, whether or not my hand will go up, or whether I will make or not make a sound – these are very tangible things. And for all this one needs to live the body above all'. She gets up to the stage with no desire to ideate, or make a statement, or even structure any particular movement. In fact, the structure comes through improvisation over time. 'Ideas are simple; they can be in three lines. The performance is never about the message or the point. It is about the form or shape of experience I arrive at between you and me' (Dogra 2019). This primacy of performance and its physicality reminds one of what Lehmann says of the body in theatre: 'Despite all efforts to capture the expressive potential of the body in a logic, grammar or rhetoric, the aura of physical presence remains the point of theatre where the ... fading of all signification occurs ... in favour of ... an actor's "presence", of charisma or "vibrancy"' (2006: 95).

The show keeps moving between vision, science and the everyday world, making the performer move seamlessly between these three different domains. Dogra does not round off any part of her narrative (imaginative or scientific) in one such domain within a demarcated timeframe and then pass on to another and complete it. The portion of the narrative the performer is developing at one point in time and space may get discontinued abruptly, as if 'cutting short the experience of the spectator and returning them to the chair' (Dogra 2019), to develop another fragment in another time and space, thus destroying sequence and causality. Performing a vision entirely through the body is arguably the toughest challenge for a performer. The patient's vision of herself standing at the edge of a black hole, for instance, blurs for her the distinction between the real and the unreal, making her attempt jumping into the hole of her death dream. But for the performer, it had to secure the authenticity of performance reality through energetic and nuanced movement rather than through narration by speech. What Dogra does to

Figure 5 *Black Hole* (2019), conceptualized and performed by Jyoti Dogra, presented by Prithvi Theatre. Photo credit: Jazeela Basheer.

achieve her feat is transgress any planned choreography or preconceived movement. It is improvised, often geometric, movements that visibilize aesthetically the dying woman's vision.

The use of sound in *Black Hole*, apart from the sound of voice, is minimal. In contemporary theatre sound is often used primarily for its 'sensorial essence' and materiality. It can be a sort of performance in itself rather than revealing of content or meaning. Dogra's chanting of the $E = mc^2$ equation or her 'singing' of Einstein's theory of relativity brings out an unusual dimension of the non-referential use of sound in theatre. She extrapolates the rhythm of mantra-chanting from Hindu rituals and mixes it with that of the Tibetan-Buddhist prayer in order to use sound as an 'independent constituent' in performance. This, however, has nothing to do with the assimilation of Buddhism and Hinduism as faiths, disapproved of by many for the two faiths' widely different positions on caste. 'The scientific formula doesn't change', says Dogra, 'but when sung, your experience of it changes' (2019). The experience for the spectator in this context is created by placing aural and visual material in a new interactive and performative relationship with each other, sometimes mutually complementary and at others contrapuntal. 'Nothing remains but energy' in the ever-changing universe seems to be the endnote to *Black Hole* in its spiritual as well as scientific sense. The performance that is otherwise ephemeral leaves behind a field of energy that is never to go away. *Black Hole* is a theatre solo setting new standards of performance-making that includes devising, storytelling, text and choreography.

5

India's Postdramatic III: Theatre-as-Event, Reality Theatre, Theatre Installations

This chapter discusses a cluster of productions where the story element is nearly absent and theatre as soundscape, live art, docudrama and real-time-action takes over. It discusses theatre-as-event (Grover's *Downtime*, 2014), 'theatre of the real' (Anuradha Kapur and Ein Lall's *Antigone Project*, 2003–4), and theatre as performance-installation (Muzamil Bhawani's *Active Space*, 2012; Zuleikha Chaudhari's *Some Stage Directions for Henrik Ibsen's* John Gabriel Borkman, 2009, and *Propositions: On Text and Space I*, 2010).

Theatre-as-event

In theatre-as-event, the signs are no longer separable, to quote Lehmann, from their 'embeddedness in the *event* and the *situation* of theatre in general'. In other words, the use of signs is no more distinguishable from the event '*within* the [very] frame' of performance; instead, they appear as 'presented reality' (Lehmann 2006: 104). This is different from the transparency/disruption polarity discussed in the section on *Peer Gynt* (Chapter 3) in the context of the sign's visibility/invisibility informing perception and meaning-making. But the sign in the present case is nothing different from the event itself, to reiterate, or the event from the sign itself. The two are co-imbricated; only the framing of what happens and how that is presented to the spectator qualifies it as theatre and performance. Here the plan is to bring together people in an interactive session and produce a shared event that the dramatic theatre cannot afford for its tendency to create an illusory world and for the fourth wall. In the postdramatic theatre of events, real-time action (one may also call it 'activities') is what constitutes the 'plot'. It executes acts that are real in the performance space with no reference to the outside and acquire their reality status in the very moment they happen, without necessarily *meaning* anything. Or, at the most, the very experience of the event/act is its own meaning. Theatre-as-event prioritizes the principle of participation and works on 'the physical, affective and spatial relationship between actors and spectators', highlighting 'presence (the doing in the real) as opposed to re-presentation (the mimesis of the fictive)' (Lehmann 2006: 104). There are also instances where no line exists between actors and spectators, where the latter become participants and, thereby, doers and performers.

'In this a motif of modernism lives on', says Lehmann (104). The classical avant-gardes also extended theatre into various kinds of events, such as political demonstrations, debate and public action. But the way of doing theatre-as-event has changed with time and history. Event as action/activity meant in those days a radical revaluation of prevalent values and conditions. Contemporary action art does not, however, focus on changing the world, as Lehmann maintains, but instead aims at producing '*events, exceptions* and moments of *deviation*' (2006: 105). But in these very moments of exception and deviation, I would argue, may lie the potential for political provocation in forms of breaks and ruptures in everyday routine performance. By bringing into play its 'event-ness' as intervention/disruption in routine activities and experience, postdramatic theatre can also throw the audience as participant into 'a provocative situation' (106). We should not here separate 'event' from 'situation': theatre-as-event turns into a situational site where players and spectator-participants can have no knowledge of the event outside of its event-ness. Moreover, an event/situation may offer a different experience to each individual participant. This redefines the relationship between spectators and the theatrical 'happenings' because the framing and organization of the event brings a significant shift in our understanding of theatre from work to an ongoing process, changing the ethics and aesthetics of performance-making radically. 'Work' with an implied preconceptuality and closure is replaced by the randomness and open-endedness of 'event' that creates a situation very different from that in dramatic theatre. The theatre-event thus underlines the processuality of an onsite happening which might have been partly pre-organized but which, at the same time, defies predictability. The director of such theatre is often the curator of a site-specific performance actually, negotiating between action/activity, time and (public) space. Erika Fischer-Lichte believes that performance as event also exists 'independent of its creator and recipient'. For 'we are dealing with an *event* that involves everybody – albeit to different degrees and in different capacities' (in Woolf 2013: 38). Her position on the event-character of theatre is that such theatre nearly dissolves the distinction between art form and other forms of social interaction where performers (doers) and spectators together create an interactive space and collaborate in doing and witnessing things simultaneously across 'material, social, political and economic relations' (Doherty 2009). However, theatre-as-event may also have a director or curator and thus still be different from a raw social event.

For this segment I chose a three-part project titled *Downtime* (2014), conceptualized by Amitesh Grover with Frank Oberhäußer, and jointly produced by Goethe-Institut/Max Mueller Bhavan, New Delhi, and Heimathafen Neukölln, Berlin. I discuss the first two sections, where there are no actors or spectators but only participants who are assigned different activities for themselves as well as for one another. These activities or acts are more important in themselves than their outcome, a process without any predetermined course or closure. Grover 'directs, curates, and collaborates to create performance situations', his blog says (2017: online). He has evolved a format called 'Performapedia' (performance as a mode of knowing and experiencing) which invites the public through auditions to participate in different forms of activity – sleeping, mourning, re/telling, walking and so on – a format of performance that Lehmann might not have anticipated but which adequately qualifies for the postdramatic today. Those activities, carried out live or sometimes technologically (technology has its own liveness, though), 'unleash a new set of possibilities and alignments into play', Grover writes, 'only when the performative – the "act" itself – is activated' (ibid.). His interest is also in performances held outdoors, which include 'promenade shows' with audience-participants travelling from one location to another (Grover 2010: online). Grover believes that in our times art is the only human-gathering form left, almost an echo of Nicolas Bourriaud's argument that the participatory performances and theatre events, which invent 'ways of being together', are 'forms of interaction that go beyond the inevitability of the families, ghettos of technological user-friendliness' (Bourriaud 2002: 60). Some gatherings, especially those organized in elite enclaves, do not, however, build a wide social network or 'democratic opportunity' for an egalitarian discourse in the way socially engaged theatre of earlier times would, but may ensue instead from what Jen Harvie calls prioritization of self-interest in a world of crass commercialization (2013: 2). But in a neoliberal society, managed by the media, art mostly links humans via commerce (in a broader sense) and technology. The gatherings it facilitates, to use Bourriaud's words, lead to 'the freeing-up of inter-human communications' (2002: 60) and redefine theatre as a community event within a changed socioeconomic structure. This may also include contemporary social movements, organized digitally, and the arts and performances that emerge out of them.

Grover no less builds on Alan Badiou's concept of 'encounter' to create a large part of his theatre-as-event. Modifying Badiou's definition of encounter and relating it to Grover's kind of theatre, we may say that for theatre to be a genuine encounter, 'we must always be able to assume that it is ... a possible adventure' (Badiou 2014: online). It is experience-in-progress in that the encounter is 'a beginning' of what one does not know yet. And the theatre built on this premise is a theatre of yet-to-be. Grover also turns to Heidegger's concept of 'praxical knowledge or handlability', which argues – as he puts it – that 'it is through the handling of materials, methods, tools and ideas in practice' that we come to know the world and that art (in this case, performance) becomes an experience that 'defies the logic of representationalism' (Grover 2016: online). Grover's theatre-as-event is an invitation to participate, a performative moment where any truth-claim is made only through interaction and confrontation, and where the truth in question is 'predicated on its transience' (ibid.). Grover hardly wants to do the dramatic theatre any more by inviting people to a world of fiction. He would instead gather them to curate in a chosen space activities that they perform in everyday life without being aware of their performativity: house parties, city walks, museum visits and even emergency drills. The invitees are not asked to do 'a rehearsed series of occurrences', Grover notes, but to re-contextualize an everyday activity like sleeping or walking. In this re-contextualization participants discover the 'eventfulness of sleep [or walking] as we-do-not-know-it' (ibid.). The invitees/participants selected through a

Figure 6 *Sleep Series* III (2014), conceptualized and directed by Amitesh Grover and Frank Oberhausser, produced by Heimathafen Berlin and Goethe-Institut India. Photo credit: Amitesh Grover.

long, gruelling 'audition' process are briefed on the context and nature of the event that they will perform or the tasks they are required to accomplish. After the event is over, their responses are recorded, individually as well as collectively, which again becomes an act of performance in itself.

Downtime (2014)

The invitation for one part of *Downtime* reads:

> For its first event, SLEEP-SURFERS: Would you like to sleep like someone else? Would you like to author someone else's sleep? Be a part of a special gathering of Sleep-Surfers. You play the role of a visitor, visiting a temporary museum of sleep. Or, lend your sleep to a visitor for one night. Either way, you observe, you record, you encounter a different sleep for one night.
>
> Grover 2016: online

SLEEP-SURFERS (Sleep Series I)

SLEEP-SURFERS asks the participants to perform sleeping, an activity they carry out every night without being aware of it. But here it becomes performative because of its 'staging' as an event and in a context different from the everyday one. SLEEP-SURFERS maintains no difference between actors and spectators, experts and non-experts – which means it has no passive, non-performing audiences who would come to the theatre for the pleasure of watching a series of fictive events unfolding before them. Although the entire event has been planned by the director/curator, it does not turn into performance-as-representation since the performer-participants are not imitating the act of sleeping as an actor would on the 'dramatic' stage. The *performance* takes place as an event that they had never performed before the way they do now and in a form that they had never thought of earlier. While 'the activity of sleeping' remains the main focus, 'the changing contexts' in which it is presently performed – 'in [an] alien surrounding, in solitude, in public, with a partner, or with a community – reveal[s] a "hidden truth" centred in the activity', writes Grover (2016: online). Whether it is to sleep over in the host's house, or to perform 'sleeping practices' different from one's own, or to 'interview a homeless expert sleeper' – the invitation offers 'a counter-representational model' based on some regular activities but not in the familiar setting. The invitation to this event redefines the relationship between the sleeper and the environment, asking them to engage materially with 'the space reserved for sleep – private, public, and networked' (ibid.).

Sleep, according to Grover, has become a private activity and, therefore, a non-sight, in recent history. Sleep-surfing intrudes into this private space to establish a relationship between sleep-surfers (participants as visitors) and sleep-hosts (participants as hosts) and explore how sleep, apparently a non-performative activity, is also an act of performance. The event took place in two cities, Berlin and Delhi, simultaneously. Sleep-surfers were invited to perform a stranger's sleep, while sleep-hosts were asked to author the surfer's sleep, Grover clarifies (2016: online). He auditioned the applicants for the events – and only twenty were chosen: ten hosts and ten surfers. In each city, the surfers assembled at a designated place and were taken to the houses of their respective hosts. These houses were carefully selected across the city – each different from the other – 'a hostel, single occupancy, low-income housing, a new-mother's home, a non-national's apartment, high-income house' (ibid.). The surfers were introduced to their respective hosts and given a guided tour of the house, the venue of sleep performance. Instructions were already handed in to the surfers who now acquire a sense of place and people and a better idea of the work assigned to them. The details of the host's bedroom are pre-recorded to archive the factors that would influence the surfer's sleep – such as the carpet on the floor, the small bedside table (on which are bedtime books, a reading lamp and a bottle of water), the bed, the fireplace, the showpieces, the layout of the room and so on. After familiarizing themselves thoroughly with the host's night routine, the surfer retires to their bedroom and listens to an hour-long audio track that 'contain[s] a series of provocations – gestures and questions that the [visitor/surfer is] asked to respond to while lying in the host's bed' (ibid.). The audio instructions or those in print are bits of information or pieces of texts that do not translate into fake action but lead to real-time activities that change the visitor's experience of sleeping. The process is simulation at both physical and technological levels, and therefore mimicking in some sense, but ultimately far from the process of building action or character in the traditional theatrical way. In this wholly complex system of action and communication, the live and the virtual, the original and the copy meet in a non-mimetic manner.

The next morning all surfers and their hosts meet over a joint breakfast and share their experiences with one another. One surfer had recorded the breathing rhythm of his host on his cell phone and tried to simulate it while performing the host's sleep, thus making a small archive of the surfer–host relationship for one night and implying by extension the formation of the 'self' in the active presence of the other, society being the larger unit. Another surfer sought to follow, in performing her host's sleep, the sleeping pattern of the mother of a newborn who would wake up every now and then to tend to the baby and again go back to sleep. Grover seeks to understand how 'the intermittent sleep became the dominant narrative of the surfer's waking life during the day'. In analysing her experience, Grover refers in his *Performapedia* to Henri Lefebvre's 'idea of rhythms as the founding bases of the sleeping body' in *Rhythmanalysis* (1992), a book that explores sleep in terms of biological, experiential, spatiotemporal and everyday routine rhythms. Rhythm here does not necessarily mean an ideal alignment of individual needs and activities, but implies recurring 'sleep waves' that are nonetheless shaped by a complex network of social and material relations. Other surfers pointed out the differences between their own bedrooms and their hosts' in setting and ambience, which significantly impacted their sleep for the night. The pattern of sleep performed and experienced by each participant in the project was different from the regular pattern they would have in their own places, and this made each aware of the relationship that exists between the sleeper, their body, the place they sleep in and the new waves of activities they perform. In the 'museum of sleep' that each bedroom turned into, filled with divergent objects, artefacts and the (performing) sleeper's body, we have a radically new language of performance (Grover 2016: online). In such performances, acting is activity and action is performing someone else's body in one's own. SLEEP-SURFERS as a performed event leaves behind a manual of sleep studies that records and collects data from the sleeping subject and demonstrates the making of the everyday in a broader sense, its performative character in other words.

SLEEP-WALK (Sleep Series II)

Now consider the invitation for the second event, SLEEP-WALK:

> Is there a survivor's manual to sleeping in Delhi without money or shelter? A local sleep entrepreneur walks you through one of the many concealed, improvised sleeping places – performing a survivor's manual for finding a safe sleeping spot in Delhi.
>
> Grover 2016: online

The subject for the second event in *Downtime*, SLEEP-WALK, may be described as an exploration of the relationship of sleep to space, cityscape, architecture, public property and the like. It is important to note that Lehmann himself included theatre-as-a-walk in his panorama of postdramatic theatre later, although he did not develop on it. Walking through a city, he writes, may 'come under the concept of theater'; only 'the focus of attention shift[s] away from the final theater product towards the process or the "situation" of theater as a social, live form of praxis that connects and involves every participant in the theater event, actors and visitors alike' (Lehmann 2016: online). Grover's 'Sleep-walk' is partly different from a lone walker – as in *En Route* – trekking through a city where she, as Tomlin would have it, 'becomes the actor of [her] own performance' and 'simultaneously ... the active spectator, or author of meaning, who evokes the narratives that the surrounding landscape is now required to perform' (Tomlin 2016: 148). The present collaborative project, in Grover's own words, 'mapped the communal sleeping spaces in Delhi and Berlin by inviting an "expert" to lead a guided walk' (2016: online).

The walks are, however, very different in the two cities in which they are conducted. In Berlin, Hannah Ahlheim, a sleep researcher, conducted 'a lecture walk' by inviting the audience inside a hundred-year-old women's hostel, which had never before admitted men into the building. Giving the invitees a tour of it, she focused on the 'relationship architecture and the interior arrangement ... had with its temporary inhabitants: single women who came to study, work or just visit the city, and needed to sleep' (Grover 2016: online). Ahlheim explained how gender played an extremely important role in designing the whole space indoors. But the boarders made certain interventions by changing or modifying some parts of the building from inside to make it suitable to their varied sleeping schedules. Most of them were working in factories that had three eight-hour-long shifts in those days and many were sharing rooms or beds exclusively for sleeping at different times. The objective of the project was to make the visitor-spectators see how the culture of sleep, gender, working schedule, place and space share a performative relationship with one another.

On the other hand, the visitors/participants were later taken to a showroom of Savoir Beds, a company that claims to produce one of the most comfortable and costliest handcrafted sleep mattresses in the world. They were also told that a significant part of the labour force is from South Asia, especially from India – which, as Grover notes, had a remarkable resonance since the other part of the project was taking place the same day in India, in Delhi in particular. The proprietors explained to the visitors/walkers the details relating to the sleep market, thereby giving them an idea of the interface between class, comfort levels of sleep, and material and design of the mattress. Ahlheim in her sleep research connects the sleep industry to economy, sociology, work pattern and individual identity. Her basic point is that sleep is externally determined. Until the late nineteenth century there was little or no research on sleep and the belief was that only people performing mental labour need to sleep whereas those doing menial jobs need only some rest to relax their muscles. More importantly, it was believed that sleep is a natural, spontaneous activity that has nothing to do with any external factors. Both sleep and wakefulness became a 'strategic resource' in the twentieth century that was manipulated in different ways for greater productivity – whether in warfare or in commerce. As 'flexitime' became an option of labour in the post-Fordist era, specialized articles of comfort, often advised by medics, flooded the market and added a new dimension of excess to consumerism in a late capitalist society. The mattress company that Ahlheim took the walkers to advertises their mattress as 'dreams realised'. A 30,000 USD bed, made from natural materials like Mongolian goat fur, exposes the flip side of the discovery of sleep as a performative act (see Ahlheim 2017: online).

In New Delhi, by contrast, Ranjit, a poor local sleep entrepreneur, was invited as an 'expert' to stage a guided walk for a group of participants to the Iron Bridge (more than a hundred years old and located in Old Delhi), where sleep mafias run an informal sleep industry for about 800 homeless sleepers. The site is first shown to the walkers on Google Maps. Himself used to sleeping for years in improvised places, Ranjit's job is to find a safe sleeping place for the homeless on the outskirts of the city, Grover informs them. Sleep acquires an important sociopolitical meaning when seen in relation to the everyday lives of the urban poor. The walk was conducted for nearly an hour, at dusk, just before the sleepers returned 'home' (Grover 2016: online). Ranjit tells the walkers that the places in which a homeless person in Delhi could sleep include various types of shelters, depending on the season and the sleeper's ability to pay. For example, when there are clouds overhead, the best place to sleep is under a flyover. Next to that are the Hume pipes dumped by the Public Works Department on the roadside to be used for making sewers. One can also get into them and sleep for the night. Then he brings the group of walkers close to the Iron Bridge and shows a more elaborate arrangement of makeshift rooms with cinemas (enclosures fitted with TVs and CD players) where people watch films before going to sleep. Making such 'rooms' under the bridge their dwelling places, they have also improvised many ways of earning around the site, such as selling tea from temporary stalls, pulling rickshaws, and collecting coins and coconuts from the riverbed that were thrown into the waters by believers in hopes of good luck. Then the walkers are shown the sandy surrounds where people spread tarpaulins and lie down for a good night's sleep in summer, especially when it does not rain. 'Ranjit spoke about improvisations and subversions that he and his cohort perform each day to make their surrounding more amenable to sleeping', Grover notes (ibid.).

Ranjit's narrative also raises questions about class in many ways – for example, 'what it means to "visit" the disenfranchised' and whether these visitors would ever have come to this place had it not been for this performance walk (Grover 2016: online). Grover's self-criticality as curator of the project is evident in the question above, an abiding trait in his works that also sometimes makes the participant-spectators aware of their 'complicity' in what he does/shows or in how they react to it. *Gnomonicity*, for instance, has consenting spectators throw their shadow on the white screen before them to make the live but illegally streamed CCTV feeds visible on it, thus vexing the question of ethics in the curating of contemporary performances. The extended question in the context of Ranjit's guided tour could be whether a gathering of people for a performance event or the selection of a particular site for it in any case exploits the condition of a deprivileged class of people for the benefit of 'entrepreneurized' artists. However, it is not only that there were no tickets for the Sleep Series – Grover selected the participants through a questionnaire and then curated them for the walk – but SLEEP-WALK confronts a privileged class of viewers with a world of sordid reality that they had never experienced before.

The people involved in the walk are obviously not actors even though the walk was 'framed and theatricalized by the performance situation' (Carlson 2015: 592). They are walkers/viewers/participants exposed to a site 'as if it were a theatre' or a live installation narrating the everyday of an unenviable section of people that we have little touch with. What Marvin Carlson maintains in his book on postdramatic theatre and performance largely holds true for some parts of Grover's Sleep Series: 'it is the non-mimetic framed as if it were the mimetic. Remove the frame, and not only mimesis disappears, but so does theatre itself, and what remains is life' (ibid.: 593). The activities that go on under the Iron Bridge and in its surrounds do not become a performance until the walkers go to the site and watch them. Watching also becomes an inward journey for the viewers, a 'witnessing' they 'perform' (Hughes n.d.: online) through their interactive encounter with the setting, atmosphere and real people in action.

Reality theatre

There is one kind of documentary theatre in recent times which Ulrike Garde and Meg Mumford call 'Postdramatic Reality Theatre'. This theatre type presents real 'contemporary people and their lives on stage, either in person, or in a carefully scripted text based on real-life interviews and documents' or in a combination of both (Garde and Mumford 2013: 147). It is 'a challenge to the traditional concept of mimesis', Marvin Carlson writes, 'and of the theatre world as a fictional construct distinctly separated from everyday life and its surroundings' (2015: 577). The performance created in this sort of theatre gives us a porous world where real-life people, their stories, their lives and places 'invade and are invaded by the frame of the stage' (Garde and Mumford 2013: 148). This theatre is also called 'verbatim theatre' in the UK and continental Europe since it may be heavily based on oral testimonies and not on documents as in tribunal theatre, while it is known as 'dramaturgy of the real' (Martin 2010) and 'ethnotheatre' (Saldaña 2011) in the US. Carol Martin prefers the term 'theatre of the real' to describe inclusively 'documentary theatre as well as docudrama, verbatim theatre, reality-based theatre, theatre of witness ... non-fiction theatre, and theatre of fact' (in Radosavljević 2013: 128). To Daniel Schulze, however, 'documentary theatre' may be 'the umbrella term for all plays and performances that stake a claim to using documentary material in Esch-van Kan's and Weiss' sense' (Schulze 2018: 192).

Tomlin observes that the revival of documentary theatre in the twenty-first century, especially when it deals with contentious issues, sounds somewhat paradoxical in the context of prevalent scepticism towards the social or political 'real'. The facticity of events and the access to information that forms knowledge, rendered problematic by the turn of events post-9/11 increasing public distrust towards political leaders and media houses, and conflicting public testimonies about an event, made representation of the real a challenge to theatre-makers (Tomlin 2016: 115–16). The theatre-makers of India have also confronted this challenge in the new millennium. The multiple stories around the scam-ridden United Progressive Alliance (UPA II) government, the post-Godhra carnage of 2002, the miscarriage of justice, and the post-truth regime inaugurated in 2014 by the National Democratic Alliance (NDA) government in the centre bear testimony to my claim. When the truth-value of documents and actions comes to be challenged either because of their suspected distortion or for its loss in the 'Naturalist glut of images' (Lehmann 2006: 144), what remains of them is only their 'indexical value', to quote Janelle Reinelt, 'the corroboration that something happened, that events took place' (in Schulze 2018: 191). While theatre's need for a return to reality from its fictive 'cosmos' is felt heavily considering the rampant camouflaging of facts in the outside world, there is hardly any widely acceptable way to rescue the truth owing to its current unprecedented mediation in different forms. Being an aesthetic category, twenty-first-century theatre's authenticity, as Funk et al. note, lies more in the 'matter of form and style in which authenticity is realized as a performative *effect*' (in Schulze 2018: 195). This effect, however, is not feasible, Schulze writes, referring to Funk et al., without 'the persona of the witness' (Schulze 2018: 196). The witness may be an actual person/artist present at the site of a happening or visiting it after the event is over and gathering information from people and available documents.

Contemporary reality theatre thus differs from the documentary theatres of the 1920s or their revisions in the 1960s and 1970s when the 'real' was more determinate to enable a critique of its distortion or concealment – which is why those works had elements of idealism and optimism about them. Here is a shift from 'the conventional dramaturgy of realism of the left-oriented twentieth-century documentary theatre', as Duška Radosavljević argues after Martin, to the 'strategies of the postmodern' (Radosavljević 2013: 128). The charge of lying doubly is sometimes levelled against contemporary theatre of the real on the grounds that it claims to 'document' reality on the basis of not-so-reliable testimonies and in a mixed medium where digital images partly structure reality. However, the use of mediums such as video footage of landscape, buildings and people may in fact exempt testimony-based yet semi-fictional performances from the compulsion to prove the authenticity of material which otherwise refers to some disturbing external 'reality'. In an age of doctored evidences, such theatre is free from the anxiety to educate the audience or advocate a particular ideology. The audience also knows that the presentation of 'real' people and incidents has undergone remediation for aesthetic reasons and, therefore, leaves the distinction between the fictive and the 'real' somewhat blurred. Postdramatic reality theatre eventually seeks authenticity in the mode of presentation. Having disabused itself of any capacity for an inviolable truth-claim, theatre locates itself in the irreconcilability of the desire to unravel truth and the impossibility of doing so because of reality's indeterminate status.

However, the real as a 'co-player' brought into the fictive cosmos in its presumed 'irreducible facticity' may not be able to escape the chain of signification, although it is also more than what Ryan A. Hatch calls a 'real *proper* to semblance' (Hatch 2019: 135–6). It can often be encountered as a 'surplus' in its traumatic effect on the spectator's experience and thus disrupt the frame of staged action, without which, paradoxically, no theatre is theatre. That is not all. As no pure presence is conceivable in postdramatic theatre without creating the tangibility of an experiential reality of what is presented, any dramatic framing of the fictive that conceals its own strategies of illusion-making is all the more deceiving. Hatch's interrogation of Lehmann's configuration of the real in postdramatic theatre is not invalid because that 'real' cannot stay unmediated by the order of 'theatrical semblance', but only *partly* valid because Lehmann (2006: 134) speaks of 'an *intentionally* unmediated experience' (italics mine) and therefore does not rule out the possibility of the failure of that intention or of the irreducible real's mediation by the fictive within the symbolic order on stage. In this liminality of the irrupted real and the fictional real is much of the contemporary dramaturgy of the real with its indexicality, including India's own.

The theatre of India has seen of late the emergence of diverse forms of reality theatre. Kapur and Lall's *The Antigone Project* (2003–04), Amitesh Grover's *Sleep-Walk* (2014) and Zuleikha Chaudhari's *Rehearsing the Witness: The Bhawal Court Case* (2015–18) merit special mention. While Grover's work has already been discussed under the rubric of 'theatre-as-event', Kapur and Lall's will be closely studied here. It is a matter of regret, though, that for space constraints *Rehearsing the Witness* – which brilliantly explores the idea of experimenting with historical material in forms of rehearsal, exhibition and performance-installation – could not be included in this book. The emergence of the kind of (reality) theatre that *The Antigone Project* is, was largely in response to the vitriolic campaign by the far right for India as a Hindu *rashtra* (state). Secularism was defined in post-independence India as the state's non-interference in matters of faith. But in practice the state's indirect involvement in religious issues by way of its avowed *equal support* to all religions has put neutrality at the risk of being tilted towards the dominant religio-cultural community. While any meddling with the nation's religious pluralism was construed in the Nehruvian archaeology of independent India as religious intolerance, majoritarian (and therefore culturally and politically Hindu) nationalism has been accepted as normative under the current ruling regime. The political party that presided over the state of affairs in 2002 Gujarat and is in the centre now has always used its aggressive propagandist machinery to quash all dissent. Lack of evidence and miscarriage of justice resulted in the acquittal of a large number of the post-Godhra accused in Gujarat, and the pattern repeats itself across the country today. Reality in such a situation not only becomes elusive but even very difficult for the artists to probe for the threat to their personal safety.

The Antigone Project (2003/2004)

In reaction to the post-Godhra pogrom in Gujarat in 2002, which saw the alleged state-sponsored killing of over two thousand Muslims and large-scale destruction of their property and sacred sites, theatre director Anuradha Kapur and video artist Ein Lall collaborated to make *The Antigone Project* (2003-4), 'using some text from Brecht's *Antigone* [1948] spliced with documentary footage of the riots, and filmed testimony of the victims' (Mee and Foley 2011: 420). It opened at the Max Mueller Bhavan, New Delhi, in 2003 and then featured at the NSD-organized Bharat Rang Mahotsav (BRM) in 2004. A major reason why Brecht chose Hölderlin's translation of the play is the latter's 'implicit resistance to a classicist view of tragedy' (Duarte 2017: online). Kapur and Lall preferred Brecht's adaptation of *Antigone* for their own work probably for the same reason and also because Brecht's adaptation did not directly transpose the mythical into the political (Duarte 2017: online) in the sense that it was already a de-mythicized tale. Based on the notions of the artist witnessing an event and the survivor testifying to it, Kapur observes, the project used at another level witness and testimony (from Gujarat) as material and made it the principal 'language of the production' (Kapur 2011: 419). The storyline from *The Antigone of Sophocles*, known to most of the (educated) audience, and the film footage, fairly familiar to local spectators, do away with the element of suspense that characterizes the progression of events in the dramatic theatre. Kapur and Lall's project belongs to the kind of theatre that can be considered both as 'verbatim practic[e]' that takes liberties with interview transcripts and testimonies in terms of directorial 'adding, cutting and editing' (Schulze 2018: 192) and as 'semi-fictional documentary performance' that reworks fictional source material to address the present 'reality' (Tim Etchells, in Tomlin 2016: 114). Whatever is 'dramatic' within that source material is broken down into non-dramatic elements that facilitate the *presentation* of contemporary political reality that is at once commented on and left to the audience for interpretation.

While Brecht begins his theatre with a conversation between Antigone and her sister on the Second World War, *The Antigone Project* opens with a video image of a body lying on the ground, suggestive of many such corpses awaiting burial in 2002 Gujarat. While the *fabel* on stage has Antigone battling against Creon to bury her brother killed in the war and Creon speaking the language of power, the eight-by-twelve-foot screen behind the mound of sand upstage, which resembles an unfilled grave, projects footage made of the Gujarat carnage. Alternately, the footage is projected on the human figures on stage and their shadows fall on the images on screen – creating a new dynamic of relationship between the stage and the world, the outside and the inside. The switching of onstage action and video footage, or the occasional simultaneity of both, leaves it to the audience to connect them. As the fiction is not 'dramatized', so is the external reality brought into the performance space not claimed to be conclusive because the testimonies recorded in the studio are also projected, for artistic purpose, with the visuals shot on the ground.

Relay of news, often without views, about the events that happened marks the production. The third live figure, sitting most of the time in a chair placed between two video screens on the stage and reciting the choral lines from Brecht, represents what Ein Lall calls 'objective news casting'. According to Lall, this figure conveys 'what Kreon [*sic*] does and what Antigone does, but I don't take sides. I keep my distance' (in Phillips-Krug 2004: 9). Kapur has a somewhat different take on the choric figure: 'The chorus should be like a commentator, maybe television, maybe radio, maybe the newspaper, maybe a bureaucrat. Somebody who rallies information and moves in his reaction from the safe to the sympathetic' (ibid.: 8). Both Lall and Kapur are right at the same time. The desire for action and a state of non-action, involvement and critical detachment simultaneously characterize the project. Keeping the people's memories of loss alive, or recuperating them, is what defines for Lall the objective of the project, while exploring 'the possibilities of resistance within that context' is not dismissed altogether. This is apparent in the very presentation of Antigone. In fact, Antigone and Ismene are brought together in one figure, to use Lall's words again. 'Antigone speaks as the active one who wants to do something, but there is also that Ismene voice in her which says "No, you can't do anything"' (ibid.: 10). This is a sort of 'strategic ambiguity' (Antje Dietze) that implies neither a dismissal of activism in theatre nor a naïve acceptance of theatre's transformative power. The testimonies of survivors, appearing as a video feed, also serve a choric and documentary function at another level, although memories are not infallible and when individuals recall the past, their remembrances tend to make 'sense of what ... happened to them ... and thus take on a form of protective remembering' which is, however, not self-deception (Macintyre 2019: 5). The testimonies expose a condition, as a documentary film does, but generating states rather than action.

Let us quickly review what led to the post-Godhra anti-Muslim campaign. Fifty-nine passengers aboard the Sabarmati Express died in a sudden fire in one of its coaches in February 2002. Those killed in the fire were claimed to be pious Hindu volunteers (*kar sevaks*) returning from a pilgrimage to Ayodhya and burnt alive by the Muslims in retaliation for the demolition of the Babri Masjid in 1992. The pogrom that continued for weeks and even months in a row made the situation on the ground more horrific and the truth more elusive. The problem about the transparency of the 'public sphere', a contradiction in liberal democracy, is that today's Creons are, as Lall says, 'democratically elected people ... assuming the proportions of tyrants, not the open tyranny of Hitler' (in Phillips-Krug 2004: 11). The camouflage they maintain, the institutions they abuse and the media houses that support the powers-that-be often make the truth irrecoverable. Consequently, activism in theatre has acquired new dimensions by inventing 'new forms of socially critical artistic practice' (Dietze 2013: 144) by doing theatre politically, as Lehmann would say, rather than doing political theatre. Instead of pitching a particular ideology or depending on metanarratives of liberation (including Marxist), Kapur and Lall's work creates a situation where the audience reflects on fragments of fiction on stage as well as on real interviews and testimonies, before coming to any interpretation of the unbearable.

The Antigone Project was conceived to expose the ideology of India's far right and the unholy alliance between the state machinery and the political party in power. Yet the performance is not dialectical except in its textual material. There is little scope for heroic resistance to power when it is crudely but surreptitiously exercised. The testimonies of Gujarat victims, presented in the form of recorded video material, rupture the dramatic rendering of the on-stage narrative in dialogue. Furthermore, while the documentary footage lends credibility to the stage events, its presentational format opens up room for questions about its explicitness. The action (post-Godhra killings) is over by the time the show opens. The experience offered to the audience is, as Carlson would say, more or less 'atmospheric and associative' (in Barnett 2013: 63). There is representation, symbolism and referencing of political/ historical reality; but none of them is continuous and direct – rather each is more connotative than denotative, more oblique than straight. Antigone is a Muslim woman and Creon, Narendra Modi (the then chief minister of Gujarat), says Kapur (2011: 420). But the identification is rather implicit even as Antigone appears in a burqa or even when the burial scene on stage is accompanied by the documentary footage of a vandalized mosque because the Thebes and Gujarat narratives run parallel to, rather than merge into, each other. Brecht's text becomes in this project linguistic material among other performance elements without dictating terms for the present context and its explication.

The Antigone Project spreads the dialectic over an expansive, multi-layered landscape rather than eschewing dialectics altogether and presents the Gujarat situation with political provocation through dramaturgy but charting no course of heroic counter/action. The spectacle of Antigone descending 'into the ordinary', into the crowd of Gujarat victims, via documentary footage mixes real-life pain with performance but stops short of elevating suffering to what Kapur calls 'the [heroic] heights of tragic drama' (Kapur 2011: 421). Kapur's remarks come close to what Lehmann says of tragedy in our time: '[T]ragedy in our time no longer has to [be] ... an outlook on life' but can be 'a certain artistic approach to and rendering of it' (Lehmann 2013: 89, 94). *The Antigone Project*, to borrow words from Borowski and Sugiera in another context, attempts to dismantle the 'tragic myth' itself and introduces 'a clash of sensibilities' and views through aesthetic strategies in place of the traditional development of conflict (2013: 74). The Brecht text in Kapur and Lall's project does not 'float ... freely' because its 'dynamics of delivery' are clearly demarcated, as Barnett would have it, since 'a power relation' lies at the centre of it. But, as the production shows, a text, even when 'linked to ... dialectical tensions', can be performed non-dialectically (Barnett 2013: 56).

The use of media in *The Antigone Project* does not contaminate theatre's purity, but rather introduces into it a new 'aesthetics of form', to quote Patrice Pavis, 'the process of semiotic transformation from one form to another', resulting in the 'emergence of meaning' (in Tasić 2011: 123) that is different from the meaning generated by the conventional mode/s of representation. The production begins with a video projection of what Lall describes as 'a beautiful [male] body, not mutilated by war' (in Phillips-Krug 2004: 8). First, it is shown as a whole, then in close-ups – the head, the feet, the navel and the nose – the focus moving up and down the whole length of the laid-out body. It was very important for Lall to show the body unravaged. 'It should be the memory of a precious body of the brother', she says, 'the memory of a whole man'. The close-up of the head slips off, if not transforms, into a heap of sand onstage to which Antigone comes running to take possession of it. 'With the sand two things were achieved', says Lall: the unburied body is lying on rather than under it and thus exposed to dogs and vultures; and the possibility that one could 'grasp a fistful of sand and say, "This is what I live by"' (ibid.). In comparison to the 'epic proportion and the human scale of the body', Kapur adds, Antigone is shown to be 'fragile, frail, starting with small things and then moving to the larger ones' (ibid.). While the exchange between Antigone and Creon tends to build a fictive scene, the video material deconstructs much of the illusion by multiplying visuals of the genocide on the screen, thus increasing the audience's perceptual intimacy with what is shown rather than encouraging interpretation of textual material.

The media coverage of the vandalism and violence shows that the bodies of the dead, or the individuals even in death, belonged to the state, which could do to the deceased whatever it liked. The survivors seldom had any chance to perform the last rites for their kin, and their own lives were under threat. When this real in its facticity enters into the performance space, it affects the fictive real and is in turn affected by it. The outcast Antigone is reminiscent of the thousands of Muslims who were killed or spared their lives to languish in refugee camps because they 'did not' belong to India, 'the land of the Hindus'. Part of the footage about the camps is projected over Antigone as she now stands in her white attire between the giant screen and the mound of sand. The camps are filled with refugees who will have to leave the makeshift accommodation soon since it will be pulled down and all supplies to the homeless stopped in order to either starve them to death or force them to flee the state. The inscriptions on the body of mediatized images, at the same time, change the traditional understanding of mimesis in theatre, and with it, of the usage of theatrical signs in general. In one of the video installations, to use Kapur's words, 'screen 1 showed close-ups of vandalized interiors of [Muslim] homes while screen 2 showed a multiple projection in which the camera followed a young schoolgirl as she walked disconsolately through the gutted ruins of what had once been her neighbourhood in the suburbs of Ahmedabad' (Kapur 2011: 420–1). The images, some superimposed on the figure of Antigone, show parts of Gujarat drowned in blood and engulfed by fire, while the story told onstage is that of Creon's Thebes, the apparent disjunct provoking the audience/spectator to contemplate on both similarities and dissimilarities between the two frames of reference. The body in this scene becomes a bearer of images relating to memories of its abuse and mutilation.

Besides documentary footage, painting and music accompany, if not aid, the live performance on stage, framing the 'authenticity' issue intertextually and intermedially. They also make the project 'Indian' in image-making and soundscape. On the video screen appears the picture of old Muslim men sitting near a mosque in good times, while the choric figure alludes to a chariot voyage (which reminds one of Modi's Gaurav Rath Yatra after the carnage) and expresses Creon's concern over its reception among the people who might have got tired from the war but who must not yet give up the fight against 'enemies' within the country. The painting mentioned above is by artist Bhupen Khakhar, titled *Muslims Around a Mosque* (oil on canvas, 2001), which, when contrasted with the video footage about the vandalized mosques in Ahmedabad, nostalgically shows that in the past there existed some space for those people meeting regularly for lazy, intimate conversations. On the other hand, Gulam Mohammed Sheikh's oil-on-canvas painting, *Returning Home After Long Absence* (1969–73), slowly and almost imperceptibly superimposed on the documentary footage of Gujarat's largest refugee camp, Lall notes, underscores the minority community's unrealized dream to belong here (in Phillips-Krug 2004: 9). The constant oscillation between, or simultaneity of, the aesthetically rendered authentic and the expressly fictive in this work keeps the spectator engaged in working out their own 'conclusions' about what is real about the material used as well as about its presentation. At the formal level, particularly, it shows how the crisis of 'dramatic' representation can be overcome through a new sign system, by bringing in other forms of art as autonomous or complementary practices.

The production begins with a short musical piece from Philip Glass which, according to Lall, 'seemed to universalize the brother's body' (in Phillips-Krug 2004: 8) and ends with a tiny quotation from Mukul Shivputra. There is another quotation from Pakistani *sufi* singer Abida Parvin, devised from Bulleh Shah's lyrics, when Antigone exits as if to seek out death for herself. The selection of music, vocal as well as instrumental, from both classical Indian and Pakistani *sufi* traditions, seems part of a scheme to dismiss the politicization of faith in the subcontinent. To achieve this, *The Antigone*

Project uses multiple aesthetic forms not accommodated into the discipline of theatre before. The choric figure also condemns all violence in the name of religion, as the performance comes to an end, making 'witnessing' a potential act of intervention.

Theatre installations

Installations have been a significant part of modern art since the 1960s and more so since the 1990s when the relationship between space and viewer received greater importance. However, the genre of performance-installation, 'the theatre equivalent of installation' (Carlson 2015: 588), gained popularity in the 1970s, cross-fertilizing 'visual art environments and the performing arts' (Levine 2016: online). It enables the spectator to experience 'three-dimensional artworks' and live performance by moving within them (Carlson 2015: 588). Installation art might have been an offshoot of visual arts, but it has recently developed itself by aligning with a variety of performing and performance arts. Canonical plays have also been produced as performance-installations (or 'theatre immersion'), Punchdrunk's *Sleep No More* (based on *Macbeth*) being one. The blending of the narrative, the performative, the visual and the digital has created installations that present events by incorporating the spectator in the 'shaping ... of the performance' (ibid.). Visual arts – such as painting, sculpture, textile arts and scenography – have always been strong in India alongside its rich performance tradition. They now meet in theatre installations. Broadening the scope of the term 'theatre', Indian theatre-makers and artists are experimenting with new kinds of performance that combine several art forms, sometimes using the text but in non-representational ways.

This section discusses two performance-installations that offer a 'reflection on particular themes instead of a dramatic action', as Lehmann would say, and are, therefore, suggestive of 'the landscape of postdramatic theatre' (2006: 112). They are more visual presentations of theatrical or non-theatrical texts, in part or whole, than thematic or narrative representations. They unfold like pictures or artworks that the spectator walks through and around, becoming 'pictorial or object-like presentations of reality' with a flexible dimension of time about them (134). They also share grounds with the theatre of situation, offering the spectator an atmosphere which is nothing without their presence in it. The spectator's gaze is invited to dynamize the 'durational stasis' of the curated atmosphere (157). The performance-installations so far produced in India either have texts to base themselves on, or have been crafted out of events directly experienced by the artists and mixed with their imagination working on things of emotional and archival value to them. I consider these installations as theatre because there is a spatial and temporal framing even in their attempted transcendence of time and space. Besides, the difference between performance-/theatre-installation and other kinds of artworks like painting or installations on show in the museum is that the former is not 'a display of separate, individual' exhibits in most cases. The focus on providing an intense performative experience for the viewer is a dominant trait in such theatre installations. As Anuradha Kapur notes, such 'installations are experiential as theatre is – because [they] share time and space with the viewer; they invite the viewer into the environment' and 'seek the spectator's attention at a register different from functional objects usually embedded in the mise-en-scène' (Kapur 2019c: 54) as well as from visual artworks. Below are close discussions of two productions only, although a whole monograph may be devoted to the study in the area.

Some Stage Directions for Henrik Ibsen's John Gabriel Borkman (2009) and *Propositions: On Text and Space I* (2010)

These two interrelated projects of Zuleikha Chaudhari's merit special attention as illustrations of India's theatre-as-installation in the new century, although her subsequent works (not discussed here through space constraints) make further departures in form. *Some Stage Directions* is a play-cum-installation project she created for the 2009 Ibsen Theatre Festival in Delhi, with stage directions from the Ibsen text as its 'spine'. Having moved out of the proscenium in 2005 with *On Seeing*, Chaudhari says, she continued to 'work with texts that were descriptive rather than dialogic' and subsequently incorporated the viewer physically in her performance. *Some Stage Directions* developed from her 'formal interest in textual descriptions as images'. 'The production was conceived as a series of images', Chaudhari continues, and 'developed as descriptions of place, people and actions and as directions for performers and viewers' (2019: 56). Interested in visual arts, she had wanted since 2005 to understand performance's relationship to 'time, spectatorship and meaning-making' (Chaudhari 2017). Monologues composed of select 'stage directions' take over dramatic dialogues in her adaptation of Ibsen's play at its first stage – and she thinks that a character's speeches, when crafted thus and put together, provide 'a juxtaposition of experience as inhabited and felt with experience as landscape' (ibid.). The textual delivery in the reworked piece, the spoken stage directions, leaves the drama out of the source text and creates a performative aesthetic that puts the audience and the text in an interactive relationship.

In *Some Stage Directions*, she stuck to the four-act structure of Ibsen's play, but in general 'used the stage directions from the play as the spoken text because they seemed to communicate the action and emotional subtext of the scenes' (Chaudhari 2017). Specifically, in Act Two, the stage directions are the texts spoken by the actors onstage, while in Act One, the conversation/dialogue between the twin sisters is turned into monologues. From this experimentation two questions arose, which she tried to answer before dropping actors/performers out of the installation: 'What do spoken stage directions convey?' and 'What does a dialogue-turned-monologue do?' The first may be considered Chaudhari's attempt to turn the literary into descriptions of 'a painting in motion' as well as 'a painting as movement and action' (ibid.). As regards monologues replacing dialogues, she says: 'The whole piece [a broken-down play] looks like people not talking to each other really', but each describing their feeling or action through a string of words and sentences that were not supposed to be spoken thus. When put in sequence and spoken, they sound like 'psychological inner landscapes – an internal monologue – or a [character's] direct communication with the audience about the self' (ibid.). Shuddhabrata Sengupta of the Raqs Media Collective, who rewrote portions of the Ibsen script for Chaudhari as descriptive texts or annotations, notes that they did not discard the text but used its verbal and non-verbal, theatrical and non-theatrical properties for its performative effect:

> We wanted to work very closely with the text, except the text we chose to work with was not the dialogue, but the stage directions. You can say that this was a first because the actors spoke the stage directions as if they were a theatrical text. And something happens when you pay such close attention to parts of the text that were not intended to be spoken ... [but] meant to be internalized by the actors. But we did the opposite. The dialogues and spoken text were internalized, while the stage instructions were externalized.
>
> Sengupta 2012b: 52–3

Apart from the 'action' through spoken texts from stage directions, the production has enough spectacular opulence in the visual text (words drop like snow on the acrylic screen) and in the setting with the look-through screen dividing the stage into two halves lengthwise. Spatial experiment counts as a contributory factor here. On either side of the divide actors deliver speeches or build up fragments of gestures, suggesting cumulatively 'a state of being' (Chaudhari 2017). Owing to the framing of the space on each side by panels of tube-lights (characteristic of Chaudhuri's work), the stage partitions the very act of watching. Sitting on one side the spectator can see only a section of the action, with a parallel or minor action taking place on the other side and appearing opaque. This splitting of perspective is significant to the project primarily because it takes 'two views of the same thing simultaneously' (ibid.): it refers to progress and construction in a kind of mirror relationship to Borkman's romantic beginning and development and, at the same time, shows the dissolution of the dream and the dreamer. Borkman's death is 'performed' in three forms: an original text/dialogue from the Ibsen play, the act rewritten as a description of a state and the Raqs text describing the dying body of Borkman as a dying industrial town. The final image is that of snow that keeps falling, covering everything. While the picture of a dying city provides a distanced view of the outside, Borkman's words spoken from inside his head present a view of his inner crisis (ibid.). Actors also talk to each other 'like snow falling', and the white paint on one side of the acrylic screen, splashed with water, runs down. The last image is that of snowing, which completes the death scene.

Propositions: On Text and Space I (developed at Khoj Studios, New Delhi, as part of Chaudhari's 2010–12 series) is a sequel to *Some Stage Directions* and built on the select material from the reworked Ibsen play. The focus now is 'on thinking about the role of the performer in a live theatre experience' (Chaudhari 2017). The interest in the role of the performer came from Heiner Müller. The Müller performer was a medium, who 'communicated text as an image', Chaudhari says. The performer, for her, had to have 'a transparent quality – a mediator between the text (images and ideas in a play) and the viewer'. This, in turn, led her to think about 'how we experience all the other elements of theatre ... when the performer is removed'. Her interest in theatre lighting, in her own words, thus 'developed into lighting structures and, therefore, scenography' (Chaudhari 2017). Consequently, *Propositions* became a venture into exploring what happens when one walks into the frame of theatre as a form of painting. Visual art ensures a 'democratic process', but theatre does not, so far as we understand it in its dramatic sense, because, as she notes, 'it has a beginning, a middle and an end even when it does not seem to have this [structural organization]'. Chaudhari wanted to do an installation that would be about 'a moment in time', where one 'can spend hours looking at it', reflecting on the translation of an idea into an image or a series of images. She craved in her work for a fluidity that would leave 'the choice to the spectator ... to come, to watch, to do something or not to do anything, to stay or to go' (Chaudhari 2017), thus shifting the meaning-making process from the director or actor to the spectator. *Some Stage Directions* might not have fulfilled that desire, but it is certainly a turning point in her career as a theatre-maker and gave her the opportunity to realize her goal largely in the *Propositions* series.

Since *Propositions: On Text and Space I* as a full-scale installation builds on the last scene of the Ibsen text, we may quickly review what happens in

Figure 7 *Propositions: On Text and Space I* (2010), directed by Zuleikha Chaudhari, based on Ibsen's *John Gabriel Borkman*, texts by the Raqs Media Collective, presented by Khoj International Artists' Association, New Delhi. Photo credit: Zuleikha Chaudhari.

that scene. Borkman, the run-over man, having spent years in prison and in isolation in his sister-in-law's house, decides to go out in the night one day, chilly from snow falling, and never goes back inside. As Borkman climbs up a small hill, with Ella by his side, and looks down the river and imagines hearing the factories working during the night shift, she describes it as the dreamland of their life, now buried in snow. Borkman, long dead within, now dies physically in the night's cold. In *Propositions: On Text and Space I*, Chaudhari focuses solely on Borkman's death. The viewer enters into the description of the scene as into the frame of a picture, a superimposition of text fragments from Ibsen on acrylic sheets in rows, accompanied by audio and visual texts. *Propositions I* turns the Ibsen play into a landscape of death: the central imagery of snow constantly falling reinforces the *presence* of death and the *absence* of life. As the viewer leisurely passes through the tunnel-like corridors, Chaudhari's installation becomes an extension of a text over space, a painted landscape suspended in time. While one may need 'to distinguish between painterly and theatrical forms and to take their respective laws and rules into account', to put it in Lehmann's words, 'the peculiar *transformation from stage space into landscape . . .* recalls an inverse process in the nineteenth century when painting approximated a theatrical event' (2006: 78).

The whole process is in a broader sense a 'ritual of transformation', which, as Kantor would say, theatre by nature is. In his manifesto, 'The Theatre of Death' (1975), he writes that life can be expressed in art only through its absence, through an emptiness that implies some lack (in Gritzner 2010: 5). The death scene, which is scenographically expanded in *Propositions I* or on which the entire performance is based, portrays the lack poetically: there is no attempt to represent Borkman and his life. The spectator performs the action by letting their imagination glide over the 'scenic essay' and experiencing paradoxically an absence or lack in a state of aesthetic fullness that has no life after they leave the installation. The last scene as created by Chaudhari may also remind one of Heiner Müller. '[T]he essential thing about theatre is transformation', says Müller, 'and the last transformation is death, dying' symbolically (in Gritzner 2010: 5). 'If theatre is no longer understood as a theatre of representation', as Susan Valerie writes, then the transformation that 'takes place on stage is a transformation at play with truth' (2016: 103). The role of the spectator becomes of primal importance here, and Chaudhari did not want to 'simply deliver a result' since one has to 'walk the path to that point in order to know what one has found' following the transformation (Müller in Kluge 1996: online). *Propositions I* as an installation is rich with visual semiotics that turns the space into an area of contemplation.

Chaudhari's second series (2011–14) – *The Transparent Performer I, II and III* – developed from the *Propositions* series, 'investigating the tension between looking or watching and doing or acting – when and how do the roles of the spectator and the performer collapse' (*Marg* 2019: 56). Her recent interest in archival documents to create her work out of them also owes its roots to *Some Stage Directions* and the *Propositions* series, especially when it comes to 'the production of truth' in performance (Chaudhari 2019: 57). The Ibsen play, for Chaudhari, 'was like a document of history', which 'specifically interested me in working with archival material' for most of her subsequent productions that probe 'the relationship between people and larger events' (Chaudhari 2017).

Active Space (2012)

Muzamil Hayat Bhawani's *Active Space*, his third-year design scene-work at the National School of Drama under Amitesh Grover's supervision, is a moving effort to create a cityscape out of his traumatic memories of Srinagar in the Kashmir Valley. The city and its surrounds were devastated in the summer of 2010 as a result of escalation of the conflict between the 'crusaders of freedom' ('militants' to the Indian government) and the Indian armed forces. Back home on vacation that year, he lived through a sixteen-day curfew, not even able to meet his friends and relatives who would in peacetime invite him to lunch or dinner and for long conversations. When he could go out and travel around, after the curfew was lifted for a brief period, his eyes fell on the roadside houses with broken windowpanes bearing witness to the appalling turn of events that left many dead and a lot more injured. The commotion was precipitated by an alleged staged encounter by the security forces, in which three Kashmiri youths were killed. Massive stone-pelting became a common language of protest in the Valley and the army reacted against the mass violence. Glass in the windows shattered in the crossfire was not replaced since it would break again in the ongoing turmoil; what people did was to cover the panes with plastic bags, tattered clothes, waste paper or some other materials like file covers cut to the proper size and shape.

On his return to school in Delhi, Bhawani decided to work on this image of broken glass and started looking for a text that would match the image. He selected two texts for his purpose: Basharat Peer's *Curfewed Night* (2010) and the popular *Alice's Adventures in Wonderland* (1865) by Lewis Carroll (Charles Dodgson) – products of two very different times. The juxtaposition of the two texts and worlds is most effective since Kashmir is at once a wonderland to the tourists pouring in from different parts of the world and a prolonged 'curfewed night' for its natives caught up in the crossfire between the 'freedom fighters' and the Indian security forces, authorized by the Armed Forces (Special Powers) Act to kill indiscriminately. *Alice's Adventures in Wonderland* is a household name, a fantasy novel narrating the adventures of a young girl. One of the best examples of literary nonsense genre, its characters, events and imagery transport the reader to a dream-world of absurdity – an escapade as well as a journey through odds and an encounter with the 'blind fury' of a tyrannical monarch. Alice's adventures end with her defiance of the Queen of Hearts' threat, 'Off with his head'. Bhawani does not refer in our conversation to the ironical side of Dodgson's *wonderland* that he partly draws on, but the very making of his own work suggests the inner contradictions of a world the book projects. Furthermore, his initial juxtaposition of the two texts/worlds slowly and smoothly moves towards a sort of merging.

The Peer text, less known to the West and even to the major part of India, stemmed from the author's mixed feelings of shame and pain that each time he walked into a bookshop anywhere he came out without being able to find a book a Kashmiri had written on the contemporary realities of the Valley. Peer simultaneously acknowledges that images of the present-day Kashmir – a mixture of satire, nostalgia and poignancy – are nevertheless found in the poetical works of the great Srinagar-born Agha Shahid Ali, one of whose poems incidentally shapes another production of Bhawani's, 'Postcard from Kashmir'. But Peer's *Curfewed Night*, a hybrid text that combines memoir with reportage, 'does a great deal to bring the Kashmir conflict out of the realm of political rhetoric between India and Pakistan and into the lives of Kashmiris' (Shamsie 2010: online). The boy Peer had witnessed the daily abuse of Kashmiris, including students on their way to school or back home, by the security forces. Grown into a young man who returns to his land after his higher education in Delhi, he first undertakes a journey with great difficulty to a village where more than twenty women were gang-raped by the forces in 1991, a year after the mindless killings by paramilitary troops of numerous unarmed Kashmiris who marched out of their homes on a curfewed morning to protest against police violence. The young Peer also writes about the notorious torture centre, nicknamed Papa-2, in a chapter of the same name. The following lines are worth quoting even though they do not figure in the installation under study:

> The line of control did not run through 576 kilometres of militarized mountains ... It ran through everything a Kashmiri, an Indian and a Pakistani said, wrote, and did. ... It ran through the reels of Bollywood coming to life in dark theatres, it ran through conversations in coffee shops and on television screens showing cricket matches, it ran through families and dinner talk, it ran through whispers of lovers. And it ran through our grief, our anger, our tears, and our silence.
>
> Peer 2009: 238

Re-materialization of a situation and the non-mimetic relationship between text and scene evolve a performance aesthetic that is postdramatic. Visuals including fragments of literary texts, newspaper clips with highlighted headlines, printed cartoons and lighting designs on one hand and the sound of music on the other create a dynamic interface between elements of installation art and theatre. Bhawani bought 640 kilograms of broken glass of mixed colours for his project and joined them with glue. None of the forty-eight window panels in his installation had any glass in them, which reminds one of the ceaseless cycle of violence in the Kashmir Valley. The panes were covered with forty-eight kinds of material on which sat side by side handwritten lines from Peer and Carroll and graphics of destruction. Long columns of glass hung from a flyer overhead. The window panels, bare or fitted with text-filled sheets, are installed in different positions: some propped by frames, resembling an open book as on a holder in a library or a museum; and others slanted against a pole or hanging in clusters from above. Their

Figure 8 *Active Space* (2012), design scene-work by Muzamil Hayat Bhawani, presented by National School of Drama. Photo credit: S. Thyagarajan.

shadows fall on the floor, some coloured, describing an indescribable glow that at once has a seductive pull and suggests a sense of doom.

As one gets closer to the panels, they notice that some are filled with running rows of graphic pictures of soldiers on guard with their guns raised, over which are printed lines in fragments from *Curfewed Night* – an example of what Jürs-Munby calls 'palimpsestuous intertextuality' to mean a multi-layering of citations (2006: 8): 'The military camps and [their] operations were an invitation for a guerrilla attack. We, uneasily, expected the inevitable'. The lines that follow in the Peer text, and which are not here, read: 'A sudden bang! And then another – the sound of a Kalashnikov'. The reading is done silently; the lines remembered by the informed spectator from *Curfewed Night* surpass the lines inscribed on the installation's windowpanes, encompassing more gory details of Kashmir in the 2010s. Reading becomes an extended metaphor: if the words/lines from the Peer text represent facticity, reading through the visuals sets the imagination free to work on the material of the installation. The latter creates an alternative, tangible space for the intangibles of memory, fear and desire. The Queen's 'Hold your tongue' mannerism in *Alice's Adventures in Wonderland* chips in to flirt with the frequent police commands 'Hands up' in Kashmir, while the phrases 'border of daisies, and a willow tree' from the book's second chapter, handwritten on a newspaper clip pasted on a pane, can remind the spectator as much of the Valley's rich flora as of its highly militarized border with Pakistan-administered Kashmir (Pakistan-Occupied-Kashmir to India). The adventures of Alice, when seen/read inside Bhawani's active space, appear in contrast to the failed attempts of Kashmir's 'freedom fighters' to achieve liberation from New Delhi, a failure given the official stamp by India's abrogation of Article 370 in 2019. The installation looks like the ruins of a civilization finding re/inscription in art. Thus the work is no 'dramatic' representation of any external reality; it is rather a state of materials moulded into an artefact that is capable of generating multiple shades of meaning jostling for space.

As the text is neither read out nor delivered as dialogue, the sound conceived for the installation is very different from the acoustic character of text-based theatre productions. From the outside the installation looks like a glittering wonderland; but once one steps in – on the material laid over the floor – they are greeted by a crushing sound like broken pieces of glass being trampled on. It is a disturbing sound influencing the spectator's mood and feeling. The melodic, soothing, tinkling music heard from the outside – which, inspired by Robert Tiso's music on glass harp, suggests a sense of *glass* with an apparent magic about it – is taken over by the shattering sound inside. It is no less reminiscent of Kristallnacht, the Night of the Broken Glass in 1938 Germany that serves as the motif for Arthur Miller's play *Broken Glass* (1994). The spectator wishes that no one else produce that sound by entering the space, but paradoxically one already inside does it themself the moment they take the next step ahead. The 'materiality of sound' without any direct referentiality underscores the theatre-installation's capacity to ideate as well as influence our perception of phenomena and situation through form. A theatre aesthetic is in place where the text in its minimality enters into a non-conventional relationship with the 'material condition of the performance' (see Ovadija 2013).

Spectating through participation in the work has become a hallmark of postdramatic theatre, including installations, with 'new structures of narrative' changing spatiotemporal organization and 'modes of address' (Fensham 2012: online). The freedom given to the spectator to impregnate the space of Bhawani's installation with their imagination, memory and experience radicalizes the relationship between the piece of art, the artist and the viewer. The spectator has a vital performative role to keep the space 'active', partly co-making the installation with the theatre-maker. Rather than 'perform or else', as Jon McKenzie (in Fensham 2012: online) said a decade ago about theatre, the theatre paradigm now urges 'participate or else' (Fensham 2012: online), and participation in this respect becomes a form of performance. This participation may result in varied responses not only from different spectators but also within the same spectator because conflicting emotions, sensations, impressions and perceptions come to constitute experience inside the performance space. One thing is certain, though: the installation is all about a broken world, a paradise fallen apart – a stark contrast to medieval India's great Persian-language poet Amir Khushrow's description of Kashmir: *Agar firdaus bar roo-e zameen ast, / Hameen ast-o hameen ast-o ha-neen ast* (If there is a paradise on earth, / It is this, it is this, it is this).

6

Activism in India's Postdramatic Theatre

Activism is found to have been reconfigured in theatre across the world for diverse reasons and in varied forms. Lehmann himself revised his notion of the connect between society/politics and theatre, following the Occupy Wall Street movement, the refugee crisis in Syria, the rise of ISIS in the Middle East, and other world events discussed in the introduction. Later he locates theatre in a 'twilight zone between political activism and aesthetic practice' (Lehmann 2013: 87); but even this 'grey' zone of 'art and the political' is fairly different from political theatre as we have known it for the most part of the twentieth century and which I have briefly discussed in Chapter 1. The audience reaction to the (tragic) real is now seldom sought to be secured through a dramatic process. There are stark realities of life today outside the structure of tragedy (or dramatic theatre) that produce trauma. But in this mediatized society, conflict, the soul of drama, loses its intensity because those realities are routinely transformed into digitized spectacles (97) and thus normalized for the public while the victim keeps suffering. The unsurveyable operation of the technologically transformed state machinery frustrates consolidation of any resistance and diffuses the conflict that may have occasionally formed in individual and collective consciousness. To represent the political dialogically with its tragic potential in theatre, therefore, becomes difficult. The political now exists in the 'theatre of situation', in 'moments of performance' (89) outside drama, but not obliterating all sense of responsibility for the spectator whose experience in the changed circumstance is nevertheless produced and shaped *form*ally.

Taking her cue from Lehmann's insistence in *Tragedy and Dramatic Theatre* (2016) on the need for the 'tragic-political' to rupture 'the aesthetic framework of the theatre event', and yet critical of his 'conflation of form and politics', Tomlin (2019: 9) seeks to read contemporary theatre and performance in the tension between Ernesto Laclau and Chantal Mouffe's 'logic of equivalence' (reconfigured in her study as 'egalitarian imaginary') and the logic of autonomy as advocated by Rancière (ibid.: 2). However, her prioritization of the 'ideological imperatives of egalitarianism' (13) in theatre takes her away from her announced plan in her first chapter because Mouffe's own counter-hegemonic politics is constructed through a subversion of political consensus that recognizes and reasserts political divisions and their individual/equal importance in a radical democracy (Tambakaki 2018: online). Laclau and Mouffe's political theory is as much post-Marxist as poststructuralist; but Tomlin's 'political dramaturgies' has less of poststructuralism in it and more of a concern for collective action which requires a difficult-to-arrive-at consensus not only among the spectators in contemporary theatre but also between them and the people outside. Tomlin's revision of Rancière's 'emancipated spectator' theory, on the other hand, is important because while Rancière advocated freedom for the spectator from authoritarian state communism, she finds little relevance of the logic of autonomy if that inserts one into the neoliberal market at the expense of the principle of social justice. State communism may have been largely over, but currently there are far-right state narratives of nationalism and crony capitalism which no less require individual spectators' liberation in theatre from a lopsided, dominant politics. This autonomy can be upheld in terms of dramaturgy but must also be calibrated by the contingent logic of justice and equality, a middle ground that informs most of the political theatre today. When political dramaturgy builds on agonism rather than antagonism, the spectator has to take the final call on things presented. The sovereignty of the spectator does not necessarily make them a collaborator with the dynamics of late capitalism but may instead be used for dissensus, as in India's contemporary political theatres, on any unitary narrative of national/anti-national, insider/outsider, patriot/traitor, economic growth/slide and so on. Tomlin's dismissal of Lehmann's reading of politics in theatre as form creates another problem because when we are in the theatre, everything – including text – should come to us as form. For theatre is performance in the ultimate analysis. But form should not be mistaken for an end in itself because it is an aesthetic product of social and political *form*ations and not an outside of content (see Boyle et al. 2019: 1–19).

Activism in Indian theatre over the past couple of decades has not been the same as before. It is not that India has become a post-political society since the collapse of the USSR and the introduction of an open market economy. But the mediatization of society and the culture of hype steadily eroding the standards of veracity, the indeterminacy of the real in a 'society of the spectacle', corruption in government offices and the judiciary diluting the sanctity of institutions, and currently a right-wing political party with brute majority in Parliament and functioning autocratically have affected the activist fabric of society and the theatre in varied ways. Besides, the 'me' generation's lack of involvement in any conflictual situation, the perform-or-perish pressure of the market and the fear of draconian laws being invoked against protesters and dissenting artists alike are the other reasons why radicalism in theatre has changed its performance language as well as brought forth newer forms that evoke and provoke responses by putting the spectator/audience in an experiential situation. However, this in no way questions the seriousness of the theatre-maker who now entrusts the audience with the task of meaning-making from the plethora of powerful pointers provided in the performance.

Work in Progress: A Nationalism Project (2018)

What I call Project Nationalism was seen to be operative at the state level in *The Antigone Project*: the horrid event occurred in Gujarat, although the bloody ripples spread all over India. The post-Godhra pogrom of 2002, the systematic torture and killing of Muslims, may be taken as a campaign of the far right for India as a Hindu nation that found full sail with the BJP-led National Democratic Alliance (NDA) coming to power at the centre in 2014 and reinforced itself with the party's re-election to Parliament with an absolute majority in 2019 for another five years. The campaign had begun in the 1990s, but until 2019 the anti-Muslim politics did not appear so brazen. The moral low that this exclusionary politics reached after their second landslide victory exposed their vile ambition to stay in power by demonizing religious minorities and building the narrative of nationalism on majoritarianism in all its senses. Cow vigilantism, a term that gained its popularity following the flogging or lynching of Muslims on the pretext of beef-eating that is considered a sin to the practising Hindu, became a new game to achieve their hypernationalist goals.

Deepan Sivaraman's *Work in Progress: A Nationalism Project*, performed by the students of Ambedkar University Delhi in both India and Poland, builds around this distorted narrative of nation, bringing a new concept of theatre-making to India and changing in the process the concept of national theatre. The ideology of the ruling regime, shown to be threatening the Constitution of the Republic of India, is the target of criticism in this performance, while the possibility for ambivalent interpretation of certain entries in the Constitution itself is no less referenced in the speeches delivered by a performer who is not a dramatic character per se. Speeches, lectures, brick-and-cement construction (of the letters N-A-T-I-O-N-A-L-I-S-M) on stage, the 'irreverent' rehearsing of India's national anthem, and the absence of interpersonal or antagonistic conversation collectively build up the production which with its political overtone appears postdramatic for its performance aesthetics. The 'ideological steer' and the autonomy of interpretation run side by side (Tomlin 2019), placing the production between 'activism and aesthetic practice', between agonistic dramaturgies (Lehmann 2013: 87).

Work in Progress, scripted by Purav Goswami and Urvi Sirket, inaugurates a new mode of using text in Indian theatre. The performance begins with the historic 'Tryst with Destiny' address by India's first Prime Minister Jawaharlal Nehru on the eve of independence. There is no cardboard character called 'Nehru' here. An audio tape is 'played as if from a distance like an echo', accompanied by the sound of swarming flies that acts as a background score and indirectly builds up a contrast between the secular content of Nehru's speech and the potential aftermath of the communally divisive lectures delivered by the Hindutva brigade. The cloud-like red balloon rising up early in the show is no embellishment but designed as a patch of Nehru's text disappearing from the face of Indian politics. The constant buzzing of the flies, on the other hand, evokes a grim picture of the insects hovering over bodies of the Other killed on flimsy grounds to build India as *one* nation, allegedly in the manner of Zia-ul-Haq's Islamization of Pakistan in the 1980s. The music that plays at this point is a purposely interrupted, if not distorted, rehearsal of India's national anthem to mock obliquely the ongoing violation of the country's plural ethos. Besides words, objects, visuals and sound acquire their autonomous function in the production, creating non-literary para-texts.

The performance is full of long speeches/notes read out to the audience from a notebook; they do not form dialogue. As the performers in hazmat suits continue their construction work, a burqa-clad woman (triply marginalized by faith, gender and class) comes in to read the speeches live. The text of the first speech is a commentary on the rights and responsibilities enshrined in the Constitution and their compromised status in the realpolitik of the current regime. Such use of text, fairly characteristic of Sivaraman's work, has lent contemporary theatre in India a distinct postdramatic character. It has hardly any material for 'dramatic' action, and, for the performer, 'the "action" of speaking, reading ... without a plot ... [or] role ... represents a challenge'. The speaking is here 'accentuated above all as a "speaking to" the audience', as Lehmann would say, and the speech is marked 'as the speech of a real speaking person' (2006: 123, 127).

There are specific real events and dates referred to in the text of the first speech – there is no element of suspense in the performance since the events are already familiar to the audience through television news channels or the press. To begin with the 'ban' on beef-eating and the arbitrary mob (in)justice meted out to those who were suspected to have eaten the forbidden food, one needs to revisit the cultural history of the 'ban' and its legal status. The cow is a sacred creature in the Hindu conception of life. In the Vedas it is 'associated with Aditi, the mother of all the gods' (Winston 2015: online). Even though the superiority of the bovine over other animals in Indian (Hindu) life is actually determined in terms of its utilitarian value – the cow produces milk, cheese, butter or *ghee* and its dung is used as fuel in village hearths – it acquires a haloed status in the Hindu imaginary by being arguably associated with the Brahmins, the highest caste in the Hindu *varna* system. The slaughter of a cow, by this equation, is considered as the killing of a Brahmin. In India, on the other hand, the majority of Muslims have long eaten beef either for its lower price, or for its arguable association with certain Islamic rituals, or simply as part of their traditional cuisine. Besides, a poor section of the Muslim population is connected to the skinning of dead cows and buffaloes for leather industries in India, a low-grade profession in a deeply casteist Hindu society where there is hardly any presence of *savarnas*. By contrast, it may be noted, a large number of Indian Hindus eat beef today and that beef is a popular cuisine in the state from which director Sivaraman comes – namely Kerala.

The issue of banning the slaughter of cows/cattle happened to be contentious even during the framing of India's Constitution. After much debate in the Constituent Assembly the 'prohibition' of cow slaughter found a dubious place in the Constitution under 'Directive Principles of State Policy', difficult to be enforceable in any court. Further, the issue was not given any consideration on religious grounds; it was sought to be tentatively resolved under Article 48, 'Organisation of Agriculture and Animal Husbandry'. The article reads: 'The State shall endeavour to organise agriculture and animal husbandry on modern and scientific lines and shall, in particular, take steps for preserving and improving the breeds, and prohibiting the slaughter of cows and calves and other milch and draught cattle' (see Administration of Cattle Laws: online). This was different from, and arguably a diluted form of, the more direct and emphatic original draft of amendment 72 to Article 38-A: '... and prohibit the slaughter of cows and other useful cattle specially milch and draught cattle and their young stock' (see Constituent Assembly of India Debates: online). The total ban imposed by various states on the slaughter of all types of cattle was challenged by petitioners in 1958, but the Supreme Court upheld the ban by focusing on extra-religious (particularly economic) reasons with the rider that 'a total ban on the slaughter of she-buffaloes, bulls and bullocks (cattle or buffalo) after they ceased to be capable of yielding milk or of breeding or working as draught animals was not in the interests of the general public and was invalid'. To cut a long story short, the central government invoked in 2017 'a [2015] Supreme Court order on cattle smuggling across the Nepal border, as well as a 1960 law, the Prevention of Cruelty to Animals Act, as ... justification' for not killing the cow, while neither of the two mentions a blanket prohibition of cattle slaughter for food (Bhatia 2017: online). In reality, the mobs killed the Muslims for being Muslim, Barkha Dutt alleges, while the same holds true of the dalit boys who were abused or hacked to death on suspicion of smuggling cows across borders. To 'use the word [cow] "vigilantism" [a popular word today] to describe hate crimes', Dutt says, 'is nothing more than the hideous normalization of bigotry' (2018: online).

Readings from the Constitution of India, government policies and speeches of legislators – sometimes accompanied by their interpretation – occupy the most part of the performance. There is no attempt to impose any meaning on the audience: interpretation of any text, it is widely admitted, depends on a complex of linguistic and cultural factors that may build either a consensus or a dissensus in a given context of reception. Long readings become 'action', detaching the reader from the text and showing that the words read do not belong to her as they would to a character. The stage becomes 'auditive' and the 'soundscape' comingles with the 'textscape' (Lehmann 2006: 148). The reading highlights that 'the point of departure for the Constitution of India was representation of each of [the] heterogeneous social and cultural groups'. The burqa-clad woman refers to Dr B. R. Ambedkar, author of the Constitution, who enshrined in it the principles of justice, liberty, equality and fraternity as the primary goals of a young nation-state, and notes with concern the systematic dismantling in our times of its democratic institutions and the raising in their place of a Hindutva-inspired monolithic structure of nationalism. This is largely shown materially in terms of the brick edifice being built during the course of the performance.

The performance was inspired by the Constitution, Sivaraman says, and its distortion in present times (2016). Highly critical of the propaganda machine of the present government, he even compares it to Hitler's Germany. This may sound like an exaggeration to many, but the fascist character of the current dispensation cannot be denied. The performance here returns us to history, but as a discourse. By foregrounding the fake confidence of the revivalist historians who see India as regaining its lost glory by reliving the Hindutva ideology, different as it is from Hindu philosophy that is founded on the plurality of faith, and their parading of fiction as truth, the production problematizes the eventual writing of history. When Sivaraman refers to the distortion of history today, he probably does not look back to the past with any nostalgia or accept all accounts of pre- and post-independence India as correct and authentic. Instead, the implication, reinforced in a sense by the directness of images/visuals and speeches, is that historiography is a difficult subject, and the job of a historian is to acknowledge the importance of self-criticality and truth's relativity even as one seeks to employ their disciplinary tools as 'objectively' as possible. What the present dispensation is doing, however, is a deliberate misrepresentation of facts, a premeditated destruction of the country's democratic fabric by indulging in populist politics. On the other hand, questions may arise in the mind of the audience – though the performance does not directly raise any – about the Congress Party's political misdeeds over time that ultimately contributed to the consolidation of the BJP as a national party and, subsequently, its absolute majority in Parliament for two successive terms (2014–2019–2024). The format the performance chooses is presentational by shoring up material, including documents, directly rather than interpreting it conclusively for the audience.

The speech is different from both soliloquy and monologue; it is like 'the speaking outside of addressing an interlocutor' in the play or the self (Lehmann 2006: 196). The dialogue, if you will, is as much between 'sound and sound space' (76) as between the speaking subject and the audience. The reading is different from those performance lectures which describe 'what writing of performance might mean', as Tim Etchell observes, by talking about set construction, improvisation and performance forms (in Lehmann 2006: 9). And yet it is suggestive of the new ideas of playwriting and performing. The reading is designed to interrogate eventually the motif of the real-time construction that will be completed before the show ends. The workers shift building materials from one place to another, gather them in a changed order, and position/reposition themselves to raise the brick edifice of N-A-T-I-O-N-A-L-I-S-M, the work in progress. The (mis)use of labour and material (resources) in turning a nation-state into a party-state, and consigning it to one strong man of dubious credentials, sharply points out the disjunct between the text being read and the work done. Images, objects, movement and text – autonomous performance elements otherwise – now sync to critique the 'nationalism project' that sabotages M. K. Gandhi's idea of an India enriching itself out of its diversity. The stage direction is important at this point: the construction workers bring out a picture of Gandhi in a large shattered glass frame that looks as if it was hit by a bullet, thus alluding to the assassination of the Mahatma by Nathuram Godse, a zealot glorified by India's right-wing leaders as a patriot.

The second speech begins with a key line from the Preamble to the Constitution of India – India is a 'sovereign, socialist, secular, democratic republic' – and then takes care to distinguish the secularism in India from its Western import and practice. In the process it also highlights some clauses in the Constitution which have been fiercely debated ever since their drafting and demands the spectator to engage with them as the *construction* of nationalism goes on in the here-and-now of the performance space as well as outside. In the Nehruvian archaeology of post-independence India religion was kept apart from the public sphere, although 'secular' was not a happy word for Nehru for its possible dogmatism. But the separation referred to was crucial after the bloodbath around the religion-based partition of the subcontinent. Eventually, however, 'secularism' in India was indigenized as toleration of, and neutrality towards, all religions. This model of secularism was founded on the twin ideas of tolerance and hospitality, often claimed as an alternative equivalent for the separation of church and state. The word 'secular' was not originally incorporated in the Preamble since it was perceived, following a long debate in the Constituent Assembly, as a concept originating from Enlightenment rationality and the Protestant position on Christianity that does not suit the fabric of Indian society and culture, but the spirit of secularism was indeed upheld by the Assembly as the state's non-interference in matters of faith.

The speech uses excerpts from B. R. Ambedkar's historical interventions in the discourse on the religion–politics interface in Indian society and its practical constitutional viability for a postcolonial state. On 2 December 1948, he said:

> The religious conceptions in this country are so vast that they cover every aspect of life from birth to death. There is nothing which is not religion and if personal law is to be saved I am sure about it that in social matters we will come to a standstill ... I personally do not understand why religion should be given this vast expansive jurisdiction so as to cover the whole of life and to prevent the legislature from encroaching upon that field.
>
> Samaddar 2016: 255

Yet when Professor K. T. Shah moved an amendment on 15 November 1949, to incorporate in the Constitution the word 'secular' in addition to 'socialist', Ambedkar maintained:

> The Constitution is ... a mechanism for the purpose of regulating the work of the various organs of the state. It is not a mechanism whereby particular members or particular parties are installed in office. What should be the policy of the state, how the society should be organised in its social and economic side are matters which must be decided by the people themselves according to time and circumstances. It cannot be laid down in the Constitution itself, because that is destroying democracy altogether.
>
> Patil 2016: 20

It may be mentioned here that Article 14, read with Article 15, was already a guarantee to all citizens against any discrimination based on caste, creed and gender. Former Prime Minister Indira Gandhi, whose assassination by her Sikh bodyguards was followed by the unleashing of terror by her followers on the whole Sikh community in 1984, had incorporated the word 'secular' in the Preamble in 1976 to bolster the separation of politics and religion. Putting aside this irony of circumstance, we see that the 'contradictions' between Ambedkar's above two statements are only too superficial. He made the latter to articulate his economic rather than political philosophy. What he actually intended to say is that by merely incorporating certain words in the Constitution, the state cannot resolve critical issues for ever. But Ambedkar's position made it amply clear that India was not to become a state based on the religion of the majority.

Ashis Nandy's contribution to this area is of relevance here. Secularism in the Indian context, Nandy writes, is not the opposite of sacred but of ethnocentrism, xenophobia and fanaticism (1995: 35). It is this non-modern meaning of secularism that the anti-colonial elite used to build 'a broad social consensus against the British rule' (36). The state's tolerance of religions does not necessarily guarantee social tolerance, for which the social/political community needs to go beyond all types of parochialism. While official secularism can be 'totally insensitive to the politics of culture today', adds Nandy, 'the pathologies of religion' will always create anti-democratic forms of dominance and power. The point made by Nandy suggests that secular fundamentalism *can* become as demanding of people's faith in its impersonal, scientific and technological means of progress as zealous religiosity would in its own spiritual and moral principles. Gandhi's allegiance to both Hindu and Muslim 'ways of life', he says, and to folk theologies rather than any proselytized religion, made him a victim of bigotry – a tragic reality discussed in the third speech read by the same woman. The cultural history of India is that 'Hinduism has become a part of Indian Islam and Islam a part of Hinduism' (Nandy 1995: 54). The failure to understand this has resulted in othering the religious minorities and rationalists alike. In a postsecular world, the secular and the religious may not be seen as antithetical postulates. While faith is sometimes performed to address worldly crises, the long-held Eurocentric idea of secularism has often been subjected (at least theoretically) to engage with the hurt caused to religious minorities by its hitherto unacknowledged mechanics of exclusionary politics. But in India, the return of Hindutva as a political ideology masquerading as traditional Hinduism, arguably an inclusive spiritual philosophy, blocks the historical-material-cultural understanding of the present (see Bharucha 2017: v–xxxii).

The reading of the text is now replaced by a visual that is also a form of text, but neither read out nor delivered as speech. The woman suddenly takes off the upper half of her burqa. Inside, she is wearing a transparent body-suit, on the back of which is written, 'This Burqa was rented for the purpose of the performance' – thus highlighting the 'anti-play' character of postmodern theatre. The layering of the words, its connection to the body and the texture of the suit radicalize the use of text in Indian theatre. Further, the visuality of the text is suddenly overtaken by the sound of flies that fills the space and gets mixed with the words of an Ambedkar address to Parliament that is played on the track. The juxtaposition of the two soundscapes, the former alluding to the carcasses of cattle as well as to the corpses of people lynched to death (both attracting a swarm of flies to feed upon them) and the latter articulating the ways to keep a diverse nation together, creates a montage of verbal, auditive and visual texts. The bundles of newspapers kept in a corner, which might never be read since a canister of kerosene is symbolically placed next to them, sets another example of the innovative use of text that does not develop 'action' – the plot in other words – but acts through its own performativity.

The interface between the activist spirit critical of any ideological lopsidedness and the autonomy of interpretation available to the spectator makes the production very contemporary in form. The appendicular skeleton of a cow, with a microphone inserted into its mouth, is brought into the centre of the performance space. The 'stage' becomes a sort of 'pictural poetry' (Lehmann 2006: 72), as in Kantor's theatre, a tableau-like figuration that is very different from what might have been a dramatic representation of the flogging and lynching of people involved in cattle trade or beef-eating. The cow delivers a speech about the government's vision of a new India (Nayee Bharat) that ironically pries into people's kitchens and bedrooms and wins a general election on the hyped superiority of the bovine tribe over people marginalized by class, caste or faith. This highly performative scene provides a textual-visual critique of nationalism which, based on exclusionary politics, continues to impress the majority of the Indian population. Most ironically, the BJP got voted back to power in 2019 on the basis of a country-wide divisive electoral campaign. In response to the question often asked these days, whether theatre can produce at all, Sivaraman's presentation of the real may be said to have left a more radical impact on the audience than any dramatic work could have by immersing them in an illusionist atmosphere and giving them a processed meaning.

The entire show takes place as 'work in progress'. The band plays out the national anthem, as noted above, but in an intermittent way. It seems it is being rehearsed for a full performance later. This serves two purposes at once. First, it circumvents censorship in a time when 'all forms of protest', as the director puts it, are interpreted as 'anti-national' (Sivaraman 2018b: online) – especially those condemning the state's contravention of the foundational values of modern Indian society. Secondly, it dismisses the traditional dramatic model of a well-rehearsed show. To elaborate on the second, Sivaraman's theatre breaks the illusionist nature of the performance environment in different ways. The overriding image of a rehearsal generating a recurring sense of incompleteness as the music is played by the band gives the impression that the action as such is not being performed (see Lehmann 2006: 107), but preparations for it are underway. This impression is created despite rehearsals preceding the show. What happens before the spectators has an immediacy and presence in its processuality very different, by virtue of its self-referentiality, from the immediacy of the dramatic type. The spectator is 'given the chance to feel their presence' (Fensham: online) in the absence of 'a closed action' (Lehmann 2006: 108) and in the activities of workers as performers rather than characters.

At the end, the woman-as-text-reader reminds us of what is enshrined in the Preamble to the Constitution of India: 'WE, THE PEOPLE OF INDIA, having solemnly resolved to constitute India into a SOVEREIGN SOCIALIST SECULAR DEMOCRATIC REPUBLIC and to secure to all its citizens: JUSTICE, social, economic and political; LIBERTY of thought, expression, belief, faith and worship; EQUALITY of status and of opportunity; and to promote among them all FRATERNITY assuring the dignity of the individual and the unity and integrity of the Nation ...' While she reads the above lines from the Preamble, she is blindfolded as if she is not allowed to read on. She is left alone by the time she comes to 'IN OUR CONSTITUENT ASSEMBLY this twenty-sixth day of November, 1949, do HEREBY ADOPT, ENACT AND GIVE TO OURSELVES THIS CONSTITUTION'. Her microphone is turned off. The stage direction reads: 'She tries to move through the constructed text "NATIONALISM" ... [and] falls several times, sometimes breaking the text as well'. It is difficult to dismantle the structure of power; but in her fall, which ironically damages part of the edifice, lurks the resistance that always inheres in the fault lines of power itself. Between 'the performativity of doing and non-doing' (Defraeye 2007: 646), telling and non-telling is the activism of the production that consists not in representing, to put it in Lehmann's words, but in creating a political reality by evaluating its own mode of representation (in Frljić 2011: 134).

Dark Things (2018/2019)

Dark Things, performed by the students of Ambedkar University Delhi, goes beyond the dramatic conventions of acting, staging and storytelling, and anchors in the aesthetic-political interstices of the postdramatic. It 'narrates' the lives of people forced out of their land by war or poverty, migrant labourers and industrial/post-industrial workers by interlacing diverse disciplines and performance languages – lectures on labour and citizenship, live readings from poems and music (South Asian raga to African jazz), video installations and real-time work by people in hazmat suits. Based on Ari Sitas's script for an oratorio and directed jointly by Anuradha Kapur and Deepan Sivaraman, *Dark Things* created 'a learning factory whose process of construction has been as important as the final work itself' (from the brochure). The production is wrought between an egalitarian steer critiquing the logic of late capitalism and an aesthetic methodology preferring presentational realism that does not alienate the audience from the outer world but accentuates the experiential reality of it.

Dark Things does not abandon text. However, the text is not only treated as *one* of the performance elements but also presented in a way different from its function as the origin of meaning in dramatic theatre. The original text by Ari Sitas, a long poetic rumination on the labour practices of the present-day silk-route underbelly, was shaped for performance by dramaturge Purav Goswami and Sitas himself. The performance (text) developed through extrapolations from and improvisations on the scenes in Sitas and meetings with actors/performers and other members of the production team (Goswami 2019). Sitas joined the rehearsal process at the last stage and was actively involved in working on the performance text, sometimes by writing new lines at short notice, as part of the collaborative project coordinated by Sumangala Damodaran. And it was he who finally came up with the title for the production. Goswami, it may be noted, mostly retains Sitas's poetry dealing with the harsh social reality. While poetry is an expressive mode for 'the artist's lyrical soul' (Ovadija 2013: 24), in *Dark Things* it is also part of the soundscape (comprising saxophone and guitar music and all the cacophony of sounds including sirens) that creates the pre- and post-industrial labour world with its materiality and performativity on one hand and its peripheral referentiality on the other. On a ticker tape the following words appear:

I saw cattle herds darken the sun, mother.
I saw people walking into the brightest nothing.
What kind of a night is this?

Contrasted with these verse lines, the 'speech' of a refugee breaking out of the line and walking towards the audience is a string of meaningless sounds because she is an inscrutable and, therefore, unwelcomed alien to the land that her boat has brought her to. Her gibberish creates a new 'text' of sound out of the social context (Ovadija 2013: 3–8). The alternation between the poetic text on screen (as visual icons) and the verses uttered by characters (as aural conduits), between the spoken text and the soundscape, continues through the show.

Rather than playing the reconstructed script mimetically, *Dark Things* rebuilds the text through movement of objects and activities of 'characters' as planned by the directors in collaboration with actor-performers. Closer to Meyerhold's biomechanical style of acting, which as a forerunner of (Western) physical theatre relies more on movement and motion than language and illusion, *Dark Things* moves away from the Stanislavsky system of getting into the skin of the character and towards the presentational style of performing. Action also develops through markings and choreography. As a small truck comes speeding into the centre of the open space from the right of stage, on the large screen on a scaffold at the back (Thrissur Production, 2019) or on the wall of a large building (AUD production, 2018) is projected the world map that shows the routes of refugee influx across continents. Two people, traffickers of refugees as well as organ traders, jump off the truck, while a man at work marks an 'X' on the ground. The worker writes the word 'STERN' alongside the 'X' mark and draws more such X's which are joined by the Fixers with two sticks, each with a piece of water-soaked sponge attached to one end, thus delivering 'a choreographed text'. The element of suspense takes a new form as the spectators struggle to figure out what is being drawn/written on the ground. As the joining of the X's reveals the pattern of a ship, on the screen a massive video projection pops up of a boat overloaded with refugees swaying in the sea. This partly evokes the memory of a performance installation called 'The Ocean as Transit Space between Life and Death': the installation 'begins with the scene of an overloaded boat on the Mediterranean. The passengers stand motionless for the whole of the crossing, the bodies pressed together form a piece of solid cargo, too much movement would capsize the boat' (Hurtzig 2017: online). I do not cite it as an instance of intertextuality, even in the sense of artists consciously referencing one another's work, but the project certainly helps us find in *Dark Things* a method more or less common to performance-installations – pictorial presentation of reality.

The text in *Dark Things* is often cast on the body, not the body articulating the text. The long-perceived dichotomy between word and body (or the conceptual and the visceral) in theatre is replaced – as it were – not by a synthesis of the two but by their synaesthetic presentation. The refugees return (to the performance space) holding a number of folded cloth tents that have letters printed on each of them. They first move to the centre of the space, forming a square, and then change their formation into the shape of a boat, staring at the audience. They sway on their feet like a boat sailing over strong waves, appearing as a tableau or a '*gestic sculpture*' (Lehmann 2006: 80) that makes the dramatic disappear. Slowly they break the formation and stand in a diagonal order across the playing ground. The tent cloths held steadfastly to their bodies, and the letters on their surface now arranged in sequence, the performers appear to be 'embodying' the letters, words and finally the sentence '*ONCE UPON A TIME THERE WAS PEACE*'. The text in *Dark Things* is also seen in the form of a video featuring a refugee narrating his ordeal and seeking the world's attention to his plight.

The production transits from the refugee crisis outside of India to the citizenship question back home. The political critique of India's hypernationalist narrative, produced and circulated as it is by the BJP-led government, is apparent here, while the dramaturgy of real-action-in-real-time confronts the spectator with the risk and responsibility of decision-making. The refugees set up makeshift tents and sit inside like prisoners, holding out their I-cards and reading aloud their identity details. These are the real AUD (Ambedkar University Delhi) students who introduce themselves according to what is printed on their cards. 'It's an age of tallying', says Anuradha Kapur in an interview. 'So what would one present if they were asked to prove identity? Little cards, but we didn't want a fictional set of people and addresses' (Kapur 2019b). The citizenship issue has taken a most grave turn with the 2019 publication of the draft National Register of Citizens (NRC) for Assam excluding almost two million people residing in the state, most of whom are bona fide Indian citizens in all probability. The descendants of people who had migrated to India from the erstwhile East Pakistan – that is, before the creation of Bangladesh in 1971 – or from West Pakistan during the partition in 1947 and received Indian citizenship subsequently, have the burden placed on themselves to prove their national identity by criteria too dubious to fulfil. The Citizenship Amendment Act (CAA) 2019 mandates that only the religious minorities (Muslims excluded) who can prove that they fled the neighbouring Muslim-majority countries for religious persecution or in fear of it and entered India by 31 December 2014 are eligible for Indian citizenship. However, the histories of exchange of people between India and Pakistan post-partition and the influx of refugees from Bangladesh post-1971 are very different. Who is an Indian citizen and who is not has thus become a contentious issue that defies any easy legal solution. The scene referred to above, when viewed in the light of recent political realities or electoral politics, looks almost prophetic while making spectating a critical act of engagement. There seems no easy way to reach a consensus on the citizenship issue. The tension between the ideological steer that is directed against the state's arbitrariness and the audience-as-public need for interpretation on a case-to-case basis runs through the scene.

When it comes to labour, *Dark Things* accommodates both the 'immaterial' sphere of work within 'globalizing networks' (Jackson 2013: 166) of the neoliberal market and the materially affective labour of a pre-technologized sphere that continues to partly characterize the third world. The presence of a JCB excavator, the huge iron skeleton of a hammer, pick-up vans and other objects in a sprawling performance space builds an archive of knowledge, to use Scott Johnson's phrase, from 'manual behaviors' (Johnson 2009). Multiple issues are intertwined to find a form that prefers physical staging, and also celebrates, as Deepan Sivaraman says, labour within and outside of the performance area. A quotation from the production brochure may not be out of place here: '*Dark Things* is a collaborative weaving together of bits of hardship from the new frontiers of work and suffering in the 21st Century. This frontier of cell-phones, silk and hazmat suits ... signif[ies] a world out of joint and out of moral kilter'. It not only exposes the operative dynamics of late capitalism but self-reflexively shows theatre's laborious process of constructing its own world. Does *Dark Things* operate under the Brechtian vision of 'labour and necessity'? If it does, it does not let the Brechtian approach to reality-behind-representation determine a whole social system or its 'base' unidirectionally. *Dark Things* does not take 'society', as Laclau and Mouffe would say, as a 'self-defined totality' (Jackson 2013: 171). It recognizes the Brechtian value of 'necessity' but sees labour imbricated with other contingencies that now create the 'base' and are in 'irresoluble tension' with one another (see ibid.: 172–3). This is the reason why the production has incomplete narratives of migrancy and labour asking for different patterns of perception and understanding, artistic engagement and planning, beyond ideologically deterministic meaning-making.

As the text was restructured through a series of meetings and workshops involving the directors, performers and also Sitas himself at some points, it was 'quickly decided that it had to be done in a constructivist style' (Kapur 2019b), but with no room for propaganda or historical determinism and class reductionism that are central to the Marxist approach to life and labour. I asked Kapur why they wanted constructivism for their production about a century after it emerged in post-revolutionary Russia, and subsequently died down. 'Because of a consideration of labour', she said, 'of the underside of labour, of footloose labour as in a developing economy like India today' (ibid.). Falling like a screw in a neoliberal global production site is labour, Kapur maintains, just as using a hammer in an industry is labour, too. When one mode of labour becomes obsolete, another usually emerges depending on the economic system in which a particular module of labour functions. *Dark Things*, however, exposes diverse patterns of labour inflected by the crosscurrents of migration, trafficking, organ trading, identity politics, global networking and so on. In the mixed labour market of post-1991 India, where industrial and deindustrialized labour coexist, Fordism operates alongside post-Fordism. While the Fordist economy has migrant labourers in construction sites and heavy industries, the post-Fordist economy requires skilled labour, but with no guarantee of job security or fixed work hours. (Neo)constructivism in this context seems an appropriate form to deal with both these patterns of labour as a 'theme'. *Dark Things* does not directly fall under the political category of the symbolic/'conditional' as practised by Meyerhold in his constructivist theatre, but the emphasis on the self-reflexivity of theatre-making, physical acting and positioning of the spectator as an active viewer are definitely reminiscent of his stagecraft that has been contemporized by artistic concerns for the socioeconomic complexities of our times.

Labour is made both image and reality. Rather than structuring the story of manual scavengers, a common item on the 'local' page of newspapers, in terms of dialogue between characters, *Dark Things* performs their labour in its materiality and corporeality, making it neither fully 'suppositional' nor wholly real-time action. The hazardous, subhuman act of scavenging is demonstrated in such a way as to insert the spectators into the very environment of this particular type of labour. Six scavengers drag six metal drums to the middle of the performance space and start twirling them on their bases, creating a harsh metallic sound. As this movement stops, they each get inside a drum. Six more people carry one large canister of clean water and another small canister of mud each. They hand in the canisters to the people inside, slowly push them down until they disappear from sight, and put the lids over the drums. When the six soiled people rise up for air, nearly choking, they wash themselves with soap and water from the larger canisters. Except for the scavengers' verbal complaints about their quality of life to a reporter, there is hardly any text in the scene that would describe their travails or recommend any remedy. The sensorial reality provokes the spectator to contemplate different narratives of dissent, but not necessarily with any hope for resolution. That such theatre is neither revolutionary in the Marxist sense nor elite/formalist 'presentism', based on an 'aesthetic of indifference' (Karahasan's phrase), clearly comes through in this episode. It is processual, letting the spectator build their own critique of economic exploitation in conjunction with the other narratives of caste, access to children's education, civic planning and the transparency of government work. The labour that goes into the act of scavenging and remains unnoticed by the public, the risk involved, the daily drudgery and the subhuman status of the workers (ironically treated as 'human waste' in a profiteering society) are at once materially performed and aestheticized in a manner that exposes our political apathy towards their condition but stops short of calling for action.

A different frontier of labour is brought in, in the fifth scene. From behind the audience gallery to the right of the performance space, a glass box is rolled in by two men. Inside the box is a worker seated in a chair before a desk with a soldering machine and a couple of motherboards on it. On top of the box is a female performer who sings live, the lyrics projected on screen. By placing the singer atop the box and simultaneously drawing attention to its interior, the scene not only enables both vertical and horizontal spectating but implies the shocking contrast between the stifling work condition inside the electronic plants and the paradoxical freedom outside in jumping out of the multi-storeyed workplace. Multiple mediums and props are at play here – words, created objects, movement, music and video – with no attempt to synthesize the sensory responses, generated by them individually, or the fragments of the narrative. The songs as adapted from Xu Lizhi's poems by Sitas and incorporated by Goswami comment on the mass suicide of workers at Foxconn, a 1.4 square-mile flagship iPhone plant just outside of Shenzhen. Lizhi wrote his poems before he killed himself. Post-Fordist high-performance work thus takes exploitation to a new height. As the song goes on, two things happen: large cannonballs are hurled across the performance space with a loud thud, underscoring at once their own heaviness and the unbearable workload at Foxconn; and three workers to the left of the stage perform a choreography of repeated falls like tiny loose screws falling off a gadget. The body is used as a locus of energetic movement with little preconceived meaning inscribed on it. This new political dramaturgy proposes new relations 'between actions, bodies and narration beyond causality, linearity and absolute closure' (Boenisch 2013: 115).

The political logic of egalitarianism informing the theatre-maker's intention comes through in a form that would build an '*affective* impact' on the spectator, an autonomous individual as well as part of a 'collective audience' (Tomlin 2019: 15). A man using a soldering machine, screws falling, cannonballs being thrown across, workers falling on the ground – in all of this we see energized signifiers that build up real-time action, light or heavy, producing an engaging experience of performance *and* only a tentative process of signification that does not communicate a mimetically processed meaning. While the thematic representation of social reality is resisted, a new 'real' comes into being in form. This is Lehmann's 'double diagnosis', as Brandon Woolf would say, the oblique appearance of the political in theatre that is not 'translatable or re-translatable into the logic, syntax, and terminology of the political discourse of social reality' (2013: 43). Woolf calls it 'theatre's (negative) political potential', which being 'much more indirect, much more unpredictable' (44) is very different from realistic political theatre. In the subtlety of this negative political, the ideological does not die but is instead given a new life dramaturgically. Spectating becomes responding to the tangible in space, an 'artistic interpellation' (Tomlin 2019: 2), and construing meaning out of the political provocation made in the production, meaning that may not converge with the intention propelling the performance.

There is also a narrative of industrial labour that coexists with post-Fordist labour in the third world. The whole scene is an event in its concreteness and there-ness, and therefore carries an intense experiential quality for the spectator. Suddenly the sirens go off, followed by the projection of the following text on screen:

> Blessed is the hammer,
> That hammers in our homes.
> Some work through the day,
> Some work through the night,
> Some stay here for weeks,
> Making home.

Several workers arrive carrying the massive iron frame of a hammer. As they grapple with it in a bid to position it, from the left of stage a crane approaches and lowers its hook. The hammer is placed onto it, a hard physical act, and is lifted by the crane. The workers applaud and whistle as the hammer is pulled to a height and drawn away. The manoeuvring of the JCB excavator/crane and the lifting of the heavy hammer frame is an extremely risky job *actually* performed there, rendering tangible the hardness and potential danger involved in any (heavy) industrial work. This scene makes it amply clear that 'we shake off our common conceptions of form as mere ornamentation', to put it in the words of Boyle et al., 'or as something that seals an artwork off from society'. Form is the 'simultaneous entwinement of the overlapping social mediations that give shape to theatre, and which theatre [also] shapes in turn' (Boyle et al. 2019: 1). The scene sounds Brechtian by stressing theatre's engagement with 'bourgeois apparatuses', as Woolf would argue after Benjamin, and its need to see its position vis-à-vis the 'production relations' of its time. Yet it is post-Brechtian in its primary interest in formal and technical innovation *within* the 'relations of *theatrical* production' (Woolf 2013: 37). The strong experiential element in the scene, which predominantly operates at the level of form, also intersects with activism as an ideological-political bulwark against exploitation. The performance cannot be discussed in its entirety for space constraints. It ends with a hazmat-clad worker in a postwar site, collecting scrap for sale to capitalist powers, recording her story on a typewriter and reading it out simultaneously.

Mimesis as imitation and faithful representation is largely denounced. The affective impact on the audience is created through a new 'politics of perception', a radicalization of 'sign usage' and a dismissal of 'rational preconsiderations' in favour of sense perceptions generating from the concreteness of performance situation (Lehmann 2006: 186). These perceptions help the spectator interpret the happening on stage independently rather than accepting the interpretation coming straight from it. The ideological imperatives, however, are never absent from such dramaturgy; but they are now calibrated, if not limited, by the democratic logic of plurality where freedom is a prerequisite for the (individual) spectator to negotiate an agonistic space and create meaning for themselves. The refugee crisis and organ trade, suicide of exploited labourers and warfare for profit are 'dark things' produced by global capitalism in connivance with hegemonic cultural and ethnic policies of the state or local governing bodies. If the 'ideological conformity' demanded by the historical Marxist project is no longer an effective way to engage 'diverse and multiple relations of inequality' (Tomlin 2019: 1), the activist intent informing any production requires a new political dramaturgy capable of navigating this multiplicity and its contingency rather than falling back on any grand egalitarian narrative of liberation. The 'political dramaturgies' employed in *Dark Things* generate a palimpsestic spectatorship that redefines activism in theatre and *also* asks if any theatre can exist outside of the social and political structures it engages with and questions.

The production is an expansive, multi-layered show which 'drama's literary form (namely dialogue) and its content' simply cannot hold (Boyle et al. 2019: 3). *Dark Things* yields more performance experience than interpretation through the (staged) text. This theatreness, however, does not mean 'theatre for theatre's sake' but shifts the focus from the untenable coupling of theatre and thematized politics on to the 'dissonance' in their relationship. It situates politics in the very experience of doing and participating in theatre that obliquely deals with extra-theatrical reality in terms of form. It replaces theatre's primary concern with textuality and mimetic representation with a focus on process and construction. This is a kind of formalism that is neither medium-specific nor characterized by political apathy. Closely connected to social and political formations, it appears postdramatic in its *presentation* (see Boyle et al. 2019: 12). The political offstage and the political onstage now meet in a more fluid and interactive relationship.

CONCLUSION

Postdrama and Theatre-Making in India

The re-theatricalization of theatre has freed it from the 'literary, photographic or filmic representations of worlds' by focusing on the 'aesthetic means of theatricality' (Lehmann 2006: 51). Consequently, *theatre-making* as a *process* has gained prominence worldwide since the 1980s, and in India, particularly, since the 1990s when women directors took over the theatre scene and changed the stale (read: realistic as well as exotic) language of theatre. The *making* of theatre shifted the emphasis from work to event, from stage translation of a literary/dramatic text to intermedial adaptation and devising, from the dialogical/dialectical development of plot to theatre solos, scenography and performance-installation, from fictional rendering of the real to 'dramaturgy of the real', and from conventional political theatre to the doing of theatre politically. W. B. Worthen dismisses the back-to-literary-dramatist movement around Shakespeare, which criticizes the conferring on the 'Bard' 'the man of theatre' status. Worthen contends that a literary text, when put to performance, creates 'the problematic performatives of the stage' rather than controlling the performance or mandating interpretation as a logo-centric activity (in Radosavljević 2013: 19–20). However, my contention is that this understanding of performance moves us further towards the theatreness of theatre as distinguished from drama, diversifying the relationship of text and performance, encouraging the writing of new texts for the contemporary stage and widening theatre's scope by making the boundaries between theatre and other performance forms porous.

Lehmann prefers the word 'theatre' over 'performance' for his thesis on postdrama ('postdramatic *theatre*') but notes how the 'new theatre' multiplied the ways and possibilities of making itself predominantly performative in the late twentieth century. Interestingly, the productions of our times have brought theatre and performance in such interactive, reciprocal terms that one cannot be viewed as a category/genre separate from the other. Today they are both theatre *and* performance – 'a field in between' (Lehmann 2006: 134). Richard Schechner's description of theatre as a subgenre of performance has yielded place to the concept of theatre-as-performance. Yet it is *theatre* ultimately because the word 'performance' also means 'performance art', especially in German, and, more importantly, the postdramatic has not wholly aligned itself – or become synonymous – with 'action art', particularly in India. However, the mode of writing and the medium of storytelling in the subcontinent have acquired a self-reflexivity that is very different from the representational forms of dramatic theatre ruling the Indian stage for more than a century until the 1990s. The broadening scope of theatre-as-performance often blurs the line between the real and the fictive. Theatre has been made in India as events, performance-installations, 'landscaped scenography' (Kapur) and cross-media performances in more recent times. The processuality of making, and not the product, augmented by the emergence of the postdramatic comes to us in multiple iterations, demonstrating the constant re/thinking of theatre beyond text or with a new kind of text that transcends its literariness. Theatre-making in India, as elsewhere today, has encouraged collaboration among artists of different genres and disciplines.

Theatre-making in contemporary India as a multi-layered process has been adequately discussed from postdramatic perspectives in the previous chapters. Here I intend to review it briefly under the separate heads of devising, writing, dramaturging and directing (inclusive of curating), although contemporary practice often demands of a theatre-maker 'multi-professionalization' that is different from specialization in one particular field of the art and builds on the ability to move freely between its individual units and layers (Radosavljević 2013: 22). For each head, with the exception of the last, I choose one production, not discussed in any of the preceding chapters, to demonstrate how these different yet interconnected departments of theatre delineate 'the extra-aesthetic *in* the aesthetic' (Lehmann 2006: 103), redefine presence on stage, claim authenticity of presentation and reconfigure the political in performance.

Devising has a long history in relation to theatre-making. A performance can be devised out of a pre-existing play text, a work of fiction or non-fiction, or even without any text existing before it. Much of postdramatic theatre is devised performance in the last sense. But it is not correct to say that contemporary theatre is necessarily non-textual or a pre-existing text cannot be devised for a postdramatic performance. While devising emerged in the UK in the latter half of the twentieth century and in the US about the same time under the name of 'collaborative creation' (Radosavljević 2013: 59), devising remains part of India's centuries-old performance tradition – its present theatrical dimension being only decades old, though. I would like to argue that the genealogical distinction Radosavljević makes between aesthetic-methodological and political modes of devising is not always tenable (ibid.). Devising can be a political reaction as much against the superior position enjoyed by the playwright and/or the director over others in dramatic theatre as against the aesthetic methodology of theatre-making *according to* a fixed play text. In devised theatre in India, adaptation of non-theatrical text, collective decision-making, collaborative improvisation and directorial supervision often go together to make an aesthetic logic that goes beyond representational realism. Political and creative methodologies combine in productions such as Kirti Jain's *Baghdad Burning* (2008) and *Aur Kitne Tukde* (already discussed) to make theatre-making non-dramatic. The conventional dichotomy between text and performance, body and mind, acting and non-acting, theatre and technology dissolves in India's contemporary 'anti-foundational[ist]' (Julia Wilson) theatrical performances (in Radosavljević 2013: 61). Below I discuss Jain's *Baghdad Burning* which goes against the grain of anxiety often expressed by veteran Indian theatre-makers and scholars that contemporary theatre 'trivialize[s] the text or "reduce[s]" the text to performance' and that such 'reduction' also trivializes 'the total physicality of the performative body' (Bandyopadhyay 2012: 4).

Baghdad Burning (2008) is a devised play that methodologically could have happened at least a decade before it actually took place, except for the fact that the Iraq war, which it is primarily based on, occurred in 2003. The storyline of *Baghdad Burning* is 'non-narrative', or the narrative in the play has been 'displaced through process-making', says Jain in an interview with the author (Jain 2016). The play is occasioned by the director's chancing upon the Riverbend blog created in 2003 and her visit to Afghanistan in 2006 where she had a first-hand experience of what a war-torn country looks like. While the blog contains entries of everyday life in Baghdad during the Iraq war on one hand and of American hypocrisies on the other, the visit to Afghanistan firmed up Jain's resolve to work on a performance that would be an arraignment of 'the policemen of the world' (Jain 2017). Nevertheless, it is the blog that lends complexity to *Baghdad Burning* because of its capacity to record the travails of the Iraqis with wit and courage as well as comment on American machinations with wry humour and satire. These two approaches brought to the stage two different modes of treatment, realistic and stylized, respectively (Jain 2019b). The anonymity of the blogger also influenced the devising of the play. 'Riverbend' is 'a fictitious name' under which the blog was put up. All efforts were made to reach out to the blogger but failed. The mere *assumption* that it was an Iraqi woman created 'some discomfort ... about the point of view' for the production (Jain 2019b). The blogger, therefore, has no name and is only dimly seen drafting her account on a laptop and simultaneously reading out what she writes.

The political is performed onstage both as farce and as strong physical images of occupation, violence, insecurity, surveillance, loss of rights and ownership. With a group of actors of mixed ethnic backgrounds Jain began her improvisations. She worked with them on short segments of the blog to create a kind of physical ritual about the ideas of torture and dispossession through repetitive actions. The actors, especially those from Assam and other north-eastern states, came up with haunting images out of their direct personal experience. Jain sat down with her group to select the sequences that they wanted to use in the play, maintaining a good balance between the segments on everyday suffering during the war and those containing political commentary. The script was written by a performer in the team, Supriya Shukla, keeping in mind the improvisations as well as the tonality of the blog that was completely devoid of any self-pity. She did an extremely competent first draft, Jain says, which was being constantly revised during rehearsals (Jain 2017).

After the individual scenes were roughly devised, the director started working on their structure, sequence and the atmosphere that could be evoked with the use of music and objects. During this devising, an improvisatory process, different kinds of reference materials were added to the production from newspapers, television channels and various official and unofficial sources. These were not part of the blog but interpolations that would serve as parallel texts and actions on stage. In a sequence, for instance, where a woman is looking for her missing brother and fears that he has been picked up by the army to be killed, corporeal images were created of naked bodies piled one on top of another, which were considerably influenced by reports of the treatment of prisoners in Guatemala prisons. The task in scene-making was also to consider the details of what people would do in such situations – such as sleeping with their shoes on, or keeping their bags packed or worrying constantly about their identity documents.

The play energizes the signs of terror in the conflict zone by devising actions that are vigorously somatic rather than aid dialogic plot development. These actions are not only serious but replete with sarcasm and sardonic humour. The victims' response to the Iraq war at one point is in the form of a devised game. A brother wakes up his sister in the middle of the night and begins a betting quiz of sorts that requires the participant to intuitively name the place where US planes are dropping bombs. Baudrillard's description of the 1991 Iraq war as a television soap for viewers safely secure in their distant homes takes an inverted dimension here: the war onsite has become so much part of the victims' daily life that they now copy (play) it as a game indoors. The movement of the body, the choreography required for the game and the performative mimesis of the war's fury make the scene affective and politically significant. On the other hand, a jubilant man appears in flamboyant casuals and sunglasses, dancing madly, announcing the 'holy war' on terror and inviting all present to join the coalition forces for the liberation of their country. The Bush administration props up their elite sycophants of Iraqi origins as rotational presidents for the war-ravaged country in the name of providing democratic leadership. The leaders enter, walking in a line, and sit on a bench, next to one another. They sway from side to side as the music plays on, cross their legs (the right across the left, the left across the right), and then give an electoral campaign speech each, paralleled by an offstage commentary on their inglorious track records. The play is not without dramatic representation; but the element of devising and the presence of physicality in image-making mark it off from the long-held realism of dramatic theatre in India. The non-dramatic language that is predominant in the production was in fact explored by Jain and her fellow female theatre-makers as early as the 1990s, a theatre language that in its own way paved the way for India's postdramatic a decade later.

To discuss the writing of text for the postdramatic stage one needs to look back, as Radosavljević does, to the changing relationship between text and performance. If text as a 'preexistent and fixed' element (Pavis) entered into European theatre in the seventeenth century (in Radosavljević 2013: 6) and into Indian theatre via the colonial route in the late nineteenth century, the figure of the playwright became central to dramatic theatre in Europe nearly two hundred years later and in India after the beginning of the twentieth century. Shanta Gokhale's book, *Playwright at the Centre* (2000), indeed considers the playwright figure to be central to the modern (Marathi) stage. A play in this perspective is treated as a stage illustration of the text and the playwright as an author and artist enjoying the best of the stage as well as the print world. The relationship between text and performance, which became increasingly unstable following the emergence of the director figure in nineteenth-century Europe, gave way to non-mimetic use of text with the emergence of modern drama that attached greater importance to form by the middle of the twentieth century and to the doing of theatre as self-reflexive performance a few decades down the line. Even as theatre in India turned postdramatic by 'downgrading drama' (Puchner 2011: 293) and connecting itself to various art forms, it has not ceased to be 'textual art' (Fischer-Lichte 1999: 170). I shall briefly discuss the text of *Ravanama* (2011) which solo artist Maya Krishna Rao wrote herself for her solo performance.

The text under discussion is written in the form of stage directions and monologues for the performer who explores through improvised movement and contemporized Kathakali choreographies the multi-dimensional relationship between Ravana, the villain-hero of the Ramayana, and Sita, whom he had stolen away from Ayodhya (the fabled birthplace of Lord Rama and currently a small town in Uttar Pradesh, India) to the mythical Lanka (Sri Lanka today). The text in its interface with a camera and a laptop is there for Rao to construct a multi-layered stage reality, but without losing its own value:

> For me, the discovery of so many stories associated with Ravana drove me to take the stories onto the floor and discover how these stories may collide with one another. Elements from different stories became the building blocks for fresh stories to be created through improvisation. I recorded these improvisations on camera. I also started putting down on my laptop the kind of interpretations that seemed to be emerging. The laptop played such an important role in the process of devising that I finally put it on stage. It was as if my computer was one of the mediums to 'get to' Ravana, the character.
>
> Rao 2016

The self-reflexive text opens with Rao asking herself why she, even as she drinks her tea and reads the morning newspaper, suddenly thinks of Ravana towards whom she as a person and performer has always felt drawn. The text at this stage, apart from those questions in verse, mostly comprises stage directions for the solo performer: '*WARM UP – vvvvvvv . . . lover . . . fffffff . . . mmmmmm . . . (go to mirror . . . Silence . . . wear strip robe . . . Rejected, scorned, pushed away, (in mirror) Your hair . . . your feet . . . your breasts . . . your eyes . . . won't you . . . from me . . . clothes . . . jewellery . . . a pan* [beetle leaf] *to eat and stain your lips? (take off one sock . . . Light . . .)*'.

As the performer muses over one of the versions of the Ravana–Sita story, the stage directions in elliptical prose nuance her movement: '*wait!! Horn – look . . . hand shake . . . hold . . . take off socks . . . Pipe – hand shake . . . Stree staccato . . . slap hand, shift mudra to left and stroke face with right (drums) . . . run back . . . turn around, see feet touch feet . . . breasts . . . hair . . . drums . . . other side hair . . . throw hair at her . . . run back for sari (high pipe) . . . put on sari, pleats . . . reject . . . bangles . . . reject pan*'. The story could begin thus, Rao suggests addressing her spectators frontally – the text complementing her gestures again: 'Ravana, Mandodari . . . / Gave birth to a long-prayed for baby girl / But with a curse that / Once she grew to be a woman, / She would be the cause of her father – / Ravana's death'. 'When I am doing this improvisation', Rao tells the author, her obsession with 'Ravana also rattled me – so who was Sita and how come she wasn't finding a place in my story-making?!' (Rao 2016). The story comes to the audience as a process, showing the simultaneity of authoring and telling where movement and technology become important mediums of articulation besides word. The story, which is many in one, is finally brought to its own lack and contradictions. Sita is required to paint the figure of Ravana but wonders how, since she has never seen any part of him other than his feet. Sita may not know the answer also because she is not certain of her feelings towards Ravana, but Rao as the performing artist does it for Sita through the changing of costumes, improvised movement and the use of digital media. The text as a staged discourse (between the performer and the spectator) on the modalities of storytelling and role-playing brings a new turn to the writing for theatre and performance.

'Dramaturgy', etymologically, means 'playmaking, not just playwriting' – though the two words are often conflated. Bharata Muni's millennia-old *Natyashastra* is the first Asian (Hindu) 'treatise on dramaturgy and histrionics' that deals, among other things, with the divine origins of drama and the theory of *rasa* that can be perceived by a detached contemplation 'of a life experience or emotion' (Seturaman 1989: 584) represented through gestures, postures and intonation. The definition and function of dramaturgy, the word being first used in Europe in the eighteenth century to mean a theatrical function or process for the development of a play, have constantly changed over the nineteenth and twentieth centuries in consonance with the shifting notions of theatre and performance – from realist-naturalist to avant-garde to postdramatic. Modern Indian theatre has not been outside of this changing topography, though the dramaturge is a European invention and (dramatic) theatre in India had no separate place for the figure until the late twentieth century.

A 'new dramaturgy' has made its way into theatre-making following the interrogation of (dramatic) theatre as 'fake', to argue after Marina Abramović (in Danan 2014: 4), and the welcoming of performance as 'real'. While 'real effect', juxtaposed as it is with 'effect of the real' (Danan 2014: 4), is claimed to constitute 'true reality' (Abramović, in ibid.) in theatre, theatre has also gone beyond theatre by expanding its interdisciplinary character and diversifying its performative rigour. This changed (and changing) approach to theatre, which no longer shares an adversarial relationship with performance, has brought radical revisions of conventional dramaturgy. The new dramaturgy, which is often described as 'porous dramaturgy' for its liaison with other art and performance forms, may not still take theatre totally beyond representation. But 'the power of the present' with its performative energy makes representation appear as 'a second crop to be harvested by the spectator' (Danan 2014: 4). The new dramaturgy provides the spectator with what Jean-Luc Nancy calls 'experience of the sense' (in Danan 2014: 9).

The role of the dramaturge has thus changed and, notably, the director can also be the 'theatre writer' (Danan 2014: 12) today, collating and editing texts from various sources for a multi-layered performance. Moreover, dramaturgy is not any longer 'restricted only to the domain of writing for the stage', Radosavljević notes. With dramaturgy, 'anything goes, so long as the artwork being created – text-based or not – is crafted with rigour, intelligence, intuition and attention to detail' (2013: 103). Theatre in India has not remained outside of this global practice. *409 Ramkinkars* (2015), conceptualized by Vivan Sundaram and executed by a large group of arts practitioners including theatre-maker Anuradha Kapur, is an example where dramaturgy is 'not a separated category' (Kapur 2019b) but connected to directing, scenography and devising in a synergistic spirit.

409 Ramkinkars, presented by Vivadi Cultural Society at the Indira Gandhi National Centre for the Arts (IGNCA), New Delhi, is in fact a cross-fertilization of forms – 'sculptural installation, landscaped scenography, improvisatory as well as immersive performance, a learning play, and … "promenade" theatre' (Kapur 2017b: 128). 'A multi-authored project variously imagined by … writers, scenographers, theatre makers, sculptors, academics' (ibid.: 117), it becomes what Synne Behrndt would call a 'dramaturgy of process' (in Radosavljević 2013: 101) laid over 4,000 square metres of IGNCA's grounds and buildings. A tribute to Ramkinkar Baij's versatile talent as painter, sculptor and theatre actor, *409 Ramkinkars* is an interdisciplinary, open-ended performance. Artist Sundaram says: 'Just as site specific installations take from architecture the plan and structure of objects in space, theatre is present within installation practice as a performative *mise-en-scene*'. Conceived as 'installation art and theatre [as] twinned genres' (Sundaram 2016: online), the project moves closer, as Carlson would say, 'to the postdramatic both by abandoning the conventional text and by allowing spectators much more control in the shaping and experiencing of the performance' (2015: online).

The dramaturgy in *409 Ramkinkars* shows how representation can be largely avoided by narrating a life and career only 'glancingly' (Kapur) and incorporating the spectators in the very process of art-making. I would cite two instances to prove my point. First, the actor-performer (or the performing sculptor) who throws cement on the half-finished replica of Baij's sculpture, *The Santhal Family*, has done all the work by himself. He had spent twenty long days working on *his* sculpture before the show began, and he resumes his action *now* by throwing cement, as Baij would do, on the armature to complete the sculpture *here* in the performing space. As he does it, he also ascribes a new dimension to the original. In the process 'the *actioning* of sculpture in concrete (as sculpting material) was bodied forth' (Kapur 2017b: 124) and rescued from being a mere category of imitation since it becomes his own work in progress. 'What was sought to be materialized in *performative action* was the labour required to throw concrete, shape and fix it on an iron armature – which was Ramkinkar's elected mode of work' (Kapur 2017b: 124). My second example is the miniatures of Baij's work, as many as 409 of

Figure 9 *409 Ramkinkars* (2015), conceptualized by Vivan Sundaram and executed by a large group of arts practitioners, produced by Vivadi Cultural Society. Photo credit: S. Thyagarajan.

them, which are not replicas but reinterpretations. The terracotta miniatures, made by many hands over nearly two years, draw the spectator's attention to these special 'copies' that are no less original by trying not to mimic the (first) original. While *The Mill Call*, another of Baij's sculptures, seeks to capture the hurried yet delightful movement of people on their way to work in the mill, the mass of miniatures, on a gallery 2 to 48 inches off the ground, multiplies the energy and abandon of the original as if to pay tribute to Baij's art. 'Pressed against the walls of the foyer, the spectators could not see any figure individually; the sculpted mass became a miniaturized pageant staged as if in an amphitheatre or as a collective marching through a square or street', writes Kapur (ibid.: 122). The 'One and the Many' segment, which showcases the miniatures, thus cites the 'world' outside but creates a performative reality for its own art life without being naïvely mimetic.

One could still say, as Carlson does, that 'the removing of the controlling text does not involve a removal of the mimetic as well' because 'the body must [also] be ... set free to register as purely performative' (2015: 588). First, *409 Ramkinkars* does not banish text. The everyday of a Santhal village is presented by interweaving text with action, music and sound from different sources (including Tagore songs). 'Characters speak directly to the audience more than among themselves', says Kapur (in Nath 2015: online). If most of this is not dialogue, it is not monologue either. It is not a case of the 'actor first'. It is rather, to quote Kapur again, 'a performance-lecture' on the nature of art practice – frontally delivered and 'directly conducted with the audience' (2017b: 125). Secondly, the body in this production may not be totally freed from its mimetic role – even in the scene where Baij as man, painter and sculptor is split up into three figures played by three actors. But the production opens theatre-making to 'scrutiny and critique', says Kapur, 'so that acting in public becomes a way of interpreting the actions of both actor and spectator' (ibid.: 118). The dramaturgy here is evidently different from dramatic writing, as John Freeman would say, with its 'constatative narratology'. Instead, it is processual, provisional and performative (in Radosavljević 2013: 101).

Directing was central to Indian (dramatic) theatre throughout the twentieth century, especially since the staging in the late 1950s of Sanskrit

Figure 10 *409 Ramkinkars* (2015). Photo credit: S. Thyagarajan.

plays in Hindi translation. The Habib Tanvir-directed *Mrichchakatikam* (1958), K. N. Panikkar-directed *Madhyam Vyayog* (1979) and Ratan Thiyam-directed *Urubhangam* (1980) – the first written by Sudraka and the last two by Bhasa – are some of such productions primarily known by the names of their directors. Directing became more popular with the emergence of modern realist theatre in the 1960s, as exemplified by the Ebrahim Alkazi-directed Dharamvir Bharati's *Andha Yug* (1962), Utpal Dutt's *Kallol* (1965) and Vijay Tendulkar's *Silence! The Court is in Session* directed by Arvind Deshpande (1967). Directing turned out to be more challenging as the anti-realist 'theatre of roots' became the alternative modern theatre in India during the 1970s and 1980s: B. V. Karanth's production of Girish Karnad's *Hayavadana* (1971) and Ratan Thiyam's *Chakravyuha* (1984), to name only two, bear testimony to this. The director enjoyed the utmost importance in the making of theatre – from interpreting characters to preparing actors to supervising the set design and lighting to choosing music – and bore sole responsibility for the success or failure of a production until the theatre in India turned collaborative in the 1990s. Directing is now working on an equal footing with performance text writers, actors/performers, designers, curators, singers, painters, digital media experts and visual and video artists. Amitesh Grover's *Downtime* (2014) and *Notes on Mourning* (2015–16), Abhilash Pillai's *Talatum* (2016) and Anuradha Kapur and Deepan Sivaraman's *Dark Things* (2018–19) are only a few of such successful collaborations. This obviously does not mean that the director figure has gone out of Indian theatre, but directing has been reconceived more as facilitating laboratory work (not strictly in the Grotowskian sense) that is experimental in its approach to theatre-making and based on sharing of knowledge produced by artists or 'experts' in other fields of performance.

Creating illusion to 'represent reality' has never been 'a serious aspect of contemporary Indian theatre', Nissar Allana observes (2012b: 40). In fact, with 'the notion of contradiction as an accepted philosophical dialectic', Allana elaborates, 'the need to recreate actual reality' in theatre has not been a part of the Indian performance tradition (40). Nevertheless, the long stay of dramatic theatre in colonial and postcolonial India made the director accept representational realism as the matrix for setting, action, acting and lighting. Since the 1990s the 'language of design' has become non-linear and directing has demanded that there be 'no fixed parameters for defining meaning' (41). Now space is more fluid or fragmented than ever before, sets architectural or plastic, characters sculptural or citations of states, and images experiential. Directing in such a context goes beyond the task of dramatizing a narrative. The nature of directing has steadily changed to prioritizing processuality and reflexivity over dramatization even as it deals with characters and events from another time and place. It aims to uphold the 'reality-status' of performance despite the material used or experience drawn on for stage(d) action being from the outside.

Direction has also become a separate category altogether with the making of theatre solos which demand a different level of expertise. As her own director, Maya Krishna Rao, for one, takes care of all the aspects of her productions that provide an alternative to group performance but avoid the hierarchized structure of dramatic theatre. She is in charge of text-writing to solo-performing to editing improvisations to making revisions, but at the same time ready to discuss issues with her videographer and musician. Different elements of theatre-as-performance receive democratic treatment in her solos. Improvised text is a hallmark of her works but never above music, movement and visuals. Attention is paid to the performer's self-presentation rather than any role-playing. Dearth of resources and lack of access to privileged sites of performance have engendered several theatre solos in India, changing the idea of theatre-making from an elaborate exercise to minimalism in performance. This minimalism, however, does not preclude emotions or narratives. With minimal art content and performance paraphernalia and the use of ordinary materials to produce a wide range of sensory perception, it creates a theatre type that has gained popularity over time (see Chayka 2020: online). Rao's choice of the solo form was, however, deliberate and thoughtful: she wanted to do theatre in a way that was not possible by working with any directors or drama schools in India of those days.

In his essay, 'There Will Be Trouble: Curating Theatre in India', Amitesh Grover points out the interesting relationship between dramaturgy, directing and curating (2020: online). He notes that Harald Szeemann, a Swiss arts curator, had once compared his work to a theatre director's. Grover also cites art theorist Beatrice von Bismarck, who more recently 'likened the process of exhibition-making' to the job of a theatre dramaturge. The curator figure has always had a secure place in organizing exhibitions of visual art works or historical artefacts in museums, but was nearly an absent figure until recently in global theatre and one that enjoyed little visibility in India before theatre festivals became a regular, popular way in the 2000s of bringing the best of domestic and international productions together. Historically, the job of the curator, as Grover observes, was 'dispersed [in] and carried out by multiple figures without' a single name to it (2020: online). In present times, however, curating theatre primarily means curating theatre festivals rather than curating a particular performance (the latter is also a practice, though). There are more than a dozen annual theatre festivals in India today, some of which accommodate besides theatrical productions exhibitions of visual art works and other kinds of performance that were not part of the theatre scene even till the end of the last century. Theatre directors are as much in demand to curate such festivals as people from other art forms. The job here is eclectic, ranging from choosing the festival theme to selecting theatre companies to be invited to preparing the daily programme to readying performers as well as spectators for the shows. Against the background of the recent (and ongoing) expansion of the scope of theatre around the world (including in India), writer and curator Florian Malzacher warns that a curator could eventually occupy the status of a meta-artist and act as a neoliberal agent (in Grover 2020: online). But this is not wholly true. Contemporary theatre festivals have given festival directors or curators ample scope to make each such event inclusive – connecting it to ongoing social conflicts, addressing the public (including but not limited to theatre-goers) and creating new realities and perceptions for them, building new cultural and artistic discourses and generating opportunities for collective activities across places (see Grover 2020: online).

There has been a lot of controversy of late about the propriety and relevance of the new language in Indian theatre since it allegedly threatens 'indigenous' performance practices. I shall cite one example. A day before the World Theatre Forum (WTF) seminar, part of NSD's Bharat Rang Mahotsav 2019, four veteran (male) theatre-makers, whose contribution to post-independence Indian theatre is recognized as significant, circulated a handout with their names printed on it. They critiqued the hierarchization (termed 'partialization' by them) of theatre forms in India over the past couple of decades and the celebration of the kind which, according to them, marginalizes the actor and the play text, and prizes technology over other performance elements. They alleged that 'theatre practice' had been turned into 'performance-making', which is not merely expensive but almost ruining small-budget, off-metropolis 'indigenous' theatres.

To answer the above doubts briefly, one may say that contemporary theatre in India takes place in a hybridized space and does not truly conform either to the conventional concept of indigenousness or to our understanding of interculturality as in the 1970s, both based on belief in the essence and exclusivity of a particular culture. I have discussed this difference elaborately in Chapter 1. I would only add here that whether or not India's 'post-colonial paranoia' (Allana 2012b: 41) can be cited to explain an anxious adherence to cultural roots, the following words of Richard Schechner hold true in our case: 'all cultures are multiple, there is no such thing as "purity"' (2013: xiii). A global modernity (and postmodernity) informs the theatres of India today, resulting in 'creative hybridity' (ibid.: xiii). One may not fully agree with Amal Allana when she says that 'a postcolonial director' needs to construct 'a performance language that would indeed reflect cultural *instability*, lack of belonging to any culture/language/ethnic group, specifically' (Allana 2013:

xix); but it is fairly proper for a theatre-maker in India to respond to the paradigm shifts in performance-making and create works that would partake of elements from around the world without making a total sacrifice of one's own rich traditions. In so doing, one must also consider the possibility of a culture's always-already mediated status. In the case of Indian theatre, it is more interesting because the wave of anti-representation came to Western theatre after its contact with the performance culture of the East. And the theatre practice in India, which turned largely 'dramatic' following the colonization of the stage in the mid-nineteenth century, started acquiring its contemporary physical, material, processual and reflexive dimensions after the 'turn to performance' in the West. However, contemporary Indian theatre is not an appendage to the Western/global postdramatic but has a hybrid aesthetic-cultural identity of its own that has an equal potential to influence the theatre outside of India today.

Allegations about reduction of text to performance and of theatre-making to performance-making have already been answered at many places in the book and earlier in this chapter, too. I would only note here, after Citron, Aronson-Lehavi and Zerbib, that if theatre borrows from performance, performance at large 'borrows the theatrical metaphor' (2014: 4). The boundaries between theatre and performance have increasingly collapsed since the 1990s in India, building new bridges between aesthetics and politics, and between aesthetic-performative methodologies. There are 'performances in/of social spaces', 'performative politics' (ibid.: 5, 7), ritualistic, activist and applied performances that not only go beyond the frames of dramatic theatre but also fall outside of conventional theatrical analyses. Theatre today includes '[e]xtra-textual and extra-theatrical components' and produces a performative effect not without but certainly beyond representation (4). It is transgressive of its traditional boundaries to perform a reality different from that in (purely) representational theatre. Hence the anxiety that theatre-making should not turn into performance-making misunderstands the nature of both theatre and performance of the twenty-first century.

Closely connected to the precedence of performance over text in contemporary theatre is the alleged marginalization of the actor. Should it suffice to say that with the 'death of character' the 'star actor' is also dead. When character ceases to be the 'motor' of dramatic structure (see Fuchs 1996), a change that started as early as the beginning of modernism in the West and reached its apex in the theatre after modernism, the emphasis shifts to the figure of the performer showing the difficulties of embodiment and the 'crisis of representation'. In Indian theatre, the word became 'wandering' and the subject 'unstable' at the turn of the twenty-first century (Kapur 2001: 5). Theatre being freed from logocentricity, the challenge for the 'actor' is no longer to get into the skin of an integral character as a vehicle for dramatic action but navigate a difficult space between imitation/representation and action/presentation.

It is not true either that scenography or visual dramaturgy (which, to those detractors of postdrama, is reducible to 'technology') is always expensive and ornamental. A created object on stage or lighting designs, when not taken as a device merely to illustrate part of a text scenically, is also scenography that can develop a theatrical situation intrinsically (Sivaraman 2016). Scenography, according to Sivaraman, can, at the same time, 'explor[e] space while collaborating with various art disciplines' (2013: online). In *409 Ramkinkars*, for example, scenography establishes itself as a 'performance design' on a sprawling campus in its own right. It is 'a multi-sensorial and dynamic' scenography which is both contributory to and constitutive of theatrical action generating immersive experience (McKinney and Palmer 2017: 5). In a multi-lingual country like India, the new visual language in theatre, that includes the new media, should find takers also because it helps get over linguistic hurdles. Scenographic theatre is going to stay more for the reason that the television and Android phones have made deep inroads into different parts of the country and no theatre can possibly exist long by abstaining totally from contemporary visual culture. I do not, however, include in this category the big-budget shows of companies like the Mobile Theatre of Assam and the Kingdom of Dreams in Gurgaon (NCR) because they exploit visual extravaganzas largely for commercial reasons. How theatre and the new visual culture can be complementary to each other today, instead of the latter being a threat to the former, is evident in Abhilash Pillai's stage adaptation of *Midnight's Children* (2005). Fragmentation of the nation, disintegration of families and communities, amnesia and incoherent chronicling find a different language in the production that comprises film footage of historical events, video shots of places and people, and a stage whose rear raised part resembles the movie screen. Scenography is here very much integrated into theatre-making.

Most importantly, a blanket rejection of postdramatic forms is neither possible nor desirable. We need to acknowledge that 'postdramatic' is no longer a European theatre paradigm exclusively. It has become a vital part of performance culture worldwide, though not without regional modalities. The twenty-first-century world, riven as it is with ethnic conflicts and refugee crisis, recession and unemployment, hypernationalism and divisive/exclusionary politics, has forced postdramatic theatre to expand its *form* to accommodate the political in a new way. Form is now understood in relation to prevalent or emerging material conditions, global as well as regional, affecting art-making. Nicholas Rideout faults Lehmann's thesis on re/presentation on the ground that it traces the postdramatic exclusively to the emergence of the 'media society' without connecting it to the relations of production in the late capitalist system. Rideout attempts to correct this 'misreading' by arguing after Fredric Jameson how the dominant information technology, or the 'media' in one word, is a product of late capitalism to sustain and augment itself against the possibility of its own systemic crises (Rideout 2019: 98–102). I do not, however, find Lehmann's thesis on changing theatre forms and Jameson's on changing forms of production influencing the arts or cultural forms to be inimical to each other. Theatre-makers have found it most difficult to represent external reality on the stage especially since the 1970s, exactly when the television and information technology captured the market. Reality loses its determinate status in times of wholesale mediatization that directly aids the prolonged wave of late capitalism, which is currently an odd mix of neoliberalism, crony capitalism, corporate–Hindutva alliance and censorship in India. Rideout's logic of production and Lehmann's question of representation are in fact co-imbricated. The changes in forms of theatre ensue from such massive 'structural transformations in society itself' as cited above (Boyle et al. 2019: 16). What is important for us to understand is that as it is not possible to make theatre by ignoring its formal situatedness in politico-economic conditions including the means of communication, so is it necessary to make the audience see this connection in the very act of performance-making. Postdramatic theatre does not revolutionize society but can *form*ally ensure that the discourses on issues do not die out, endowing the spectator with the responsibility of finding the connection between the politics of theatre and the theatre of politics. Several theatrical productions in India since the 1990s, whether or not their makers and theatre scholars identify them as postdramatic, have inaugurated a new discourse on social and political reality primarily in terms of form. These productions are certainly postdramatic, if only India's own.

References

Administration of Cattle Laws. https://dahd.nic.in/node/86828.
Ahlheim, Hannah. 2017. 'Losing Control – Gaining Control: Hannah Ahlheim Talks about Sleep Research'. 23 November 2017. http://www.nachhaltig-beleuchten.de/blog/en/losing-control-gaining-control-hannah-ahlheim-talks-about-sleep-research/.
Alexandrowicz, Conrad. 2015. 'Dancing the Page: Reflections on Staging Poetic Text'. *Studies in Theatre and Performance* 35, no. 2: 120–39.
Allana, Amal, ed. 2013. 'Introduction'. In *The Act of Becoming: Actors Speak*, xvii–xxiii. New Delhi: National School of Drama.
Allana, Nissar. 2012a. 'Festival Director's Message'. *Ibsen Festival Proceedings*. Delhi: Dramatic Art and Design.
Allana, Nissar. 2012b. 'Redefining the Actor'. *Theatre India* 1: 36–43.
Ambrose, Cohen. 2015. 'A "Paradox of Expression": Bertolt Brecht's Verfremdungseffekt in Performance'. PhD diss., University of Montana. https://scholarworks.umt.edu/cgi/viewcontent.cgi?article=5490&context=etd.
Appadurai, Arjun. 1996. *Modernity at Large: Cultural Dimensions of Globalization*. Minneapolis: University of Minnesota Press.
Aronson, Arnold. 2017. 'Foreword'. In *Scenography Expanded*, edited by Joslin McKinney and Scott Palmer, xiii–xvi. London: Bloomsbury Methuen.
Awasthi, Suresh. 2001. *Performance Tradition in India*. New Delhi: National Book Trust.
Babbage, Frances. 2018. *Adaptation in Contemporary Theatre: Performing Literature*. London: Bloomsbury Methuen.
Badiou, Alain. 2014. 'Alain Badiou: "People Cling onto Identities . . . It is a World Opposed to the Encounter"'. Interview by Clément Petitjean. Verso blog, 14 April 2014. https://www.versobooks.com/blogs/1557-alain-badiou-people-cling-onto-identities-it-is-a-world-opposed-to-the-encounter.
Bandyopadhyay, Samik. 2012. 'Note from the Guest Editor'. *Theatre India* 1: 4–5.
Bannerji, Himani. 1984. 'Language and Liberation: A Study of Political Theatre in West Bengal'. *Ariel* 15, no. 4: 131–44.
Barnett, David. 2013. 'Performing Dialectics in an Age of Uncertainty, or: Why Post-Brechtian ≠ Postdramatic'. In *Postdramatic Theatre and the Political*, edited by Karen Jürs-Munby, Jerome Carroll and Steve Giles, 47–66. London: Bloomsbury Methuen.
Baudrillard, Jean. 1995. *The Gulf War Did Not Take Place*, translated and with an introduction by Paul Patton. Bloomington: Indiana University Press.
Baudrillard, Jean. 1988. *Selected Writings*, edited by Mark Poster, 166–84. Stanford: Stanford University Press. https://web.stanford.edu/class/history34q/readings/Baudrillard/Baudrillard_Simulacra.html.

Berger, Cara. 2016. '"Knowledge and Taste Go Together": Postdramatic Theatre, Écriture Féminine, and Feminist Politics'. *Journal of Dramatic Theory and Criticism* 30, no. 2: 39–60.

Bevir, Mark. 2013. 'Meaning, Truth, and Phenomenology'. In *Presence: Philosophy, History, and Cultural Theory for the Twenty-First Century*, edited by Ranjan Ghosh and Ethan Kleinberg, 45–61. Ithaca: Cornell University Press.

Bharucha, Rustom. 2017. 'Foreword'. In *Performing the Secular: Religion, Representation and Politics*, edited by Milija Gluhovic and Jisha Menon, v–xxii. London: Palgrave Macmillan.

Bhatia, Gautam. 2017. 'Cow Slaughter and the Constitution'. *The Hindu*, 31 May 2017. https://www.thehindu.com/opinion/lead/cow-slaughter-and-the-constitution/article18683942.ece.

Boenisch, Peter M. 2013. 'Spectres of Subjectivity: On the Fetish of Identity in (Post-) Postdramatic Choreography'. In *Postdramatic Theatre and the Political*, edited by Karen Jürs-Munby, Jerome Carroll and Steve Giles, 111–28. London: Bloomsbury Methuen.

Borowski, Mateusz, and Malgorzata Sugiera, eds. 2007. 'Preface'. In *Fictional Realities / Real Fictions. Contemporary Theatre in Search of a New Mimetic Paradigm*, vii–xxviii. Cambridge: Cambridge Scholars Publishing.

Borowski, Mateusz, and Malgorzata Sugiera, eds. 2010. 'Introduction'. In *Worlds in Words: Storytelling in Contemporary Theatre and Playwriting*, 2–12. Cambridge: Cambridge Scholars Publishing.

Borowski, Mateusz, and Malgorzata Sugiera. 2013. 'Political Fictions and Fictionalisations: History as Material for Postdramatic Theatre'. In *Postdramatic Theatre and the Political*, edited by Karen Jürs-Munby, Jerome Carroll and Steve Giles, 67–86. London: Bloomsbury Methuen.

Bose, Santanu. 2016. Interview by author. 16 November 2016. Unpublished.

Bose, Santanu. 2019. WhatsApp message to author. 20 January 2019.

Bourriaud, Nicolas. 2002. *Relational Aesthetics*. Translated by Simon Pleasance and Fronza Woods. Paris: Les Presses du Réel.

Boyle, Michael Shane, Matt Cornish and Brandon Woolf, eds. 2019. *Postdramatic Theatre and Form*. London: Bloomsbury Methuen.

Brecht, Bertolt. 2015. 'The Job'. In *The Collected Short Stories of Bertolt Brecht*, edited by John Willett and Ralph Manheim, 158–62. New York: Bloomsbury.

Brejzek, Thea. 2017. 'Between Symbolic Representation and New Critical Realism: Architecture as Scenography and Scenography as Architecture'. In *Scenography Expanded*, edited by Joslin McKinney and Scott Palmer, 63–78. London: Bloomsbury Methuen.

Carlson, Marvin. 2015. 'Postdramatic Theatre and Postdramatic Performance'. *Revista Brasileira de Estudos da Presença (Brazilian Journal on Presence Studies)* 5, no. 3: 577–95. https://www.scielo.br/pdf/rbep/v5n3/2237-2660-rbep-5-03-00577.pdf.

Carroll, Jerome. 2013. 'Phenomenology and the Postdramatic: A Case Study of Three Plays by Ewald Palmetshofer'. In *Postdramatic Theatre and the Political*, edited by Karen Jürs-Munby, Jerome Carroll and Steve Giles, 233–54. London: Bloomsbury Methuen.

Case, Sue-Ellen. 1983. 'From Bertolt Brecht to Heiner Müller'. *Performing Arts Journal* 7, no. 1: 94–102.

Chand, Shweta. 2011. 'India Divided over Legacy: Glasnost, Gandhi, Grouchy Marx'. *Russia Beyond*, 29 March 2011. https://www.rbth.com/articles/2011/03/29/india_divided_over_legacy_glasnost_gandhi_grouchy_marx_12339.

Chaudhari, Zuleikha. 2017. Interview by author. 18 January 2017. Unpublished.

Chaudhari, Zuleikha. 2019. 'India's Postdramatic: Conversations with Theatre-Makers and a Critique'. Interview by Ashis Sengupta. *Marg* 70, no. 3: 46–63.

Chayka, Kyle. 2020. 'What We Get Wrong About Minimalism'. *New York Times*, 24 January 2020. https://www.nytimes.com/2020/01/24/opinion/sunday/minimalism-definition-history.html.

Cherian, Anita. 2012. 'Policies of Sangeet Natak Akademi and National School of Drama'. http://theatreforum.in/static/upload/docs/anita.pdf.

Chowdhry, Neelam Mansingh. 1998. 'Unpeeling the Layers within Yourself'. *Seagull Theatre Quarterly* 17: 3–21.

Chowdhry, Neelam Mansingh. 2019. 'India's Postdramatic: Conversations with Theatre-Makers and a Critique'. Interview by Ashis Sengupta. *Marg* 70, no. 3: 46–63.

Citron, Atay, Sharon Aronson-Lehavi and David Zerbib, eds. 2014. 'Introduction'. In *Performance Studies in Motion*, 1–14. London: Bloomsbury Methuen.

Clark, C. C. 1920. 'Symbolism in the Theatre'. *The Sewanee Review* 28, no. 2: 228–40.

Clough, Patricia T., and Jena Halley, eds. 2007. *The Affective Turn: Theorizing Social*. Durham, NC: Duke University Press.

Company, The. 2007. 'Kitchen Katha'. https://thecompanychandigarh.wordpress.com/kitchen-katha/.

Constituent Assembly of India Debates (Proceedings), vol. vii, 24 November 1948: http://loksabhaph.nic.in/writereaddata/cadebatefiles/C24_11948.pdf.

Cooke, Grayson. 2010. 'Start Making Sense: Live Audio-Visual Media Performance'. *International Journal of Performance Arts and Digital Media* 6, no. 2: 193–208.

Cooley, Charles Horton. 1902. *Human Nature and the Social Order*. New York: Charles Scribner's Sons.

Craik, Jennifer (2005). 'Dilemmas in Policy Support for the Arts and Cultural Sector', *Australian Journal of Public Administration* 64, no. 4: 6–19.

Dalmia, Vasudha. 2009. *Poetic, Plays and Performances*. New Delhi: Oxford University Press.

Danan, Joseph. 2014. 'Dramaturgy in "Postdramatic" Times'. In *New Dramaturgy: International Perspectives on Theory and Practice*, edited by Katalin Trencsényi and Bernadette Cochrane, 3–17. London: Bloomsbury Methuen.

Defraeye, Piet. 2007. Review of *Postdramatic Theatre*, by Hans-Thies Lehmann. *Modern Drama* 50, no. 4: 644–7.

Deshpande, Sudhanva, K. V. Akshara and Sameera Iyengar, eds. 2009. 'Introduction'. In *Our Stage: Pleasures and Perils of Theatre Practice in India*, 11–16. New Delhi: Tulika Books.

Dietze, Antje. 2013. 'Christoph Schlingensief's *Rocky Dutschke,' 68*: A Reassessment of Activism in Theatre'. In *Postdramatic Theatre and the Political*, edited by Karen Jürs-Munby, Jerome Carroll and Steve Giles, 129–46. London: Bloomsbury Methuen.

Dogra, Jyoti. 2019. Interview by author. 27 April 2019. Unpublished.

Dogra, Jyoti. 2020. Email to author. 1 February 2020.

Doherty, Claire. 2009. *Situation: Documents of Contemporary Art*. Cambridge, MA: MIT Press.

Duarte, Bruno C. 2017. 'Rhythm and Structure: Brecht's Antigone in Performance'. *Performance Philosophy Journal* 2, no. 2. https://www.performancephilosophy.org/journal/article/view/95/141.

Dutt, Barkha. 2018. 'Opinion: Will Modi Stop India's Cow Terrorists from Killing Muslims?' *Washington Post*, 25 July 2018. https://www.washingtonpost.com/news/global-opinions/wp/2018/07/24/will-modi-stop-indias-cow-terrorists-from-killing-muslims.

Eagleton, Terry. 2003. *Literary Theory: An Introduction*. Minneapolis: University of Minnesota Press.

Fensham, Rachel. 2012. 'Postdramatic Spectatorship: Participate or Else'. *Critical Stages: The IATC Webjournal* 7 (December). http://www.critical-stages.org/7/postdramatic-spectatorship-participate-or-else/.

Ferrato, Yolanda. 2014. 'Telling Stories Across Forms: Interview with Brian Quirt'. In *New Dramaturgy: International Perspectives on Theory and Practice*, edited by Katalin Trencsényi and Bernadette Cochrane, 53–67. London: Bloomsbury Methuen.

Fischer-Lichte, Erika. 1999. 'From Text to Performance: The Rise of Theatre Studies as an Academic Discipline in Germany'. *Theatre Research International* 24, no. 2: 168–78.

Fischer-Lichte, Erika. 2005. *Theatre, Sacrifice, Ritual*. London: Routledge.

Friedman, Dan, ed. 2007. 'Introduction'. In *The Cultural Politics of Heiner Müller*, 1–9. Cambridge: Cambridge Scholars Publishing.

Frljić, Oliver. 2011. 'Postdramatic Theatre and Political Theatre'. In *Dramatic and Postdramatic Theatre Ten Years After*, edited by Ivan Medenica, 129–36. Belgrade: Faculty of Dramatic Arts.

Fuchs, Elinor. 1996. *The Death of Character: Perspectives on Theater after Modernism*. Bloomington: Indiana University Press.

Fuchs, Elinor. 2008a. 'Lost in Translation'. *TDR: The Drama Review* 52, no. 4: 13–20.

Fuchs, Elinor. 2008b. 'Review of *Postdramatic Theatre*, by Hans-Thies Lehmann'. *TDR: The Drama Review* 52, no. 2: 178–83.

Fuchs, Elinor. 2011. 'Postdramatic Theatre and the Persistence of the "Fictive Cosmos": A View from America'. In *Dramatic and Postdramatic Theatre Ten*

Years After, edited by Ivan Medenica, 63–72. Belgrade: Faculty of Dramatic Arts.

Fuchs, Elinor. 2019. 'Drama: The Szondi Connection'. In *Postdramatic Theatre and Form*, edited by Michael Shane Boyle, Matt Cornish and Brandon Woolf, 20–30. London: Bloomsbury Methuen.

Garde, Ulrike, and Meg Mumford. 2013. 'Postdramatic Reality Theatre and Productive Insecurity: Destabilizing Encounters with the Unfamiliar in Theatre from Sydney and Australia'. In *Postdramatic Theatre and the Political*, edited by Karen Jürs-Munby, Jerome Carroll and Steve Giles, 147–64. London: Bloomsbury Methuen.

Genette, Gérard. 1997. *Palimpsests: Literature in the Second Degree*, translated by Channa Newman and Claude Doubinsky. Lincoln: University of Nebraska Press.

Giannachi, Gabriella, Nick Kaye and Michael Shanks, eds. 2012. 'Introduction: Archeologies of Presence'. In *Archeologies of Presence: Art, Performance and the Persistence of Being*, 1–26. Abingdon: Routledge.

Glaser, Elaine. 2014. 'Bring Back Ideology: Fukuyama's "end of history" 25 years on'. *Guardian*, 21 March 2014. https://www.theguardian.com/books/2014/mar/21/bring-back-ideology-fukuyama-end-history-25-years-on.

Goswami, Purav. 2019. WhatsApp message to author. 24 February 2019.

Gritzner, Karoline, ed. 2010. 'Introduction'. In *Eroticism and Death in Theatre and Performance*, 1–11. Hatfield: University of Hertfordshire Press.

Grover, Amitesh. 2010. 'Amitesh Grover, Performance Maker and New Media Artist'. *Yourstory*, 5 July 2010. https://yourstory.com/2010/07/amitesh-grover-performance-maker-new-media-artist/.

Grover, Amitesh. 2014. 'Performance, Entre Nous'. 30 January 2012. http://amiteshgrover.blogspot.com/2014/09/performance-entre-nous.html.

Grover, Amitesh. 2016. 'Audience-as-performer: Identities, roles and experience as archive'. Presented at the University of Exeter (Drama Department) Conference on Audience, Experience, Desire. January 2016. https://static1.squarespace.com/static/5a6086f0d74cff47a5d9d983/t/5a7d8a5371c10b289b7b2ca0/1518176852901/Performapedia_Audience_As_Performer.pdf.

Grover, Amitesh. 2017. 'Artist Statement'. https://amiteshgrover.com/bio.php.

Grover, Amitesh. 2019. 'India's Postdramatic: Conversations with Theatre-Makers and a Critique'. Interview by Ashis Sengupta. *Marg* 70, no. 3: 46–63.

Grover, Amitesh. 2020. 'There Will Be Trouble: Curating Theatre in India: Amitesh Grover'. *Hakara Journal*, 15 May 2020. https://www.hakara.in/amitesh-grover-3/.

Grusin, Richard. 2015. 'Radical Mediation'. *Critical Inquiry* 42: 124–48.

Hadjioannou, Markos, and George Rodosthenous. 2011. 'In Between Stage and Screen: The Intermedial in Katie Mitchell's ... *Some Trace of Her*'. *International Journal of Performance Arts and Digital Media* 7, no. 1: 43–59.

Hadley, Bree, Anuradha Kapur, Clarissa Ruiz and Sheena Wrigley. 2013. 'Vision, Viability and Value: Three Perspectives on the Performing Arts Across

Cultures, Context and Nations'. *Performance Research* 18, no. 2: 95–101. https://doi.org/10.1080/13528165.2013.807173.

Haksar, Anamika. 2019. 'India's Postdramatic: Conversations with Theatre-Makers and a Critique'. Interview by Ashis Sengupta. *Marg* 70, no. 3: 46–6.

Harvie, Jen. 2013. *Fair Play: Art, Performance and Neoliberalism*. Basingstoke: Palgrave Macmillan.

Hatch, Rayan Anthony. 2019. 'Galleries: Resituating the Postdramatic Real'. In *Postdramatic Theatre and Form*, edited by Michael Shane Boyle, Matt Cornish and Brandon Woolf, 131–46. London: Bloomsbury Methuen.

Heddon, Deirdre, and Jane Milling. 2006/2016. *Devising Performance: A Critical History*. Houndmills: Palgrave Macmillan.

Hughes, Erika. n.d. 'Performing Witnessing: Dramatic Engagement, Trauma, and Museum Installations'. University of Portsmouth. https://core.ac.uk/download/pdf/157862133.pdf.

Hurtzig, Hannah. 2017. 'Mobile Akademie Berlin'. http://www.mobileacademy-berlin.com/englisch/2017/hamburg-2017-the-immobilized.html.

Ilić, Vlatko. 2011. 'Everyone Repeats the Same Rhetorical Question: Do We Still Need Theatre?' In *Dramatic and Postdramatic Theatre Ten Years After*, edited by Ivan Medenica, 137–49. Belgrade: Faculty of Dramatic Arts.

In Transit. 2002. UnDo.Net, 29 May 2002. http://1995-2015.undo.net/it/mostra/9524.

Jackson, Shannon. 2013. 'Postdramatic Labour in The Builder Association's *Alladeen*'. In *Postdramatic Theatre and the Political*, edited by Karen Jürs-Munby, Jerome Carroll and Steve Giles, 165–88. London: Bloomsbury Methuen.

Jäger, Ludwig. 2010. 'Epistemology of Disruptions'. In *Beyond the Screen: Transformations of Literary Structures, Interlaces and Genres*, edited by Jörgan Schäfer and Peter Gendolla, 71–94. Bielefeld: Transcript-Verlag.

Jain, Kirti. 2001. 'Different Concerns, Striking Similarities'. *Theatre India* 3: 22–7.

Jain, Kirti. 2016. Interview by Ashis Sengupta. 17 November 2016. Unpublished.

Jain, Kirti. 2017. Email to author. 22 March 2017.

Jain, Kirti. 2019a. 'Intersections of Practice and Pedagogy: The National School of Drama'. *Marg* 70, no. 3: 24–35.

Jain, Kirti. 2019b. Emails to author. 9 February and 29 December 2019.

Johnson, Dominic. 2012. *Theatre and the Visual*. Houndmills: Palgrave Macmillan.

Johnson, Scott. 2009. *Neoconstructivism: The New Science of Cognitive Development*. Oxford: Oxford University Press.

Jürs-Munby, Karen. 2006. 'Introduction'. In *Postdramatic Theatre*, by Hans-Thies Lehmann, 1–15. London: Routledge.

Jürs-Munby, Karen. 2013. 'Parasitic Politics: Elfriede Jelinek's "Secondary Dramas"'. In *Postdramatic Theatre and the Political*, edited by Karen Jürs-Munby, Jerome Carroll and Steve Giles, 209–32. London: Bloomsbury Methuen.

Jürs-Munby, Karen, Jerome Carroll and Steve Giles, eds. 2013. 'Introduction'. In *Postdramatic Theatre and the Political*, 1–30. London: Bloomsbury Methuen.

Kapur, Anuradha. 2001. 'A Wandering Word, an Unstable Subject...' *Theatre India* 3: 5–12.
Kapur, Anuradha. 2010. 'Resembling the Modern: An Indian Theatre Map Since Independence'. In *Modern Indian Theatre: A Reader*, edited by Nandi Bhatia, 41–55. Delhi: Oxford India Paperbacks.
Kapur, Anuradha. 2011. 'The Antigone Project'. In *Antigone on the Contemporary World Stage*, edited by Erin B. Mee and Helene P. Foley, 415–27. Oxford: Oxford University Press.
Kapur, Anuradha. 2016. Interview by Ashis Sengupta. 13 November 2016. Unpublished.
Kapur, Anuradha. 2016/17. 'Interweaving Performance Cultures'. Freie Universität Berlin. https://www.geisteswissenschaften.fu-berlin.de/en/v/interweaving-performance-cultures/fellows/fellows_2016_2017/anuradha_kapur/index.html.
Kapur, Anuradha. 2017a. Interview by Ashis Sengupta. 7 April 2017. Unpublished.
Kapur, Anuradha. 2017b. 'Traversing Sites, Traversing History: Practising Citizenship through Art'. In *Gendered Citizenship: Manifestations and Performance*, edited by Bishnupriya Dutt, Janelle Reinelt and Srikhla Sahai, 117–44. Basingstoke: Palgrave Macmillan.
Kapur, Anuradha. 2019a. 'Genealogy and Overwriting'. *Marg* 70, no. 3: 16–23.
Kapur, Anuradha. 2019b. Interview by Ashis Sengupta. 4 January 2019. Unpublished.
Kapur, Anuradha. 2019c. 'India's Postdramatic: Conversations with Theatre-Makers and a Critique'. Interview by Ashis Sengupta. *Marg* 70, no. 3: 46–63.
Kapur, Anuradha. n.d. 'Workshop Theatre MA Alumni'. University of Leeds, https://www.leeds.ac.uk/arts/info/125107/workshop_theatre/1933/workshop_theatre_ma_alumni
Karnad, Girish. 1994. 'Author's Introduction'. *Three Plays: Naga-Mandala, Hayavadana, Tughlaq*, 1–18. New Delhi: Oxford University Press.
Kester, Grant H. 2011. *The One and the Many: Contemporary Collaborative Art in a Global Context*. Durham, NC: Duke University Press.
Khurana, Chanpreet. 2019. 'How a Cosmic Event 1.3 Billion Years Ago Inspired an Indian Artist's New Play'. *Scroll.in*, 16 January 2019. https://scroll.in/magazine/908471/how-a-cosmic-event-1-3-billion-years-ago-inspired-this-indian-artists-new-play.
Kirby, Michael. 1972. 'On Acting and Not-Acting'. *TDR: The Drama Review* 16, no. 1: 3–15.
Kluge, Alexander. 1996. 'Epic Theater and Post-Heroic Management: Conversation with Heiner Müller'. https://kluge.library.cornell.edu/conversations/mueller/film/106/transcript.
Komporaly, Jozefina. 2017. *Radical Revival as Adaptation: Theatre, Politics, Society*. London: Palgrave Macmillan.
Kringelbach, Hélène Neveu, and Jonathan Skinner, eds. 2012. 'Introduction: The Movement of Dancing Cultures'. In *Dancing Cultures: Globalization, Tourism and Identity in the Anthropology of Dance*. New York: Berghahn.

Lakhe, Amruta. 2015. 'Jyoti Dogra Sticks to Her Minimalist and Experimental Style of Production with "Notes on Chai"'. *Indian Express*, 19 February 2015. https://indianexpress.com/article/entertainment/entertainment-others/not-so-small-4/.

Landes, Donald A. 2013. *Merleau-Ponty and the Paradoxes of Expression*. London: Bloomsbury.

Lehmann, Hans-Thies. 2006. *Postdramatic Theatre*. Translated by Karen Jürs-Munby. London: Routledge.

Lehmann, Hans-Thies. 2011. '"Postdramatic Theatre", a Decade Later'. In *Dramatic and Postdramatic Theatre Ten Years After*, edited by Ivan Medenica, 31–46. Belgrade: Faculty of Dramatic Arts.

Lehmann, Hans-Thies. 2013. 'A Future for Tragedy? Remarks on the Political and the Postdramatic'. In *Postdramatic Theatre and the Political*, edited by Karen Jürs-Munby, Jerome Carroll and Steve Giles, 87–110. London: Bloomsbury Methuen.

Lehmann, Hans-Thies. 2016. 'Postdramatic'. Translated by Megan Hoetger and Aleksandr Rossman. In *In Terms of Performance*, edited by Shannon Jackson and Paula Marincola. Philadephia and Berkeley: The Pew Center for Arts & Heritage and Arts Research Center, University of California. http://intermsofperformance.site/keywords/postdramatic/hans-thies-lehmann.

Levine, David. 2016. 'Installation'. In *In Terms of Performance*, edited by Shannon Jackson and Paula Marincola. Philadephia and Berkeley: The Pew Center for Arts & Heritage and Arts Research Center, University of California. http://intermsofperformance.site/keywords/installation/david-levine.

Macintyre, Ben. 2019. 'Fallible Memory'. *The Telegraph*, 12 August 2019. Rpt. from *The Times*, London.

Madsen, Deborah Lea. 2011. 'Hybridity, Hyphenation and Mixed-Race Identities'. In *Hybridity: Forms and Figures in Literature and the Visual Arts*, edited by Vanessa Guignery, Catherine Pesso-Miquel and François Specq, 103–13. Newcastle upon Tyne: Cambridge Scholars Press.

Martin, Carol, ed. 2010. *Dramaturgy of the Real on the World Stage*. Basingstoke: Palgrave Macmillan.

Mazzilli, Mary. 2017. *Gao Xingjian's Post-Exile Plays: Transnationalism and Postdramatic Theatre*. London: Bloomsbury Methuen.

McKinney, Joslin, and Scott Palmer, eds. 2017. 'Introducing "Expanded" Scenography'. In *Scenography Expanded: An Introduction to Contemporary Performance Design*, 1–20. London: Bloomsbury Methuen.

Medenica, Ivan, ed. 2011. 'Introduction'. In *Dramatic and Postdramatic Theatre Ten Years After*, 19–30. Belgrade: Faculty of Dramatic Arts.

Mee, Erin B. 2008. *Theatre of Roots: Redirecting the Modern Indian Stage*. Calcutta: Seagull Books.

Mee, Erin B., and Helen Foley, eds. 2011. *Antigone on the Contemporary World Stage*. Oxford: Oxford University Press.

Menon, Jisha. 2013. *The Performance of Nationalism: India, Pakistan and the Memory of Partition*. Cambridge: Cambridge University Press.

Mitra, Shayoni. 2014. 'Dispatches from the Margins: Theatre in India since the 1990s'. In *Mapping South Asia Through Contemporary Theatre*, edited by Ashis Sengupta, 64–102. Houndmills: Palgrave Macmillan.
Morgan, Margot. 2013. *Politics and Theatre in Twentieth-Century Europe*. New York: Palgrave Macmillan.
Mourenza, Daniel. 2014. 'Walter Benjamin, Film and the "Anthropological-Materialist" Project'. PhD diss., University of Leeds. http://etheses.whiterose.ac.uk/8041/.
Nair, Malini. 2017. 'Maya Krishna Rao: The Argumentative Actor'. *Open Magazine*, 27 September 2017. http://www.openthemagazine.com/article/theatre/maya-krishna-rao-the-argumentative-actor.
Nandy, Ashis. 1995. 'An Anti-Secular Manifesto'. *India International Centre Quarterly* 22, no. 1: 35–64.
Nath, Dipanita. 2015. 'They Came, Saw and Kinkared'. *Indian Express*, 22 March 2015. http://indianexpress.com/article/cities/delhi/they-came-saw-kinkared/.
Nath, Dipanita. 2017. 'Rage, in her Name: Maya Krishna Rao, the Face of Protest Theatre Also Wants to Make Audience Laugh'. *Indian Express*, 23 July 2017. https://indianexpress.com/article/lifestyle/art-and-culture/actor-maya-krishna-rao-the-face-of-protest-theatre-also-wants-to-make-audience-laugh-4762861/.
Ojha, Nikhil Prasad, and Joydeep Bhattacharya. 2016. 'Liberalization in India: Glasnost? Yes. Perestroika? Not Much'. *Mint*, 5 July 2016. https://www.livemint.com/Politics/rGKBdfx5zan2Z0XKjQFGdM/Liberalization-in-India-Glasnost-Yes-Perestroika-Not-muc.html.
Orosa-Roldán, Miguel-Ángel, and Paulo-Carlos López-López. 2018. 'Postdrama Culture in Ecuador and Spain: Methodological Framework and Comparative Study'. *Comunicar* 26, no. 57: 39–47.
Ovadija, Mladen. 2013. *Dramaturgy of Sound in the Avant-garde and Postdramatic Theatre*. Montreal: McGill-Queen's University Press.
Pais, Ana. 2014. '"A Way of Listening": Interview with John Collins'. In *New Dramaturgy*, edited by Katalin Trencsényi and Bernadette Cochrane, 115–24. London: Bloomsbury Methuen.
Patil, S. H. 2016. *The Constitution, Government, and Politics in India*. New Delhi: Vikash Publishing House.
Pavis, Patrice. 2010. 'Intercultural Theatre Today'. *Forum Modernes Theater* 25, no. 1: 1–15. https://doi.org/10.1353/fmt.2010.0009.
Pecora, Vincent P. 2013. 'Be Here Now: Mimesis and the History of Representation'. In *Presence: Philosophy, History, and Cultural Theory for the Twenty-First Century*, edited by Ranjan Ghosh and Ethan Kleinberg, 26–45. Ithaca: Cornell University Press.
Peer, Basharat. 2009. *Curfewed Night*. Noida: Random House.
Phillips-Krug, Jutta. 2004. 'Narratives of Violence: The Antigone Project – An Interview with Ein Lall and Anuradha Kapur'. *Mahagonny.com: The Brecht Yearbook/Das Brecht-Jahrbuch* 29: 7–14. https://search.library.wisc.edu/digital/AA3IL7RKGT4KXA8C/pages/ADG4PNIKISY5FH8U.

Pillai, Abhilash. 2011. 'New Act on Stage'. Interview by G. S. Paul. *The Hindu*, 8 December 2011. http://www.thehindu.com/features/friday-review/theatre/new-act-on-stage/article2697578.ece.

Pillai, Abhilash. 2012. 'The Space Through Visual Language in Indian Theatre'. PhD diss., Jawaharlal Nehru University. https://shodhganga.inflibnet.ac.in/handle/10603/117728.

Pillai, Abhilash. 2014. 'Stage-Struck'. Interview by S. Gopakumar. *Bhawani Cheerath*, 5 July 2014. https://bhawanicheerath.wordpress.com/tag/abhilash-pillai/.

Pillai, Abhilash. 2017a. Interview by author. 20 January 2017. Unpublished.

Pillai, Abhilash. 2017b. 'How theatre director Abhilash Pillai pushes Indian theatre into discomfort zones'. Interview by Dipanita Nath. *Indian Express*, 24 May 2017. http://indianexpress.com/article/lifestyle/how-theatre-director-abhilash-pillai-takes-his-plays-and-audience-into-discomfort-zones/.

Pillai, Abhilash. 2019. 'India's Postdramatic: Conversations with Theatre-Makers and a Critique'. Interview by Ashis Sengupta. *Marg* 70, no. 3: 46–63.

Poll, Melissa. 2018. *Robert Lepage's Scenographic Dramaturgy: The Aesthetic Signature at Work*. New York: Springer/Palgrave Macmillan.

Power, Cormac. 2006. 'Presence in Play: A Critique of Theories of Presence in the Theatre'. PhD diss., University of Glasgow. http://theses.gla.ac.uk/3428/.

Prakash, Brahma. 2010. Review of *Theatre of Roots: Redirecting the Modern Indian Stage*, by Erin B. Mee. *Asian Theatre Journal* 27, no. 1: 175–9.

Prasanna. *Indian Method in Acting*. 2013. New Delhi: National School of Drama.

Pratap, Anita. 2002. *Island of Blood: Frontline Reports from Sri Lanka, Afghanistan and Other South Asian Flashpoints*. Gurgaon: Penguin.

PTI. 2017. 'Rise in Protectionism Threatens Gains from Globalisation: Narendra Modi', 7 July 2017. https://economictimes.indiatimes.com/news/economy/foreign-trade/rise-in-protectionism-threatens-gains-from-globalisation-narendra-modi/articleshow/59493716.cms.

Puchner, Martin. 2011. 'Drama and Performance: Toward a Theory of Adaptation'. *Common Knowledge* 17, no. 2: 292–305.

Punjani, Deepa. 2018. 'Initial Thoughts on the Curious Case of Postdramatic Theatre in the Indian Context'. *Critical Stages: The IATC Journal* 18. http://www.critical-stages.org/18/initial-thoughts-on-the-curious-case-of-postdramatic-theatre-in-the-indian-context/.

Punjani, Deepa. n.d. '*Notes on Chai*: Play Review'. *Mumbai Theatre Guide*, http://www.mumbaitheatreguide.com/dramas/reviews/notes-on-chai-others-play-reviews.asp.

Radosavljević, Duška. 2013. *Theatre-Making: Interplay Between Text and Performance in the 21st Century*. Basingstoke: Palgrave Macmillan.

Ramnarayan, Gowri. 2004. 'The Bhakti Poet of Our Times'. *The Hindu*, 5 September 2004. https://www.thehindu.com/todays-paper/tp-features/tp-literaryreview/the-bhakti-poet-of-our-times/article28499552.ece.

Ramnarayan, Gowri. 2012. 'From Text to Performance'. *Theatre India* 1 (January): 6–13.

Ramnarayan, Gowri. 2017a. Brochure for the 2017 production of *Dark Horse*.
Ramnarayan, Gowri. 2017b. 'Stage to Come Alive with Fictional Tale'. Interview by Aishwarya Upadhye. *The Times of India*, 4 August. https://timesofindia. indiatimes.com/city/pune/stage-to-come-alive-with-fictional-tale-of-2-writers/articleshow/59909277.cms.
Rang Swarn Festival. 2003. '*Kitchen Katha*, play in Punjabi'. http://www.indiaculture.nic.in/sites/default/files/events/005a-sanchayan-31072015.pdf.
Rao, Maya Krishna. 2013. 'Maya Krishna Rao: Engaged Theatricality'. In *The Act of Becoming: Actors Talk*, edited by Amal Allana, 262–73. New Delhi: National School of Drama.
Rao, Maya Krishna. 2016. Interview by author. 14 November 2016. Unpublished.
Rao, Maya Krishna. n.d. Blogspot. http://mayakrishnarao.blogspot.com/p/multi-media.html.
Rao, Maya Krishna. 2019. 'India's Postdramatic: Conversations with Theatre-Makers and a Critique'. Interview by Ashis Sengupta. *Marg* 70, no. 3: 46–63.
Rao, Phalguni. 2019. 'Jyoti Dogra on Her Play *The Black Hole*, Drawing Connections between Life and Science on Stage – Living News', *Firstpost*, 3 March 2019. https://www.firstpost.com/living/jyoti-dogra-on-her-play-the-black-hole-drawing-connections-between-life-and-science-on-stage-6170411.html.
Rashid, Parbina. 2002. 'Neelam Mansingh's "Kitchen Katha" comes on stage'. *Tribune India*, 15 June 2002. http://www.tribuneindia.com/2002/20020615/cth2.html.
Ray, Bharati. 2005. *Women of India: Colonial and Post-colonial Periods*. New Delhi: Sage.
Ray, Girindranarayn. 2018. *Thinking Theory: Issues, Perspectives, Politics*. Kolkata: Alphabet Books.
Ray, Shreya. 2016. 'NSD Theatre Festival: Light to Fade'. *Open Magazine*, 25 February 2016. https://openthemagazine.com/art-culture/nsd-theatre-festival-light-to-fade/.
Read, Alan. 2008. *Theatre, Intimacy & Engagement: The Last Human Venue*. New York: Palgrave Macmillan.
Reilly, Kara, ed. 2018. 'Introduction'. In *Contemporary Approaches to Adaptations in Theatre*, xxi–xxviii. London: Palgrave Macmillan.
Rideout, Nicholas. 2019. 'Media: Intermission'. In *Postdramatic Theatre and Form*, edited by Michael Shane Boyle, Matt Cornish and Brandon Woolf, 96–112. London: Bloomsbury Methuen.
Saldaña, J. 2011. *Ethnotheatre: Research From Page to Stage*. Walnut Creek, CA: Left Coast Press, Inc.
Samaddar, Ranabir. 2016. *Ideas and Frameworks of Governing India*. Abingdon: Routledge.
Sanders, Julie. 2006. *Adaptation and Appropriation*. Abingdon: Routledge.
Schechner, Richard. 2013. 'Foreword'. In *The Act of Becoming: Actors Speak*, edited by Amal Allana, xi–xiii. New Delhi: National School of Drama.
Schneider, Rebecca. 2015. 'New Materialisms and Performance Studies'. *TDR: The Drama Review* 59, no. 4 (T228): 7–17.

Schulze, Daniel. 2018. *Authenticity in Contemporary Theatre and Performance: Make it Real*. London: Bloomsbury Methuen.
Sengupta, Ashis, ed. 2014. Introduction. *Mapping South Asia Through Contemporary Theatre: Essays on the Theatres of India, Pakistan, Bangladesh, Nepal and Sri Lanka*, 1–63. Houndmills: Palgrave Macmillan.
Sengupta, Ashis. 2019. 'India's Postdramatic: Conversations with Theatre-Makers and a Critique'. *Marg* 70, no. 3: 46–63.
Sengupta, Shuddhabrata. 2012a. 'At the Edge of Practices: Between and Across Art Forms and Cultures'. In *Ibsen Festival Proceedings*, 39–44. Delhi: Dramatic Art and Design Academy.
Sengupta, Shuddhabrata. 2012b. 'Discussions/Questions'. In *Ibsen Festival Proceedings*, 45–53. Delhi: Dramatic Art and Design Academy.
Seturaman, V. S., ed. 1989. *Contemporary Criticism: An Anthology*. Madras: Macmillan India.
Shamsie, Kamila. 2010. 'Review of *Curfewed Night*, by Basharat Peer'. *Guardian*, 5 June 2010. https://www.theguardian.com/books/2010/jun/05/curfewed-night-basharat-peer-review.
Shankar, Karin. 2019. 'Tracing Minor Gesture in Maya Krishna Rao's Kathakali-Influenced Performance'. *Women and Performance: A Journal of Feminist Theory* 29, no. 2: 125–45.
Shearing, David. 2017. 'Audience Immersion, Mindfulness and the Experience of Scenography'. In *Scenography Expanded*, edited by Joslin McKinney and Scott Palmer, 139–54. London: Bloomsbury Methuen.
Singh, Nonika. 2010. 'Layered Perspective'. *Tribune India*, 1 August 2010. https://www.tribuneindia.com/2010/20100801/spectrum/book6.htm.
Sivaraman, Deepan. 2012. 'The Devil's Own'. Interview by Dipanita Nath. *Indian Express*, 20 January 2012. http://archive.indianexpress.com/news/the-devil-s-own/901740/.
Sivaraman, Deepan. 2013. 'The Future of Indian Theatre'. Interview by Deepa Punjani. *Critical Stages* 8. http://www.critical-stages.org/8/the-future-of-indian-theatre-will-be-based-on-our-ability-to-intermingle-with-other-art-disciplines-interview-with-deepan-sivaraman-indian-theatre-director-and-scenographer/.
Sivaraman, Deepan. 2014. 'For Visual Language'. Interview by Deepa Ganesh. *Frontline*, 18 April 2014. https://frontline.thehindu.com/arts-and-culture/for-visual-language/article5848123.ece.
Sivaraman, Deepan. 2016. Interview by author. 29 November 2016. Unpublished.
Sivaraman, Deepan. 2017. 'Maker of Grand Spectacles'. Interview by Vikram Phukan. *Mint*, 13 January 2017. https://www.livemint.com/Leisure/d1Z9IwQUIuBPY6n8E9cWCO/Maker-of-grand-spectacles.html.
Sivaraman, Deepan. 2018a. Email to BRM, 6 December 2011; forwarded to author, 21 February 2018.
Sivaraman, Deepan. 2018b. 'Subverting the Idea of Nationalism'. Interview by Vikram Phukan. *The Hindu*, 18 July 2018. https://www.thehindu.com/entertainment/theatre/subverting-the-idea-of-nationalism/article24453449.ece.

Sivaraman, Deepan. 2019a. 'Deepan Sivaraman on Going Beyond Words'. Interview by Sohaila Kapur. *The Hindu*, 6 July 2019. https://www.thehindu.com/entertainment/theatre/theatre-director-deepan-sivaraman-on-going-beyond-words-to-embrace-the-visual-language-of-theatre/article28294845.ece.

Sivaraman, Deepan. 2019b. 'India's Postdramatic: Conversations with Theatre-Makers and a Critique'. Interview by Ashis Sengupta. *Marg* 70, no. 3: 46–63.

Smart, Jackie. 2014. 'The Feeling of Devising: Emotion and Mind in the Devising Process'. In *New Dramaturgy: International Perspectives on Theory and Practice*, edited by Katalin Trencsényi and Bernadette Cochrane, 101–14. London: Bloomsbury Methuen.

Spanos, Tony. 1995. 'The Paradoxical Metaphors of the Kitchen in Laura Esquivel's "Like Water for Chocolate"'. Translated by Tony Spanos. *Letras Femeninas* 21, no. 1: 29–36.

Stegemann, Bernd. 2008. *After Postdramatic Theatre*. Translated by Matthew R. Price. *Theatre* 39, no. 3: 11–23.

Subramanyam, Laksmi. 2002. *Muffled Voices: Women in Modern Indian Theatre*. Delhi: Har-Anand Publications.

Sukant, Deepak. 2013. 'Director Neelam Mansingh Chowdhry Explores Newer Frontiers with the London Debut of Her Opera Naciketa'. *India Today*, 7 December 2013. www.indiatoday.in/magazine/profile/story/20131209-director-neelam-mansingh-chowdhry-london-debut-of-opera-naciketa-768883-1999-11-30.

Sundaram, Vivian. 2016. '*409 Ramkinkars*: Sculptural Installation and Theatre'. *Magzter*, 8 November 2016. https://www.magzter.com/article/Art/TAKE-on-art/409-Ramkinkars-Sculptural-Installation-and-Theatre.

Tambakaki, Paulina. 2018. 'Chantal Mouffe'. *Oxford Bibliographies*, https://www.oxfordbibliographies.com/view/document/obo-9780190221911/obo-9780190221911-0067.xml.

Tasić, Ana. 2011. 'Live Video Relay in Postdramatic Theatre'. In *Dramatic and Postdramatic Theatre Ten Years After*, edited by Ivan Medenica, 119–28. Belgrade: Faculty of Dramatic Arts.

Tesche, Claudia. n.d. 'Quantum Entanglement'. *Merriam-Webster.com Dictionary*. https://www.merriam-webster.com/dictionary/quantum entanglement.

Tomlin, Liz. 2016. *Acts and Apparitions: Discourses on the Real in Performance Practice and Theory, 1990–2010*. Manchester: Manchester University Press.

Tomlin, Liz. 2019. *Political Dramaturgies and Theatre Spectatorship: Provocations for Change*. London: Bloomsbury Methuen.

Trencsényi, Katalin, and Bernadette Cochrane, eds. 2014. *New Dramaturgy*. London: Bloomsbury Methuen.

Valerie, Susan. 2016. *Actors and the Art of Performance: Under Exposure*. Translated by Laura Radosh and Alice Lagaay. Houndmills: Palgrave Macmillan.

Vanfleteren, Katrien V. 2008. 'A Postdramatic Psychoanalytical Dramaturgy'. Paper presented at the 11th International Conference of ISSEI, Language Centre, University of Helsinki, Finland, 28 July – 2 August 2008. https://

helda.helsinki.fi/bitstream/handle/10138/15245/36_VuylstekeVanfleteren.pdf.

Varney, Denise. 2007. Review of *Postdramatic Theatre*, by Hans-Thies Lehmann, translated by Karen Jürs-Munby (London: Routledge, 2006). *Performance Paradigm etc. A Journal of Performance and Contemporary Culture* 3: 135–40.

Watkinson, Philip. 2019. 'Time: Unsettling the Present'. In *Postdramatic Theatre and Form*, edited by Michael Shane Boyle, Matt Cornish and Brandon Woolf, 66–80. London: Bloomsbury Methuen.

Weigel, Sigrid. 2015. 'The Flash of Knowledge and the Temporality of Images: Walter Benjamin's Image-Based Epistemology and Its Preconditions in Visual Arts and Media History'. *Critical Inquiry* 41: 344–66.

Winston, Kimberly. 2015. 'The "Splainer": What Makes the Cow Sacred to Hindus?' *Washington Post*, 5 November 2015. https://www.washingtonpost.com/national/religion/the-splainer-what-makes-the-cow-sacred-to-hindus/2015/11/05/acdde3e2-840c-11e5-8bd2-680fff868306_story.html.

Woolf, Brandon. 2013. 'Towards a Paradoxically Parallaxical Postdramatic Politics?' In *Postdramatic Theatre and the Political*, edited by Karen Jürs-Munby, Jerome Carroll and Steve Giles, 31–46. London: Bloomsbury Methuen.

Zarrilly, Philip. 1984. *The Kathakali Complex: Actor, Performance and Structure*. New Delhi: Abhinav Publications.

Zecchini, Laetitia. 2011. 'Breaking from Origins, Hovering over Boundary Lines: Hybridity in Contemporary Indian Poetry'. In *Forms and Figures in Literature and the Visual Arts*, edited by Vanessa Guignery, Catherine Pesso-Miquel and François Specq, 237–49. Cambridge: Cambridge Scholars Publishing.

Index

409 Ramkinkars 27, 174–6, 181, 195

A Deeper Fried Jam 23
Abel, Roysten 36
Active Space 45, 117, 140–5
activism and aesthetics in contemporary theatre 11, 13, 34, 73, 75, 107, 131, 147–65
adaptations 12, 15, 17, 25, 40, 47–55
Afghanistan 76, 78–81, 169
agonism, antagonism 148
Ahlheim, Hannah 124–5
Alexandrowicz, Conrad 70
Alice in Wonderland 141, 143–4
Alkazi, Ebrahim 82, 177
Allana, Amal 105, 179
Allana, Nissar 43, 177
Allende, Isabell 56
Ambrose, Cohen 58
Antaryatra 25, 50
Antigone of Sophocles, The 130
Antigone Project, The 28, 129–35
Are You Home, Lady Macbeth 95–104
Aristotle 2
Armed Forces (Special Powers) Act (AFSPA) 141
Aronson, Arnold 89–90
audio 100, 112, 122, 139, 150
Aur Kitne Tukde 61–6
Auslander, Philip 8–9
autonomous women's movement 29–32
avant-gardes 40–2, 106–7, 118, 173
Awasthi, Suresh 69, 92
Ayodhya 78–9, 131, 171

Babbage, Frances 48
Babri Masjid 78–9, 131
Badiou, Alan 119
Baghdad Burning 61, 169

Bandyopadhyay, Samik 169
Barnett, David 132
Barthes, Roland 48
Baudrillard, Jean 35, 77, 170
Benjamin, Walter 9, 108
Berger, Carl 31–2
Berlin Wall 33
Bevir, Mark 7
Bharat Rang Mahotsav (BRM) 43, 85, 129
Bharatiya Janata Party (BJP) 149, 153, 156, 160
Bharucha, Rustom 18, 155
Bhatia, Gautam 152
Bhawani, Muzamil 45, 140–5
Black Hole 109–15
Boenisch, Peter M. 8, 163
Bolter, David 9
Borowski, Mateusz 10, 28, 68, 75–7, 132
Bose, Santanu 36–8
Bourriaud, Nicolas 11, 119
Boyle, Michael Shane, et al. 1, 10, 37, 42, 75, 148, 164–5, 182
Brecht, Bertolt 2, 20, 54, 57–8, 129–30, 132
Brejzek, Thea 90
Buddhism 115
Butalia, Urvashi 62–3, 72
Butler, Judith 31

Carlson, Marvin 126, 132, 135, 174, 176
Carroll, Jerome 27
Case, Sue-Ellen 30
Castellucci, Romeo 41
cattle slaughter in India 151–2
Chaudhari, Zuleikha 23, 26–9, 41, 43, 45, 82, 129, 136–40
choreography 159, 162, 170–1

Chowdhry, Neelam Mansingh 20, 25, 30, 32, 39, 50, 55–60
Citizenship Amendment Act (CAA) 160
Citron, Atay, et al. 180
cognition, cognitive 27–8, 32, 35, 61, 77, 93, 109–10
Cold War 33
collaborate, collaboration, collaborative productions 25, 30–2, 43, 48, 50, 60, 82, 85, 94–5, 118, 119, 124, 129, 158–9, 161, 168–9, 177, 181
collage 39, 55, 74, 79
Company, The 55–60, 85
Congress Party 153
Constituent Assembly of India debates 151, 154
Constitution of India, The 78, 149–55, 157
constructivism 161–2
Cooke, Grayson 100
cow vigilantism 149, 152
crony capitalism 148, 182
curating 126, 168, 178–9
Curfewed Night 141–3
Cut Piece 93

Dalmia, Vasudha 17–18, 22–3, 57, 107
Danan, Joseph 173
Dark Horse 67–8, 69–74
Dark Things 157–65
Debord, Guy 35, 77
de-dramatize, de-dramatization 13, 26, 67, 83, 87, 95–7
Derrida, Derridean 8–9, 52
devising, devised productions 12–13, 23, 25, 27, 30, 32, 38, 60–6, 85, 93, 95, 98, 100–1, 109, 113, 115, 167–71, 174
directing 13, 29, 168, 174, 176–8
Dogra, Jyoti 92–3, 108–15
Doherty, Claire 118

'double diagnosis' 24, 163
Downtime 23, 117, 119, 121–6
Dramatic Art and Design Academy (DADA) 43, 85
dramatic-postdramatic 'binary' 4–6, 65
dramaturgy 12, 20, 22, 30, 39, 50, 62, 69, 83, 98, 127, 128, 132, 148, 160, 163, 165, 167, 173–4, 176
'dramaturgy of the real' 69, 127–8, 167
Duarte, Bruno C 129–30

epic theatre 2
Esquivel, Laura 56, 59
event horizon 111
experiential reality 35, 63, 73, 90, 110, 128, 158
experimental theatre 24, 27, 43, 48, 98

feminist theatre 29, 32, 59
Fensham, Rachel 144, 157
festivals 23, 29, 38–44
Fischer-Lichte, Erika 4, 118, 171
flogging, lynching 149, 156
Fordist/post-Fordist society 75, 125, 162–4
formalism 10, 11, 37, 74–5, 91, 165
Friedman, Dan 33
Frljić, Oliver 157
Fuchs, Elinor 1–2, 67–8, 97, 180

Gandhi, Indira 155
Gandhi, M. K. 78, 153, 155
Gatz 67–8
Giesekam, Greg 8, 81
globalization, globalized, globalizing 12, 17, 30, 33, 35, 61, 161
'globalized performance' 17
Gnomonicity 126
Godhra, post-Godhra 127, 129, 131–2, 149
Godse, Nathuram 153
Goswami, Purav 158, 163
Grotowski, Grotowskian 40–1, 113

Index

Grover, Amitesh 23, 27–8, 35, 37–8, 43, 102–3, 119–26
Grusin, Richard A. 9
Gujarat 129–30, 132, 134, 149
Gumbrecht, Hans Ulrich 7

Haas, Birgit 31–2, 75
Habermas, Jürgen 35
Haksar, Anamika 39–40, 50
Handke, Peter 23
Harvie, Jen 119
Hatch, Rayan Anthony 128
Heads Are Meant for Walking Into 27, 104–8
Heidegger, Martin; Heideggerian 32, 120
Hindi theatre 29, 81, 177
Hindutva 72, 78–9, 150, 152, 155, 182
Hurtzig, Hannah 159
hybrid, hybridity, hybridized, hybridization 94, 101, 106, 142, 179–80
hypermediacy 8–9

Ibsen, Henrik 85–7, 136–40
Ilić, Vlatko 15–16, 35
impersonation 38, 51, 53, 92
improvisation 30–1, 48, 57, 61, 63, 93–4, 101, 104–5, 106, 113, 125, 153, 158–9, 170, 172, 178
Indian Peace Keeping Force (IPKF) 79
Indian People's Theatre Association (IPTA) 22
intercultural/inter-artistic 17–18, 22, 37, 39, 41, 49, 61, 179
intermedial theatre 8–9, 16, 39, 48–9, 51, 74, 81, 94, 100–1, 106, 167
intertextual, intertextuality 48–9, 134, 143, 159
Islamization of Pakistan 150
Island of Blood, The 67, 76–81

Jackson, Shannon 24, 161
Jáger, Ludwig 89

Jain, Kirti 29–30, 32, 42, 50, 61–6
Jameson, Fredric 182
Janatha Vimukthi Peramuna (JVP) 77, 79–80
Job, The 24–5, 50–5
Jürs-Munby, Karen 26, 28, 32, 60 81, 101, 143

Kane, Sarah 31, 68
Kantor, Tadeusz 26, 40–1, 83, 140, 156
Kapur, Anuradha 22–5, 27–38, 40, 42, 50–1
Karnad, Girish 16, 177
Kashmir 140–5
Kathakali 19–20, 93–6, 101–4
Khakhar, Bhupen 134
Kirby, Michael 98
Kitchen Katha 24–5, 55–60
Kluge, Alexander 140
Kolatkar, Arun 67, 69–74
Komporaly, Jozefina 48

Lall, Ein 23, 28, 129–34
late capitalism 10, 75, 148, 158, 161, 182
Lefebvre, Henri 123
Legend of Khasak, The 41
Lehmann, Hans-Thies 11–24, 27–8, 30–2, 34–5, 39, 41, 47–9, 53–8, 60, 62–3, 65–70, 73–7, 81–2, 86–7, 91–3, 95, 98, 101, 104, 113, 117–19, 123–4, 127–8, 131–2, 135, 139, 147–8, 150, 152–53, 156–7, 160, 163, 165, 167–8, 181–2
Levine, David 135
Liberation Tigers of Tamil Eelam (LTTE) 80
live video play 8, 95, 98–9, 101
Lizhi, Xu 163
Lukács, George 9

Macbeth, Lady 95–103
McKinney, Joslin 85–6, 88, 181

Makeup 38, 54
Malani, Nalini 50–2
Manipur(i) 22, 77, 80, 105, 108
Mazzilli, Mary 12, 21
mediation 8–9, 18, 81, 85, 90, 127–8
mediatization, mediatized 3, 8–9, 24, 34, 77–8, 81, 133, 147–8, 182
Mee, Erin B. 20–2, 129
Menon, Jisha 62–5
Midnight's Children (play) 23, 35–6, 181
Miller, J. Hillis 48
minimalism (in performance) 104, 115, 178
Mitra, Shayoni 22–3, 30, 107
monologue 56, 64–5, 137, 153
montage 55, 71, 156
Morgan, Margot 74
Mujahideen militia 80
Müller, Heiner 87, 138–40

Naciketa 39
Nandy, Ashis 155
narration, narrator 50, 52–4, 56–9, 63, 65, 92, 110, 114, 157, 163
Nath, Dipanita 85, 108, 176
National Democratic Alliance (NDA) 34, 127, 149
National School of Drama (NSD) 40, 44, 76, 94–5, 129
nationalism, hypernationalism 78, 129, 148–9, 152–3, 156–7
Natyashastra 81, 98, 173
Navalakha 32
Nehru Theatre Festival 23
neoliberal(ism) 10, 12, 34, 37, 119, 148, 161, 179, 182
new materialism 32, 105
non-dramatic 38–9, 47–66
Notes on Mourning 23, 177

open market economy 148
Ovadija, Mladen 144, 158

Pais, Ana 61
Pakistan 65, 79, 134, 142, 144, 150, 160
palimpsest(ic), palimpsestuous 22, 48–9, 87, 143, 165
Palmer, Scott 85–6, 88, 181
Panikkar, Kavalam Narayana 22, 177
parataxis 51
Parsi theatre 21, 81
partition 62–5, 154, 160
Pavis, Patrice 17, 133, 171
Pecora, Vincent P. 7
pedagogy 41–2, 71
Peer, Basharat 141
Peer Gynt 40, 44, 85–90
perception, perceptual 6–7, 24, 28, 35, 37, 49, 59, 72, 74, 77–8, 86–7, 92, 100, 104, 117, 133, 144–5, 161, 165, 179
performance art(ist) 30, 38, 45, 93, 102–3, 135, 167
'performative mimesis' 170
Phillips-Krug, Jutta 130–1, 133–4
Pillai, Abhilash 26, 35–6, 39–40, 45, 76–81
playwright 16, 19, 30–1, 50, 57, 168, 171
'political dramaturgies' 148, 163, 165
politics 148–50, 153–6, 165, 180–2
politics and postdrama 9–12
Poll, Melissa 49
post-Brechtian 2, 16, 164
postmodern theatre 3, 156
poststructuralism 3, 148
Power, Cormac 56
Prakash, Brahma 22
Prasanna 98
Pratap, Anita 76–81
predramatic 19–21, 69, 81, 98
presence 1, 6–9, 27–8, 39, 51–2, 56, 58, 62, 64, 73–4, 81, 90, 98, 100, 104–5, 114, 118, 128, 139, 157, 168, 171

present 7–8
presentation 3–4, 6–7, 13, 25, 28, 34, 41, 44, 52, 58–9, 65–7, 72, 80, 87–9, 101–2, 105, 107, 110, 128, 130, 134, 159, 165, 168, 181
promenade theatre 28, 119, 174
Propositions: On Text and Space Series 27, 45, 136, 138–40
protectionism 33
Puchner, Martin 10, 171
Punjani, Deepa 29, 109

quantum entanglement 111–12

Radcliffe line 64–5
Radosavljević, Duška 127–8, 167–9, 171, 173–4, 176
Rajan, C. R. 87
Rakesh, Mohan 22–3
Ramnarayan, Gowri 69
Rancière, Jacques 10, 147–8
Rao, Maya Krishna 23, 92–110, 171–3, 178
Raqs Media Collective 43, 137–9
rasa 22, 92, 173
Ravanama 23, 171–3
reality theatre 117, 126, 128–9
real-time action/performance 3, 13, 25, 56–7, 82, 88, 117, 153–8, 162–3
refugee crisis 147, 160, 165, 181
Rehearsing the Witness 26, 45, 129
Reinelt, Janelle 31, 75, 127
representation, representationalism 1–3, 5–9, 17–19, 23–8, 35, 47–54, 56, 58–62, 69–71, 74–5, 77–83, 89–90, 97–8, 105, 108–10, 118, 120–1, 127, 133–5, 140, 144, 156–7, 161, 163, 165, 167–9, 171, 173–4, 177, 180–2
Rideout, Nicholas 181–2
right-wing politics 72, 148, 153
Ruiz, Alan 37

Sanders, Julie 48
Sangeet Natak Akademi (SNA) 21–2
Sanskrit plays/drama/theatre 20, 22, 81, 92
scavenging 162
scenography 13, 22–3, 25, 40–1, 44, 50, 81–5, 86, 88–90, 101, 135, 138, 167–8, 174, 181
Schechner, Richard 167, 179
Schiller, Friedrich 10
Schneider, Rebecca 105–6
Schulze, Daniel 127, 130
secular(ism), postsecular(ism) 34, 72, 78, 129, 150, 153–5, 157
self-referential(ity) 3, 6, 24, 27, 49, 53, 57, 66, 101, 157
self-reflexive, self-reflexivity 5, 10, 25, 59, 66, 70, 72, 85, 87, 97–8, 102, 161, 168, 171–2
Sengupta, Ashis 80
Sengupta, Shuddhabrata 43, 137
sensory/sensorial/sensorium 10, 26, 28, 32, 35–6, 40, 56, 73–4, 100, 102, 110, 115, 162–3, 178
Shamsie, Kamila 142
Shankar, Karin 94
Shariat rule 79
Shearing, David 90
Sheikh, Gulam Mohammed 134
Shiv Sena 78
Sikh 65, 155
Silappatikaram 50
singularity 111
Sirket, Urvi 150
Sitas, Ari 158, 161, 163
Sivaraman, Deepan 149–52
Sleep-Surfing/*Sleep-Surfers* 121–3
Sleep-Walk 123–4
Smart, Jackie 61, 93
solos 13, 23, 27, 91–115, 178
somatic (text) 62–3, 170
Some Stage Directions 43, 136–8, 140
spectating 2, 13, 25, 40, 44, 54, 99, 102, 144, 160, 163–4

Sri Lanka 76–7, 79–80, 171
Stanislavsky, Konstantin 97, 159
Stegemann, Bernd 3
storytelling 25, 31, 51, 55–6, 62, 68, 83, 94, 115, 157, 168, 173
Sugiera, Malgorzata 10, 28, 68, 75–7, 132
Sundaram, Vivian 174–5
Sundari 24–5, 31, 51
Surrealist(ic) 86
Szondi, Peter 2, 10, 20

tableau 156, 160
Talātum 28, 40, 177
Tanvir, Habib 16, 177
Tasić, Ana 8–9, 81, 133
technology in theatre 29, 34–5, 37, 42–3, 47, 54, 80, 98, 106–7, 119, 169, 172, 179, 181–2
textscapes 49, 73, 152
Thackeray, Bal 78–9
theatre festivals 29, 39, 41–2, 44, 178–9
theatre installation 135–45
theatre of roots 18, 20–2, 50, 177
theatre-as-event 13, 23, 117–29
theatre-making 149, 162, 167–9, 173, 176–8, 180–1
theory of relativity 109, 115
Thiyam, Ratan 22–3, 42, 44, 177
Tomlin, Liz 3, 5–6, 8, 12, 26, 124, 127, 130, 147, 149, 163–5

trafficking 161
'tragic myth' 132
transnational 18–19, 21, 23, 42

Ubu Roi 41, 45, 83
United Progressive Alliance (UPA) 33, 127

Valerie, Susan 140
Varney, Denise 2
verbatim practice/theatre 67, 127, 130
video relay 8, 95, 99
'visual dramaturgy' 12, 20, 22, 25–6, 31, 41, 47, 67, 82, 87, 181
Vivadi Cultural Society 174–5

Watkinson, Philip 8
Weigel, Sigrid 28, 108
Wilson, Robert 20, 26, 49, 74, 83, 91, 95, 101
Wirth, Andrzej 17, 58
Woolf, Brandon 1, 10, 24, 28, 31, 118, 163–4
Work in Progress: A Nationalism Project 27, 45, 60, 149–57
World Theatre Forum (WTF) 179

Yerma 39

Zarrilly, Philip 101
Zecchini, Laetitia 72

www.ingramcontent.com/pod-product-compliance
Lightning Source LLC
Chambersburg PA
CBHW061827300426
44115CB00013B/2281